THE OFFICIAL PRICE GUIDE TO

GOLF

Collectibles

Edward Kiersh

House of Collectibles
New York

House of Collectibles and colophon are registered trademarks of Random House, Inc.

RANDOM HOUSE is a registered trademark of Random House, Inc.

This book is available for special discounts for bulk purchases for sales promotions or premiums. Special editions, including personalized covers, excerpts of existing books, and corporate imprints, can be created in large quantities for special needs. For more information, write to Special Markets/Premium Sales, 1745 Broadway, MD 6-2, New York, NY, 10019 or e-mail specialmarkets@randomhouse.com.

Please address inquiries about electronic licensing of any products for use on a network, in software, or on CD-ROM to the Subsidiary Rights Department, Random House Information Group, fax 212-572-6003.

Visit the House of Collectibles Web site: www.houseofcollectibles.com

Library of Congress Cataloging-in-Publication Data is available.

Printed in the United States of America

10 9 8 7 6 5 4 3 2 1

ISBN: 0-375-72085-5

704 5632

ACKNOWLEDGMENTS

This guidebook is shaped around the history of golf and the unique artifacts that echo the game's grandest traditions. It would not have been possible without the assistance of several experts who offered their time, wisdom, and friendship.

Passionate collector Joe Tiscornia invited me into his home and took me on a journey through time. Before his recent and tragic death, he had one of the world's most notable collections of memorabilia—particularly pre-1850s artifacts—and it was a delight to enter this time capsule with him. I'll always be indebted to him for his hospitality, his expertise, and the photos that he provided that illustrate the grandeur of golf collecting. He will be sorely missed.

Will Roberto was equally generous with his advice and dedication to this one-year project. He provided numerous photographs, price information, and even more importantly, his encouragement.

Art and pottery lover Wayne Aaron, who was struggling with personal matters throughout the writing of this book, was always there for me when I needed access to other collectors. I wish him Godspeed, and many days of happy collecting.

Mark Emerson is known as the "paper expert." He should be called "Old Reliable." By consistently offering wise counsel and friendship, he adopted this project as his own, and his offerings of many photographs are a testament to his kindness.

The "Monster Man" Jim Espinola is another golf fanatic who befriended me and made this book a reality with his insights and good cheer. My thanks also go out to Dick Donovan, Eddie Papczun, Lew Lipset, Rand Jerris, Alistair Johnston, George Fox, David Berkowitz, Dick Estey, Bob Burkett, golf course designer Michael Hurdzan, and Jeffery Ellis, who's arguably the most learned man in the world about antique clubs, and who was always there when I needed information about these beautiful collectibles. His book *The Clubmaker's Art* is a must.

Along with a labor of love, a book project is also a long journey. Such a trip demands help along the way, and people who are there to support your efforts. My wife Nancy and son Aaron were certainly my foundation, true reliable sources and confidantes always willing to invigorate my efforts. I wish to express my thanks to them, and to two people at Random House who were also instrumental in making this golf book a success. They are my editor Dorothy Harris and her assistant Lindsey Glass, who both offered valuable assistance and advice that will always be appreciated.

Edward Kiersh

CONTENTS

INTRODUCTION

Ever since Scottish gentlemen ignored King James II's warning in 1457 that the game would interfere with archery practice, golf has been a "good walk spoiled." No matter the "weapon," technological advance, or alluring terrain, man continues to be humbled, a victim of golf's many extraordinary charms.

In that battle against the "Merciless Slayer of Dreams," otherwise known as the often futile pursuit of par, golfers have armed themselves with an encyclopedic array of equipment to skirt sand traps and sink putts.

Long-nosed woods. *Lardshaft* mashies. *Falcon* and *Viking* balls. *Park Cleek* irons. *Brassies, Jiggers, Niblicks,* and *Featheries.* Many of these accoutrements, even though they're evocative of the Marquis de Sade, are historical artifacts, uniquely designed, unusual looking, and of course, highly-coveted collectibles.

In this near-limitless constellation of wooden or iron-shafted clubs and gutta-percha balls that mirror golf's 600-year evolution into a Tiger Woods–crazed sport (with an equally limitless audience), there are many rare and semi-rare items that are absolute treasures. Those duffers-*cum*-collectors who have the budgetary clout or keen eye to really score can pursue mint, near-mint, and outstanding examples of *featheries* or *Haskell* patent (rubber core) balls from the late 19th century into the early 20th century that are valued between $800 and $9,000; $300 *sand mold* tees; $950 *spring face* irons; or a *Long Spoon A. Patrick* wood priced at $2,650. These items, along with Anderson of Anstruther, Robert Forgan, and steel-shafted E.H. Winkworth Scott clubs (circa 1912) are the "caviar" of the booming golf market, iconic pieces that mirror the game's refuge for the rich origins.

Yet $1,450 Forgan *transitional* playclubs, $340 *Scareneck* drivers, and $1,950 *Blacksmith Cleek* irons (many anonymous blacksmiths manufactured clubs in the 1800s) are only part of the collecting game.

Golf became more of an Everyman pastime in the 1920s and 1930s as major American companies such as Wilson and Spalding started producing clubs. Reflecting that democratization of the sport, there are several club–ball–memorabilia niches that are within reach of enthusiasts of more modest means. Equally indicative of golf's rich history, particularly of the revolutionary change from shafts being made from steel rather than hickory in the 1920s, the *Whistler* (which made a unique noise when swung), a *Tom Morris Special* (dot-punched putter), and Cochrane's *Super Jigger* (circa 1920 iron) are all available for below $400.

This book will provide an added dimension to collecting by placing the game in its historical context. Whether found at flea markets, estate sales, or through the countless collector societies, clubs, and Internet sites available, semi-rare and moderately-valuable clubs are worth owning. Whether it is to complement a love for the game or to appreciate its rich history, these items are attractive, and they are *fun* to collect.

To get the most out of this fascinating hobby, you will need to learn the "secrets" of the collecting game, and follow certain rules that govern condition, availability, desirability, and negotiation of purchases.

As this illustrated price guide will emphasize, the first crucial step towards enjoyable—and profitable—collecting is selecting the most appealing "course" of interest.

Antique golf items include equipment, artwork, books, balls, ceramics, photos, trophies, tees, and medals. Collectors must decide which niche best suits their tastes and budget. Many enthusiasts are attracted to old clubs, so this pricing guide will picture the how-tos of acquiring collectible woods, irons, and putters, with tips on condition, rarity, negotiating sales, Internet purchases, spotting fakes or doctored clubs, and identifying special markings. Along with interspersing colorful descriptions of how certain clubs originated and profiles of illustrious clubmakers, this book will also describe the allure of antique balls, tees dating back to the 1900s, balls signed by famous golfers, tournament trophies, scorecards, and ceramics.

Too often, books of this ilk only provide a few pictures and the prices of various items. This comprehensive work will furnish rich histories of collectibles, their distinguishing characteristics, and how they can be discovered and purchased for the best price.

To further augment the art and science of collecting, this book will provide insights from the top collectors in various fields on how to secure "top condition" items. In this world, condition is key.

Other sections will feature tips from experts; a listing of the best Internet sites to facilitate access to antique dealers, publications, golf associations, and collector organizations; and a chapter devoted to the maintenance and preservation of these artifacts.

Collecting is all about *fun*. Pursuing unique clubs, balls, and memorabilia is an adrenaline rush, especially when a valuable item is found at a garage sale or flea market. Yet along with providing treasure hunt secrets, this book will put the sport of collecting within a historical-folklore context that will increase the joy of discovering rare golf collectibles.

1 COLLECTING
An Adventurous Journey Back in Time

A few years ago golf antiquities dealer David Berkowitz discovered several $5 and $10 thimble-shaped plastic sand tee molds. Dismissing their value, he gave them away to friends, only to realize a few years later that these once worthless tees were selling for $500 to $1,000.

"You could once buy all the sand tee molds you wanted for a few dollars," he said. "Now these same pieces are going for $250 to $350, and even more. It's a price explosion which dramatizes one general fact about golf collectibles: Today's junk is tomorrow's gold."

A relatively new and dynamic hobby offering specialties at many different investment levels, collecting golf artifacts certainly has a golden profit potential. Yet whether it's tees or medals, country club menus or ornate pottery, golf mementos can't be viewed merely as tangible assets, investment portfolio items, or plain profit-and-loss entries. These objects of wonderment are far more bewitching than that.

Golf memorabilia is a slice of history, capturing moments in time that evoke the unique artistry of club makers, pottery craftsmen, and ballmakers. There's no way to measure the intangible rewards they offer, except to say that these long nose clubs and Map of the World balls evoke the spirit of golf's storied past from King James and Old Tom Morris to Ben Hogan and the Golden Bear. They are an investment, yet one with a real magical power to transport collectors back in time.

How does the new collector embark on the search for these rarities?

It's critical to understand that discovering unique or valuable items often entails a search—a Sherlock Holmes–like quest—and that this exhilarating hunt can take place in a picturesque Scottish town or in an American roadside antique shop. A real adventure!

If you are the more bookish, less adventurous type (more likely to read about collecting, golf histories, course architecture, or biographies of the game's greatest players), then the better strategy is to work with a handholder. Find a trustworthy dealer to do your bidding at auctions, to network with other collectors, and to unearth scarce, reasonably priced treasures.

That approach won't be as pleasurable as venturing out alone with this reference guide, yet it is safe. It's the time-honored way that comes well-recommended by the collecting experts who graciously helped make this book possible.

But no matter how collectors go after the rich prizes (and *bargains*) that can turn up at a St. Andrews auction, flea market, estate sale, golf show, or convention, there is one common thread to these journeys of exploration. Besides being stimulating, and charged with history, they're all fun.

And potentially profitable as well, for golf antique collecting is based on one alluring principle: The supply of quality items is always decreasing, while demand continues to increase. That golden rule assures scarcity and the stability—if not the upward movement—of prices. It also guarantees that rare books, clubs, and balls will continue to possess tremendous liquidity, just in case these objects will have to be sold someday.

All of these enticements add up to one attractive, bogey-free scorecard. One that's going to keep you out of the rough, and enjoyably *in* the green.

2 UNLOCKING THE SECRETS OF SIR ISAAC NEWTON
Golf Balls

To play golf, every would-be Tiger Woods must certainly have courage, a sense of adventure, a firm grip on risk and reward, and even the mettle to tackle challenges worthy of Homer's *Odyssey*. All too often the game is a merciless comeuppance, a long day's journey into night that demands, no matter how you slice it, a big supply of B-A-L-L-S.

The bold and daring must also enter this water- and sand-tossed universe with a bag of dimpled, aerodynamically-tested spheres, otherwise known as golf balls. Here Galileo, Kepler, Sir Isaac Newton, and a host of NASA-inspired flight-distance engineers have given golfers new hope in the quest for the Promised Land.

Now that relentless, often quixotic pursuit of par takes flight with an array of super-compression, tough polymer-cored, two- or three-piece construction balls. Whether made of balata, surlyn, or some other Space-Age material ensuring "high spin" and a "softer, yielding feel," golf is in the midst of an uplifting "scientific revolution."

As the immortal Arnold Palmer said of "Newtonian" golf, "this ought to be a game for scientists, not athletes . . . give them a club and calculator, they'd shoot lower than me."

Far more emblematic of the game's rich past, "golf bawls" predating scientific spin-and-drag explanations of flight trajectories have become one of golfiana's hottest—and most expensive—items. Taking a swing at discovering these treasures demands a Sherlock Holmes eye, patience (the best historical balls are rare, seldom coming on the market), money, and a keen appreciation of the ballmaker's craft. It's sometimes dangerous business to hunt down these historical relics, as more and more counterfeiters are plying their noxious trade. Yet along with the heady satisfaction of reliving

Henley Union Jack pattern gutty ball. Red ca. 1896, very rare. *Photo courtesy of Will Roberto.*

Knife cut gutty ball ca. 1848–50, very rare. *Photo courtesy of Will Roberto.*

history, such *important* balls as William Gourlay featheries, Haskells, along with an array of patterned gutta-perchas (such as Willie Dunn Jr.'s "Stars and Stripes," a Henley with Union Jack markings, or a $35,000 Park Royal Gutty) are attracting record prices.

To make sense of this exploding market (a "pneumatic" 1906 ball was actually prone to exploding), looking back at the golf ball's "spotted past" is of paramount importance. As in any collecting field, *knowledge is power*, and appreciating the golf ball's various designs is critical to collecting.

"Balls are the game's engine," insists avid collector and ball enthusiast James Espinola, who collaborated with Kevin W. McGimpsey in the writing of *The Story of the Golf Ball* (Philip Wilson Publishers, Ltd., 2003). "The whole game is centered around the ball, for the ball is an extension of the golfer. The player hits the ball, watches the ball. The ball is a golfer in motion. It's the name of the game."

"Mr. Golf Ball" agrees. Emphasizing the ball's impact on golf equipment, David Berkowitz, the owner of 300 to 400 balls, says "every improvement starts with the ball. When feather balls became dominant, clubs were changed. They didn't change again until the gutta-percha ball came into play, and an iron club or wooden club with a little more support than the long nose club was needed. Then clubs needed to be stronger with a stronger neck. So that meant the passing of the sleek long nose, and the coming of shorter, fatter heads—the deeper-faced Bulger shape. Changes also had to be made when golf moved on to the rubber core ball. So the ball has really forced changes in the clubs. Throughout history it's always been at the center of the action."

Unknown maker Feather Ball ca. 1820 with incised owners mark "W." This ball is possibly from the Wemyss Family (Gosford Park estate near Edinburgh) or David Wallace a competitor in the Grand National Tournament—precursor to British Open. *Photo courtesy of Will Roberto.*

A D. Marshall feather ball, ca. 1930. David Marshall made featheries 1815–1830 faintly stamped "D. Marshall." The patina and condition are excellent. The angled cut of the seams is typical of the earliest featheries. The ball measures 1.74″. *Photo courtesy of Old Tom Morris Golf, L.L.C.*

That history or evolutionary journey begins in Scotland back in the 1400s. Fearing the game would interfere with his subjects' archery practice (and defense of the country), King James II tried to ban the sport. But golfers ignored his injunctions, and played with roughly hewn wooden balls.

Playing with those cumbersome objects was such a jarring experience, that ye olde golf enthusiasts devised leather-cased balls filled with uncombed wool waste flock (which in the mid-1400s balls sold for ten English pennies). While it's unknown if animal rights groups objected to the fleecing of sheep for a rich man's game, the pre-1700s *flok* ball was straight out of Charles Darwin. Hardly satisfying the demands for longer distance, it was another species doomed to extinction.

The British Royal and Ancient Golf Association, also known as Royal & Ancients, was forced to search for that "longer," more lasting and playable ball. Rich devotees of the game (which was increasingly becoming known as "the sport of the idle nobility") demanded a ball that would fly farther—and the era's most resourceful thinkers followed a predictable course of action. They again looked to pastoral barnyards for inspiration.

What greeted them didn't disappoint. Dazzled by the colorful feathers of geese, cocks, and hens, the early lords of ball aerodynamics gave new meaning to the word "stuffing," and in 1618 introduced the featherie.

One of golfiana's most highly sought collectibles (and a staple of the game for four centuries), this tightly stitched, horsehide leather-covered ball was stuffed with a "gentleman's top hat full" of boiled and softened feathers. As the goose down, cow hair, or chicken feathers dried, the leather was hammered into shape, sewn tight with twine, and painted. Each 18th and 19th century craftsman, such as the fabled William Gourlay (John C. Gourlay was also an accomplished ballmaker), or Allan Robertson, could give the ball distinctive markings, artistic nuances, and—very appealing to today's collectors—numbers indicating weight and playability. These featheries prompted the development of long-nosed concave-faced clubs with hard wooden (apple or pear) heads, but since most of these balls were similar looking, those with the maker's names or other distinguishing marks have become the most collectible.

As Jeffery Ellis, the collector and author of *The Clubmaker's Art* and *The Golf Club,* suggests, "All featheries are basically the same. With no name you can't say who made it. There's no real characteristic or trademarks to determine absolutely its maker or origins. Yet Gourlay, Robertson, they were real craftsmen who made beautiful balls. In most cases, though, you just can't tell who made the ball, and that's why a marked featherie will sell for double the price of an unmarked one—nameless balls are also easier to counterfeit—as Espinola warns, 'Fakes do not have knotholes, and the twine should be a thick rope type . . . in fakes the twine is shiny black'. These marked balls are the ones with personality, the balls with real history. But since most look alike, in this market niche the driving force of values is condition."

While Ellis feels that owning a feather ball is a real treat (as they were made by artisans with "a real story"), most of the better-made balls (those with tighter stitched seams, the extra large balls, and the "named" balls) are either squirreled away in private collections, or lost forever. If an ultra-rare, older ball does surface (whatever the condition), it sells for an astronomical price.

In this universe of five-figure relics, Tom Morris, Allan Robertson, Willie Dunn, and James C. Gourlay were the Mozarts of stitching and stuffing. Yet many featheries were flawed. Oblong rather than perfectly round, these balls became waterlogged or only lasted for a few rounds. Even worse, once a badly played shot ripped the ball's seams, feathers showered down on the golf course.

Featheries were also expensive, beyond the reach of the Common man. In effect, they stymied the game's growth, so a more affordable alternative was desperately needed.

Britannia then ruled the seas. Union Jack ships were traveling to all parts of the world, and once natural milky latex, a solid-molded rubber material, was taken from Palaquium trees in Malaysia, golf experienced its next "revolution" in 1848.

An unnamed feather ball ca. 1820, size 30. This ball has a wide center strip and original paint. *Photo courtesy of Old Tom Morris Golf, L.L.C.*

An unnamed feather ball in display case. This ca. 1840 ball was presented to the Warwick GC, England in 1916. *Photo courtesy of Old Tom Morris Golf, L.L.C.*

Hard, nonbrittle, and extremely malleable, this rubbery substance, known as gutta-percha (aka "guttie-perchie") could be boiled and easily shaped into the first one-piece, all-solid golf balls. These "gutty balls" were far stronger than featheries, and since they were cheaper to produce than leather-encased balls, their introduction prompted two seismic changes in the golf landscape. Playing the game now became more affordable for the general public, and since this new ball was very hard, wooden-headed clubs were initially abandoned for convex-shaped hickory, persimmon, or dogwood clubs, and later, iron clubs.

History is a bit unclear at this point. The first gutties could have been invented by Robert Adams Paterson, a divinity student, who according to writer and golf ball expert Kevin McGimpsey received a packing crate which was filled with items protected by gutta-percha. He might have experimented with making a few balls, but then again, as McGimpsey notes, Paterson's half brother John could also be the "father" of the gutty ball. He discovered that this latex substance could be heated, softened, and molded into round balls.

John Paterson called his smooth-surfaced ball (one of the "Holy Grails" of collecting since it was only made for a few months, and would fetch about $100,000) "Paterson's Composite Patented" and later "Paterson's New Composite." It quickly became known for its long, straight flight, though McGimpsey insists "it didn't get airborne quickly enough," and prompted what dealer Leo Kelly calls a debate between featherie traditionalists and the progressive, even "free swinging," New Guard.

Paterson's Patent ball flew further than featheries, but it also plummeted straight down. Yet the inventor's disciples discovered that once this gutty became nicked, it

7

A feather ball ca. 1840 stamped Allan. *Photo courtesy of Old Tom Morris Golf, L.L.C.*

An unnamed hand-hammered gutta-percha, ca. 1850s, painted red for winter play. *Photo courtesy of Old Tom Morris Golf, L.L.C.*

soared even straighter and longer. Impressed by these aerodynamics, ballmakers (like Robert Forgan in the 1860s, who later introduced the Bramble pattern, and William Currie and William Dunn in the 1870s) began to hand-hammer ridges and grooves, or as Kelly suggests, "to simulate cuts made by an iron golf club."

Hand-hammered balls with longitudinal lines and simple mesh patterns were the dominant trend for several years. Yet as the game attracted new adherents toward the end of the 19th century, an increasing number of club makers entered the ball market with a spate of daring designs. As McGimpsey suggests, "club makers and club professional had seen that making gutta-percha balls was a good business opportunity for very little outlay. All they needed was the raw gutta, moulds, and the painting and drying equipment."

According to Leo Kelly, the now legendary Tom Morris, Willie Park, Willie Dunn (of "Stars and Stripes" ball fame), and Alexander Henry (a gunmaker known for his grooved and rifled patterned ball which was touted, according to McGimpsey, as the "swiftest flying ball in the market . . . it flies like a bullet"), were the leaders in restyling balls with "circles, triangles, letters, and other geometric shapes." Many of the most unusual, super-rare, and intricately detailed balls are generically called "weird patterns" by collector James Espinola. Awed by the craftsmanship of these balls (made from molds), he feels the most striking items are (1) the 1897 Stars and Stripes (a salute to America, and last selling for $26,000 in mint condition, it's now valued between $70,000 and $80,000), (2) the 64 hexagonal-sided Park Royal (in 1996 it sold for $35,650, and is now estimated at $70,000), and (3) a rubber-cored Bramble

A Star Challenger, ca. 1910s in good condition. *Photo courtesy of Old Tom Morris Golf, L.L.C.*

The Wonder Ball, with an unusual diamond pattern. Scarce if not rare. *Photo courtesy of Old Tom Morris Golf, L.L.C.*

An unusual patterned Done It Rubber core similar to the Lunar. Light paint flaking, several areas darkened, name and registration clearly readable. Rare. *Photo courtesy of Old Tom Morris Golf, L.L.C.*

A Zome One, pattern of raised center circles inside of larger recessed circles, blue lettering. Mint. *Photo courtesy of Old Tom Morris Golf, L.L.C.*

by J. P. Cochrane called the Terrestrial Globe or "Map of the World" ball (only about 50 to 100 dozen of these were made, ensuring their unquestioned rarity).

"Miniature works of art, these boldly designed and sometimes odd looking balls are true visual delights," enthuses Espinola, a New Hampshire "golf fanatic" who advises the Lyon & Turnbull auction house in Edinburgh, Scotland. He owns over 200 balls, an ever-expanding golf library, and some of the rarest clubs. "They're beautiful to look at, but only a handful were made, and since they rarely, if ever, come up for sale, that guarantees incredibly high prices. These odd pattern balls, the real historical nice ones are true market blue-chips no matter what their condition."

Visually exciting, these "monsters," as Espinola lovingly dubs his exotically-patterned balls, enjoyed tremendous popularity at the turn of the 20th century. Yet echoing McGimpsey's thesis that gutty balls had "less bounding power," or actually traveled a shorter distance than featheries, Espinola insists, "The gutta-percha ball didn't work all that well."

As for collecting "real" gutta-percha balls, Leo Kelly advises collectors to use the billiard ball—and color tests—to determine a gutty's authenticity.

"Gutta-percha balls, when hit, make a clicking sound somewhat like the sound of billiard balls at impact. One way to tell if a golf ball is made of gutta-percha is to tap it against an iron club head. If it sounds (clicks) like a billiard ball does, it may be a solid gutty. (High priced items should be examined with an x-ray.)"

McGimpsey's book offers other "gutty collecting" tips. Along with describing a "cracking" sound test for gutty balls, he feels a named gutta-percha such as a Paterson "are even rarer than featheries because they were only made for a short time." Many gutty balls are not perfectly round or attractive, but McGimpsey still feels that Allan Robertson, Robert Forgan, and Tom Morris "are very collectable" ballmakers. In his book, tributes are also paid to the J. B. Halley "Ocobo," Willie Park's "exceptionally pretty" Diamond Mesh, and the Henley "Union Flag" ball.

Though prized today, gutty balls still provoked criticism. Many players felt their "clicking" sound (after the advent of iron clubs) was distracting, and gutta-percha balls were also notorious for falling apart during a round.

Always searching for that "flight-proven, greater distance wonder ball" (America in the early 1900's was entering a new age of scientific discovery), golfers-turned-inventors briefly tried to develop a hollow aluminum ball to meet the increasing clamor for a durable, affordable ball. That experiment lasted as long as a three-foot putt (McGimpsey points out that this ball "emitted a weird whistling sound"), and the next, far more noteworthy discovery in the evolutionary cycle was the rubber-cored ball.

Several inventors had produced a variant of this type of ball in the late 1890s. But none of their efforts led to mass production until Coburn Haskell collaborated with Bertram G. Work of Ohio's B. F. Goodrich Company in 1898, to design a vulcanized Indian rubber ball. Ultimately nicknamed the "Bounding Billy," for it scooted around the fairway, the one-piece "Haskell" was essentially a solid rubber core with thread wound around it and a gutta-percha covering. This "breakthrough" ball was initially expensive to produce, but it gave golfers an extra 20 yards of distance.

Once automatic winding machinery replaced the tedious hand threading of elastic around the core, the Haskell became a more affordable choice for golfers. The ball also prompted another "traditionalists versus progressives" debate, as critics of the

A Silvertown gutta-percha, two minor iron marks, 85% paint, ca. 1890s, excellent. *Photo courtesy of Old Tom Morris Golf, L.L.C.*

An unnamed gutta-percha, 98% paint, ca. 1898, mint condition. *Photo courtesy of Old Tom Morris Golf, L.L.C.*

Haskell felt it gave golfers an unfair advantage. As McGimpsey's book points out, that clamor, plus the subsequent development of other so-called "innovative" balls (such as the all-air Pneumatic, the Springvale Hawk, Kite, Ace, Roc, Swan, Buzzard, and "Ghost in the Night" Wizard) prompted the legendary Harry Vardon "to call for a return to the solid gutta-percha."

Progress again triumphed. Despite charges that the Haskell symbolized a pact with the Devil, it won new adherents once the original mesh pattern was replaced by a raised "pimply" Bramble design. The gutta-percha casing around the core was also changed to a forgiving balata (plastic synthetic), and as scores of inventors and rubber companies pursued other advancements, science opened a floodgate of real (and patently questionable) innovations.

As both Kelly and McGimpsey describe, an engineer from Leicester, England named William Taylor pioneered the "Dympl" in 1907, a "ball pitted with small circular cavities instead of being covered with the usual bramble-like protuberances."

Taylor ultimately sold the patent to A. G. Spalding, and that sale opened a Pandora's box of legal wrestling matches, as British ball companies questioned Spalding's stranglehold on the round "Dimpyl." This American sporting goods behemoth would lose that battle, as a host of companies were allowed to develop their own dimpled "Gravitators," "White Flyers," and "Spitfires."

All of these ballmakers were essentially searching for the innovation with the greatest Bernoulli effect—the energy dynamic that minimizes drag and maximizes a spinning, lifting force otherwise known as *distance*.

A Willie Park molded mesh gutty, ca. 1890s, in mint condition. The finest known example of this Open Champion's mesh ball. With the exception of very minute paint loss, the ball appears as new. *Photo courtesy of Old Tom Morris Golf, L.L.C.*

A St. Mungo Patent Colonel bramble, painted red for winter play, mint condition in partial original wrapper. *Photo courtesy of Old Tom Morris Golf, L.L.C.*

Various vulcanizing processes were initiated. Companies experimented with cork and metal cores, and during this transitional period of trial and error, all sorts of wacky fabrications, including spheres of various sizes, dimensions, and materials, were introduced.

Every company was supposedly "solving the mystery of flight" with their distinctive, dimple-patterned balls. When its compressed air center ball wasn't expanding and exploding, the Chatfield Pneumatic went "30 yards further" due to "300 pound pressure." The round dimple Avon "Arc" was the "finest" golf ball in the world, while the Beldam carried a swastika emblem. There was the curious Henley "Why-Not" ("the most perfect ball England has produced"), and arguably the oddest concoction: a devilish-looking figure swinging at a "Spirit of Magic," Martins-Birmingham "Zome Bramble Zodiac."

As suggested by McGimpsey's wonderfully illustrated book, all of these enterprising (even ballsy) hucksters hyped "the longest, winningest, swiftest, straightest, steadiest, and Olympian" rubber-cored ball. Trying to find that ideal mix of Big D (distance and durability), each ozone-layer reaching ball promised par, or some sort of stroke-saving "sensation." While much of lofty attitude talk was pure flim-flam, there's nothing imaginary about today's soaring prices.

Balls reflecting that sky's-the-limit auction spirit include a Worthington "Ocobo" with "raised O decoration" selling for $550, an original Haskell with mesh and dot markings at $5,060, a 1908 "Map of the World" with "pimples" at £10,500, a 1910 Dunlop V with large flat dimples at £1,207, a Why-Not with seven dots in circle markings for $1,400, and as McGimpsey adds, "an exceptionally rare (Alexander) Henry's rifled (rubber core) ball, circa 1903, with stamp to both poles in pristine condition, unused but with a few flakes of original paint missing. The great rarity of these balls is probably due to the fact that they did not work very well and not many of them were made."

Once World War I ended, and the public was more in the mood for playing golf, the United States Golf Association wanted one type of long-distance ball, whereas Britain's Royal and Ancient Golf Association preferred another. Worried that the other side's players would gain an unfair distance advantage, each ruling body demanded the use of their own favored dimple.

As the world moved towards another, more serious international conflagration, the heated ball debate over conflicting weights and diameters (between 1.48 and 1.76 ounces and 1.55 and 1.71 inches, respectively) sparked rounds of hard-hitting claims and counterclaims. At times the differences of opinion seemed as complicated and tangled as a lesson in nuclear physics.

But as McGimpsey notes, Spalding "claimed that adding paint to a ball could dramatically affect its performance: tests show that a variance of so much as one one-thousandth of an inch can cause a variance of 3 to 5 yards in distance or direction, the full import of the newest Spalding feature can be realized."

Not to be outdone "scientifically," the MacGregor Company introduced the "Pace-Maker dry ice center golf ball" (McGrimsey humorously points out this meant carbon dioxide gas, another "revolutionary" advance with "a special liquid center" that could *almost* be compared to a "miniature cannon"). He also recalls the Bristol golf ball with its "frozen cores," and arguably the most outlandish, the L.A. Young Golf Company's unique contribution to golf ball flight: a ball with a "pure honey center" which "has undreamed of elasticity and resilience and is not affected by climatic changes and does not evaporate."

Now these *sweet* dimpled items from the 1920s are enjoying a burst of popularity. "Feather balls got very expensive so people started to collect gutty balls, and now that they got very costly, dimpled balls have become attractive," explains Espinola. "Old dimpled balls are steadily rising in price to the point that they're now $500 to $600. So people are moving into signature (or signed) dimpled balls. Paying $10,000 to $15,000 a ball is crazy sometimes unless you're a purist, and want to keep the history of the game alive."

As on any golf course, that beauty is lined with traps and hazards. Collecting can be fun, a spirited journey back into the history of the ballmaker's art. Yet to fully enjoy that passage (which may lead to profitable investments), certain rules must be followed.

A Silver King Red Dot mesh, as new in box.
*Photo courtesy of Old Tom Morris Golf,
L.L.C.*

To stay in bounds financially, and to also appreciate the political, social, and industrial aspects of golf ball evolution, read several books, particularly McGrimsey's meticulously researched work.

Clearly an avid admirer of such unique items as the concentric ridged Faroid 75 (1933), the David Marshall feather ball (selling for £23,000 in 2001), and Willie Park's diamond mesh (1890), he advises enthusiasts to "collect everything and anything: soon you will be able to decide what to specialize in." He emphasizes that "unused cover patterns always attract a premium," and warns against removing balls from wrappers. McGrimsey also insists that "ball boxes are very collectible," and as for one definite no-no, "keep (balls) cool and out of direct sunlight."

Offering his own "dos and don'ts," James Espinola warns, "Old is terrific, but since really nice featheries rarely come on the market, be very careful. Once a ball goes to $5,000, $8,000, $10,000, $15,000, lots of people try to reproduce them, or put a name on a ball. To spot the fakes, beginners have to first read books, and really look at balls, feel them. Condition, condition, condition, is critical. See if the knotholes are there. Most of [the] time with fakes the knotholes aren't there. I'd also look at the seams, the stitching, to make sure it's nice dark brown cord. Roped twine instead of this black shiny stuff. That junk is another dead giveaway. If they're real they should appreciate (in value) every year."

Espinola also advises budding collectors to be patient and to make condition the first priority. "Try to buy or to wait for the best condition ball," he says. "Only when a ball is very rare, then condition isn't as critical. Sometimes you just have to buy the ball because it's so rare no matter what the condition is. You just have to go for the 'blue-chips' like the mint gutty balls or patent golf balls."

Espinola hasn't amassed one of the world's most fabled collections of balls, books, clubs, and medals by himself. He's sought out golfiana's leading experts, and says, "Network with collectors. Determine who the experts are, and rely on their advice when buying. They have the knowledge, and knowledge is power in this game."

"Mr. Golf Ball" echoes those sentiments. "The average person might not know how rare a ball is, how to determine condition, so newcomers should work with knowl-edgeable people who know what's going on, especially when spending a lot of money," cautions dealer David Berkowitz, who along with acquiring such rare balls as a J. P. Cochrane Map of the World and an 1896 Henley Cross, collects ephemera, ball boxes, and wrappers ("the different colors, designs, this is where you really see beautiful artwork like the little devil associated with the zodiac"). "At auctions, shows, knowledge always triumphs over money."

Berkowitz calls himself "a condition person," and while the rarity of an item is im-portant to him, he recommends, "I've passed over quite a number of balls that weren't in top condition. Sometimes you don't have a choice since there's a rare ball for sale that's one of two or three existing. You get what you can. Show patience, but there are just some unusual designs that are so rare you go for it, and hope that you can upgrade in the future."

After pointing out the dangers of buying on eBay ("a place for bargain hunters where you don't get to touch and feel items, and sellers try to run things by you"), Berkowitz urges collectors to be cautious when buying feather balls ("Guys who've seen a lot of them can tell if they're real by looking at the stitching, and the aging of the paint"). Working with those experts at auctions (or in private sales) is an important first step for new collectors, yet Berkowitz says that attending auctions and "sticking your feet into the pond by yourself" is inevitable.

"Go to as many auctions and shows as possible to learn about the market, to see what's available, but you do have to jump in at some point, and can't expect dealers to share their entire philosophy. This might lead to [buying] mistakes, but you've got to pay your dues with either purchases or overpaying. When you get into this world don't be afraid to bring balls to the party."

Those "mistakes" are easy to make, for as author and 30-year collector Jeffrey Ellis says, "Choosing between condition and rarity is tough. A feather ball is not always in the greatest condition, but it will still draw good [buying] interest because of its point in history, and rarity. If you can spend $5,000 for a feather ball, wait for a good one. If you can spend $2,500 take what you can get. There's definitely a difference between collecting for fun, and for investment."

Ellis still recommends, "Don't buy poor condition if you can afford better. Some people are impatient, they think it's a great ball, but all too often it's common. I think in terms of attractiveness [for display balls]. Is the ball original? Repainting is going on big-time. People are trying to make balls look more original, prettier. A ball might be attractive to the untrained eye, but at an auction for example, find out about that item, ask the auctioneer about its history, who owned it. Get educated."

History is crucial to Ellis, who reasons, "If you're collecting for profit, what's the point? If all you see is the money you spent that's a bad buy. Yet if you see balls as a great part of the game's early history, the element that drove the introduction or development of different clubs, then it's a great buy. While medals and trophies reflect a golfer's accomplishments, and can be very valuable, only balls and clubs remain for our examination from the early days. They are the only core elements reflecting the game's early history."

The prices of golf collectibles fluctuate. The following values are estimates offered by various experts:
MM—Mullock & Madeley
WR—Will Roberto
JE—Jeffrey Ellis

- 8 x interesting patterns rubber core golf balls incl. Avon small Heavy, Spalding triangular pattern, Colonel 29, 3 x Nimble, Goblin, the BE-UP all used but with good markings, **$112–170, MM**

- Scarce "Silver King" golf ball box for 6 (corners split) c/w hinged lid to reveal original silver King Label to the inside plus 6 various used square mesh dimple golf balls, **$225, MM**

- 4 x square mesh gutty golf balls incl. Helsby, Daisy, Silvertown, and another pattern similar to the Silvertown, all with some strike marks but retaining good shape, **$375, MM**

- Scarce "B. I." hexagonal mesh pattern rubber core ball, circa 1910, **$150, MM**

- The Pneumatic (on equator) Goodyear, Bramble, circa 1905, 50% original paint, mud-stained, no iron marks, **$1,000–1,250, WR**

- Silvertown S, large letter, 90% original paint, no iron marks, ca. 1912, good condition, **$600–700, WR**

- Spalding Dot (blue), 98% paint, a few very faint age cracks, ca. 1900s, mint, **$700–800, WR**

- Martins Zodiac, unusual pattern of circles with center studs, **$350–375, WR**

- Spalding smooth gutta ball faintly marked, ca. 1900, unused, **$1,500–1,750, WR**

- Relsby National bramble, very good condition, **$350–400, WR**

- Eclipse composition or gutty-type ball, ca. 1877–1892, oxidized, **$800–1,000, WR**

- Allaway molded mesh gutty, some iron marks, **$900–1,000, WR**

- Henley molded mesh gutty ball, **$400–600, WR**

- Why-Not Bramble by Henley's Telegraph Co., London, very good condition, **$350–400, WR**

- Willie Park molded mesh gutty, ca. 1890s in mint condition, fine example of Open Champion's mesh ball, **$6,000–8,000, WR**

- D. Marshall feather ball, ca. 1830, faintly stamped "D. Marshall," patina and condition are excellent, **$12,000–15,000, WR**

- Wonder ball, unusual diamond pattern, scarce if not rare, **$1,000–1,500, WR**

- Star Challenger, ca. 1910s, good condition, **$500–700, WR**

- Silvertown gutta-percha, minor iron marks, ca. 1890s, excellent condition, **$400–500, WR**

- St. Mungo Patent Colonel Bramble painted red for winter play, mint in original partial wrapper, **$1,000–1,500, WR**

- Unnamed hand-hammered gutta-percha, ca. 1850s, painted red for winter play, **$2,000–3,000, WR**

- Zome One, pattern of raised center circles inside of larger recessed circles, mint, **$1,500–2000, WR**

- Eclipse Gutty, ca. 1877–92, **$300–500, WR**

- Haskell remade with minor paint loss, **$700–1,000, WR**

- Reach Eagle, mesh as new in box, **$250–350, WR**

- Silver King Red Dot, mesh as new in box, **$250–350, WR**

- Springvale Falcon wrapped Bramble, fine, **$350–500, WR**

- Unnamed feather ball in display case, ca. 1840, **$3,000–4,000, WR**

- Feather ball stamped Allan, **$12,000–13,000, WR**

- W. & J. Gourlay feather ball, ca. 1840, size 32, large feather ball with equatorial ring mark with original paint, **$10,000–12,000, WR**

- T. Alexander feather ball, ca. 1790–1800, oversize ball typical of late 1700s, fine condition, **$15,000–20,000, WR**

- Haskell in used condition, **$200–250, WR**

- Eighteen Dimple ball, all but three Hagen Fifty's in unopened sleeves of three, **$125–150, WR**

- Dunlop V tan muslin ball bag, scarce, **$300–500, WR**

- Cast iron gutty ball press, ca. 1860, very good condition, **$800–1,000, WR**

- Why-Not Bramble in excellent condition, **$200–300, WR**

- The New Eureka Gutta-percha, ca. 1890s, extremely uncommon survivor from the gutty era, slight scruffing, rare, **$1,500–2,000, WR**

- Golf Ball Box: The Silvertown, ca. 1890s, leatherette cover, silver letters, very good condition, rare, **$1,500–2,000, WR**

- Arch Colonel, good condition, **$150–250, WR**

- Army & Navy No. 1, **$300–500, WR**

- Line-cut gutty, **$175–200, WR**

- Here unusual pattern balls, Chemico Triumph, Star, Heavy Colonel, **$200–250, WR**

- Set of three dimple balls, Dunlop 29, Dunlop 162, Silver King, **$300–500, WR**

- Three Bramble balls, The Colonel, The Flag, Why-Not, **$200–250, WR**

- Silvertown gutty ca. 1880s with no iron strikes and some traces of original paint, **$350–400, WR**

- Martins Zodiac with unusual ring pattern, **$300–400, WR**

- Craig Park Special Flyer Bramble gutty, **$150–175, WR**

- Ten mesh pattern including 2 Zip, 2 Colonel 29s, Colonel 1.62, Ken-Wel Meteor, **$200–225, WR**

- Three Bramble Balls, Chemico Bob, Special Argus, Challenger, **$200–250, WR**

- T. Alexander, Willie Dunn, Tod Gourlay feather balls, rare, 1800–40, cost range, **$8,000–35,000, WR**

- T. Morris, Willie Park, Gourlay feather balls, scarce, **$5,000–25,000, WR**

- Smooth gutty balls, 1850–60, only in use for ten years, rare, **$3,000–5,000, WR**

- Dunn's Stars and Stripes, ca. 1890–1900, U.S. flag pattern, rare, **$10,000–25,000, WR**

- Henley's Union Jack, ca. 1870–80, British flag pattern, rare, **$3,000–8,000, WR**

- Faroid, ca. 1920s, concentric circle pattern, rare, **$3,000–8,000, WR**

- The Link, chain pattern rubber-core ball by Helsby, circa 1910, some discoloration, **$200, MM**

- 6 x various named bramble pattern golf balls incl. Martins Zodiac Propeller, 2 x Helsby, the Dunlop, Why-Not, and the Linx, all retaining good shape, some with paint marks and others with some strike marks, **$225, MM**

- Rare 1960 Open Championship Winner's signed golf ball. Autographed Silver King golf ball used by Ken Nagle in the final round of the Centenary Open Championship, together with 1960 Open Championship program plus a scarce official list of Open Winners and another program for the 1973 Open, **$1,120, MM**

- Rhythm square mesh golf ball in original green wrapper and label, **$140, MM**

- The Admiral black cross rubber-core golf ball with the most unusual pattern of indented crosses with raised center spot, and another chain link pattern golf ball as found, **$115, MM**

- Two rare golf ball shop counter display cartons for "Trump" and "Radar" golf balls, unused colorful foldout display cards, **$95, MM**

- Marathon lattice (mesh) pattern ball from the 1920s, mint, never used, **$135, JE**

- Special 27$^{1}/_{2}$, mesh pattern gutta-percha 1890s ball has a few strike marks, paint still good, **$265, JE**

- Baby Kite Bramble cover, rubber core, no cuts, name is deep and clear, **$215, JE**

- Silvertown, mesh gutta-percha 1890s ball has a fair number of strike marks, **$200, JE**

3 STICKING IT BIG-TIME
Golf Clubs

Four men, four different love affairs, all with a common thread. Along with being consummate sleuths, ever intoxicated by the hope of landing (and preserving) an important golf relic, they're charmed by the limited number of clubs that were made during the wood shaft era.

There's the acclaimed author and art lover Jeffery B. Ellis, who's written the most masterly tome ever written about antique golf clubs. An aspiring collector must take a look at his universally hailed *The Clubmaker's Art*, and the genius of "golfers' best friends," from pre-1880s longnoses, baffing spoons, and splice neck irons, to the mechanically ingenious patent clubs, comes vividly alive. More than just a chronicle of the golf club's spirited evolution, Ellis is an art historian, making collecting—and golf folklore—come beautifully into focus.

Equally enthralled with the pursuit of rare, wonderfully designed antiquities, Will Roberto has spent 36 years ferreting out prizes in Scotland and England. An obsessive researcher and "bird dogger" who has taken many gambles on damaged clubs (to secure potentially valuable clubs at lower prices), he has assembled a stunning array of clubs that date back to the 17th and 18th centuries.

Roberto is a purist, insisting on discovering the provenance of each club, tracing its origins, and subjecting every item under consideration to one crucial test: Does it come alive when he cradles it? Does it "sing" to him?

Then there's the "Patent Club" Man, the inveterate lover of everything golf with one of the most practiced eyes in the collecting world, Jim Espinola. His unusual—even bizarre—and vast assortment of highly ingenious clubs that never delivered golfers

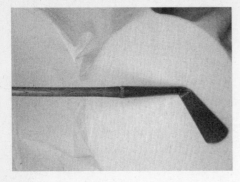

Blacksmith- or armorer-made iron ca. 1780.
Photo courtesy of Will Roberto.

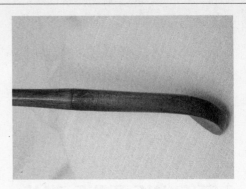

Blacksmith- or armorer-made circular track
iron ca. 1825 with owner's initials "J.T."
engraved on hosel. *Photo courtesy of Will
Roberto.*

to the Promised Land are stacked haphazardly in a room filled with remarkable old books, balls, and gleaming trophies. It barely matters that his water irons, antishank putters, rake irons, and "convex sole" brassies never lived up to their hype. Espinola is religiously devoted to his treasures, and his knowledge of "where all the bodies are buried" (as well as impossible-to-find rarities), is well-steeped in the art of investment-wise collecting.

Sparing no expense and continually willing to "pull the trigger" at auction sales in Great Britain, Dick Estey is another seasoned enthusiast. Besides adoring the pursuit of museum-quality clubs that invariably entails contacts with knowledgeable dealers and tracking down relatives of fabled players or clubmakers, he relishes the spirit of competition surrounding the acquisition of these historical art objects.

Once one of the world's greatest amateur senior golfers, collecting is Estey's way of staying competitive with some of the world's "biggest hitters."

♀ ♀ ♀

At the beginning of Jeff Ellis's well-illustrated "encyclopedia," which richly charts the history and work of golf's most legendary craftsmen, there's a preface that every aspiring collector should ponder. Quoting Garden G. Smith in the July 31, 1908, issue of *Golf Illustrated*, Ellis emphasizes his affection for these wooden shafted wonders by echoing, "There is nothing so fascinating to a golfer as his clubs. . . . Every one in his bag is a cherished friend . . . He knows them, as a shepherd his sheep. . . . Their shape, their color, their grips, even their dents and bruises, are engraved on his brain by the

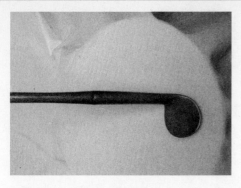

Blacksmith- or armorer-made track iron ca. 1825. *Photo courtesy of Will Roberto.*

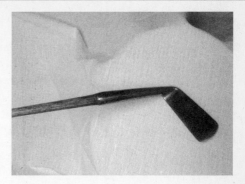

Blacksmith- or armorer-made lofting iron ca. 1840 from the Duke of Atholl (Blair castle) Collection. *Photo courtesy of Will Roberto.*

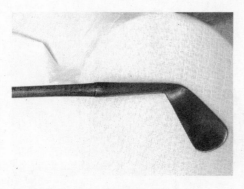

Blacksmith- or armorer-made general iron ca. 1820. *Photo courtesy of Will Roberto.*

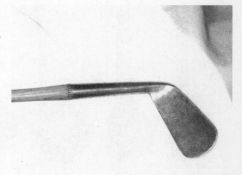

Blacksmith- or armorer-made bunker iron ca. 1840. *Photo courtesy of Will Roberto.*

burin of sweet and poignant memories. A man's clubs become almost members of his body . . ."

After 25 years of "journeying back into time" to amass what's arguably the most comprehensive collection of hand-crafted clubs from the late 1700s and early 1800s, Ellis has many of those "cherished friends." In *The Clubmaker's Art* and his equally informative *The Golf Club: 400 Years of the Good, the Beautiful & the Creative* he unmistakably details his passion for Willie Park Jr. short spoons, Old Tom Morris's fruitwood-headed play clubs, R. Forgan's forked hosel putters, and other illustrious treasures. But even more importantly for the new collector, he provides (along with

Blacksmith- or armorer-made rut iron ca. 1825 with lancewood shaft. *Photo courtesy of Will Roberto.*

Rut iron, unknown maker ca. 1860 made of brass. Shaft stamped "D.S." Club belonged to David Strath, a great player from St. Andrews in the mid-19th century. *Photo courtesy of Will Roberto.*

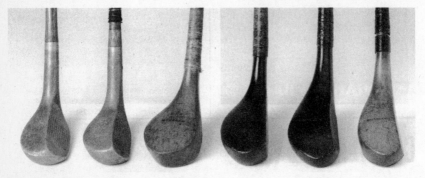

From L to R: Mills aluminum MSD# baffy; A Mills MSD2 mid spoon with shaft repair; R. Forgan blonde transitional bulger driver with original stamped shaft; R. Forgan putter ca. 1855 with large letter stamp; B. W. Day long spoon ca. 1880–5 in original condition; G. Forrester long nose brassie with original stamped shaft ca. 1885. *Photo courtesy of Old Tom Morris Golf, L.L.C.*

hundreds of enchanting photographs), an informative overview about how these clubs evolved, their pricing, and ways to outwit the scam artists.

"The key to collecting is developing an 'eye,' understanding quality, condition, and what is truly unique," stresses Ellis, who along with buying and selling clubs for clients, is a consultant to many auction houses, a renowned authenticator, and maintains the *www.antiques.com* Web site. "Developing that eye is never foolproof. The beginner has to make mistakes. Everyone will pay a certain tuition for their education. But you need that eye to know what you're looking at, to realize that something has a wonderful shape like noses (long, thin heads with slightly concave, or curved inward faces). Many people feel all of these long noses look alike. Yet they're all totally different, and it's up to the collector to learn how to spot differences (which markedly affect values)."

Ellis is clearly enthralled by long noses, insisting that "having that eye for beauty is what this pursuit is all about. You derive joy from beauty, from the knowledge that these clubs were sculptured by hand before there was electricity. While I also appreciate patent clubs (from the 1890s), nothing can equal the age, antiquity of (long nose) clubs that are 100, 200, 300 years old. So few remain, they're just fabulous (and pricey) stuff."

As Ellis insightfully points out, in that universe where "graceful and elegant clubs draw the most collector interest, everything else, such as age and condition, being equal," the names of certain clubmakers are particularly appreciated.

At the top of that distinguished list is Hugh Philp (1782–1850), the premier long nose clubmaker who's been likened to the Amati or the Stradivarius of golf.

Ellis says Philp "set the standard by which the work of other clubmakers is measured." And while approximately 190 of his clubs are known to exist (most are held by golfing organizations), "a Philp in nice condition rarely becomes available."

Yet the true collector never abandons all hope of discovering a prized rarity. As Ellis explains, finding a club from this official clubmaker to the Society of Golfers at St. Andrews "is not impossible."

"His absolutely beautiful stuff is the pinnacle, and not the hardest to find. Since he made a lot of clubs at a big golfing center (St. Andrews), you can find a nice Philp for $10,000, [with] the best examples for $20,000 and more. In either case, (just be wary of those Robert Forgan & Son putters that have the Philp stamp on them—these were made in tribute to him after his death), he was the master."

Reputed for his wonderful carvings, particularly those stamped with a distinctive "c" or a fabled thistle (only three exist), James McEwan was another maestro worthy of five-figure splurges.

"In the top three there's also John Dickson, who prior to 1850 made fabulous stuff on a par with Philp and McEwan," says Ellis, referring to one of Dickson's long and graceful baffing spoons (used to sky a ball over a hazard) that's "well worth owning if the condition is at all reasonable." "Willie Dunn, Tom Dunn, Alex Patrick also made fine stuff (though not as valuable as Philp and McEwan) and one of my real heavyweights is an A. D.—Andrew Dickson (1665-1753?)—a clubmaker in Leith. [Once a forecaddie to the Duke of York and a ballmaker,] Dickson is the first clubmaker to mark his clubs with his initials. He too was a master craftsman."

Blacksmith- or armorer-made iron putter ca. 1800–30. *Photo courtesy of Will Roberto.*

Blacksmith- or armorer-made heavy iron ca. 1780 with ash shaft. *Photo courtesy of Will Roberto.*

Prized Dicksons, McEwans, and Patricks feature "plenty of style" with exquisitely shaped fruitwood heads.

Yet awed by their rarity (of great size and weight, they were expensive to produce), Ellis is also particularly fond of his pre-1850 (typically unmarked) early irons made by blacksmiths.

Mainly used to lift feather balls out of deep-potted bunkers and high grass, these antiquities (most are owned by British or Scottish golf clubs) look extremely crude. And they were termed "reprehensible" or "destructive" for taking large divots.

But the workmanship in these early square-toed irons especially delights Ellis. An iron with a sharp blade crease, purportedly the "oldest known club in existence," sold for $1.25 million.

"While the square toe doesn't look all that special and demands a special aesthetic sensibility, this is the premier iron to own," says Ellis, the owner of 750 hickory-shafted clubs. "Each one is its own unique self. You have to know the characteristics of the early square toes (i.e., length and thickness of the hosel) that can be worth $200,000 to $300,000 to know for sure they're not fakes. And to appreciate them. I've known someone who felt one of these irons wasn't very attractive, didn't know what he was looking at, and failed to appreciate its significance. You need a prior understanding to avoid those kinds of mistakes."

To gain that knowledge, collectors must patiently examine and handle "a lot of stuff." Instead of initially attending auctions, where it's easy to lose control in emotionally-

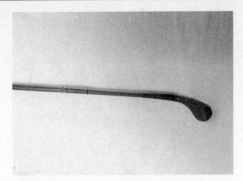

Long nose putter ca. 1780 by James McEwan. *Photo courtesy of Will Roberto.*

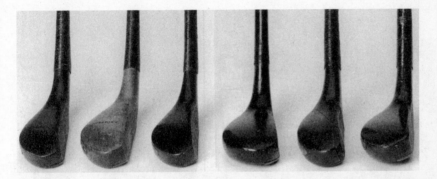

J. Anderson play club ca. 1870 with minor chip to toe; R. Simpson long nose driver with golden head ca. 1880s, replacement grip; G. Forrester play club in dark finish ca. 1870s with an elegant thin neck, possibly a lady's club, all original condition; H. Philp/R. Forgan putter with stamped shaft by R. Forgan ca. 1960 manufactured to commemorate Philp's death in 1856; M. Park playclub ca. 1875 with leather face repair, replaced shaft, grip. Faint "M."; T. Morris transitional putter with original stamped shaft and grip ca. 1895. *Photo courtesy of Old Tom Morris Golf, L.L.C.*

charged bidding contests, Ellis advises: "First understand who a Willie Dunn, James Wilson, or John Gray was [both made lofting irons], establish an intimacy with club-makers, know what's out there, and how things fit into golf history. I started my journey—and collecting is certainly an adventure—with a one-piece club, no neck joint, just solidly crafted out of one piece of wood. It had a tiny little head and I said 'wow, they played golf with these things.'"

Ellis subsequently "relived history" by acquiring clubs made or used by Tom Stewart (Bobby Jones favored his creations), David Strath (Young Tom Morris's close friend), and Willie Park (British Open winner in 1887 and 1889).

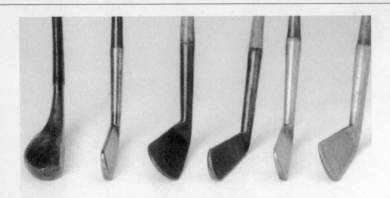

Thornwood head long nose putter ca. 1850 with bulging lead backweight; Blacksmith putting cleek ca. 1875, 4.5" hosel with greenheart shaft; lofter ca. 1860s, 4.5" hosel with T. Morris stamped shaft; blacksmith made cleek ca. 1870, 4.75" hosel with replacement grip and shaft; 1860s blacksmith cleek, 4.75" hosel; Anderson general iron with a very faint stamp marking, slightly concave, 4.5" hosel. *Photo courtesy of Old Tom Morris Golf, L.L.C.*

Maker unknown, early thornwood head putter with thin neck; J. Anderson child's putter made of beech, all original; J. Anderson playclub, scarce club from three-time Open champion; J. Beveridge putter; R. Forgan thornwood head putter in very good all original condition; R. Forgan thornwood head playclub with POW. *Photo courtesy of Old Tom Morris Golf, L.L.C.*

"If you don't know Robert Ferguson won the British Open three years in a row (1880–82), and worked the last 20 years of his life as a caddie, his club has much less value," argues Ellis. "Collecting clubs isn't Wall Street. To get into this you must enjoy, savor history. A club is only a good buy if you derive pleasure from it, if it spurs a sense of wonderment and enchantment. Even $20 clubs can have a beauty and speak to people, make an era come alive."

Maker unknown—ca. 1750 Baffy spoon stamped "J. Wilson," the owner's name. Maker from St. Andrew with same name 100 years later. James Wilson was a lawyer from Edinburgh, a friend of Thomas Jefferson, signator of the Declaration of Independence, U.S. Constitution and Justice on the first Supreme Court. Club found in Carolinas where he owned property at time of death. *Photo courtesy of Will Roberto.*

One of Ellis's favorite eras is that transitional period between long noses and steel shafted items—the mid-1870s to the 1930s—when Patent clubs epitomized the innovative and bizarre.

Whether they were golfers turned inventors, mad scientists, or just P. T. Barnum–styled charlatans, scores of clubmakers bucked tradition (and the ire of purists) to manufacture "wonder working" oddities.

Most of these unusual and highly ingenious clubs, such as the Higgs Deliverer, a rake iron with large downward teeth, and the Rudder Putter, shaped like a T with a six-inch bar, had a very short shelf life. Produced in very small numbers, these patent marked (or dated) mechanical marvels, as Ellis affirms, "are part of that neverending quest of many frustrated golfers today: to obtain a club that will make them better golfers than they are."

As we all know however, the best intentions are often a path to deviltry. The vast majority of these so-called "stroke savers" were a pure sham. They just didn't work.

"Forget their utility, there's a real passion behind the patent clubs," says Ellis. "Some golfer came up with the center-balanced, three cylinder duplex baffy, weighted alter-

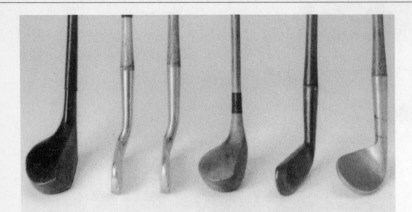

William Park Jr. splice neck brassie with stamped shaft; Spalding Kro-Flite Robt. T. Jones Jr. signature model Calamity Jane Putter; Spalding Kro-Flite Robt. T. Jones Jr. signature model Calamity Jane putter, very uncommon model; Tom Morris juvenile socket driver; an unusual D. Anderson putter; Scottish Makers Company smooth dish faced rut niblick, very uncommon mark. *Photo courtesy of Old Tom Morris Golf, L.L.C.*

Walter Hagen concave sand wedge; Spalding Gold Medal Seely Patent mashie with original stamped shaft; St. Andrew's Golf Co. anti-shank diamond-back niblick for Sprague of Boston; Schenectady putter imported by Harry J. Lee for Cupples Co. St. Louis, no bag nicking; R. Forgan anti-shank lofter with ball back weight; Jean Gassiat putter. *Photo courtesy of Old Tom Morris Golf, L.L.C.*

natively with layers of sand, cinders, and sawdust in the hope of finding a better way. Some of these inventors wanted to make money, others because they were golf nuts. In either case, there was a spirit of 'I can do better. That's why these clubs speak to me.' ([A]nd that should be a credo for all collectors; find clubs that fascinate and intrigue you.) There's real passion and emotion connected to these weird clubs."

They are also "jumping in value." A John K. Garner, triple-faced, billiard-styled putter (circa mid-1890s), a Holmac Rudder Putter with a T-frame (1920s), and other

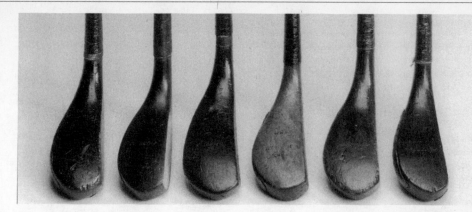

W. Park thornwood head putter, club in original used condition; Patrick beech head putter with greenheart shaft; Patrick thornwood head putter with greenheart shaft, with seldom seen St. Andrews bend; H. Philp golden thornwood head putter, good condition; J. Wilson thornwood head putter with greenheart shaft in original condition; J. Wilson thornwood head putter with green heart shaft, added lead weight to sole. *Photo courtesy of Old Tom Morris Golf, L.L.C.*

Long nose long spoon by Peter McEwan ca. 1800–20. *Photo courtesy of Will Roberto.*

highly unusual pieces are enjoying a remarkable spurt of interest. Most of these relics are now selling for $3,000 to $10,000, while the strangest looking (and arguably the most ambitious rarities) have soared to the $25,000 range.

Excited by the inventive spirit that spurred the development of Patent clubs, Ellis recently acquired a Hartford Aiming Putter (with a 12-inch rod that extends from the grip). Described as "the mother of all mechanical design," and featuring a hinged

R. Forgan long spoon with large letter stamp and POW; J. Jackson gold thornwood head putter with lead weight to sole; McEwan thornwood head spoon, featherball era club; McEwan thornwood head putter, original condition, T.

Morris large beech head putter, neck whipping replaced, refinished; T. Morris thornwood head playclub, dark stain. *Photo courtesy of Old Tom Morris Golf, L.L.C.*

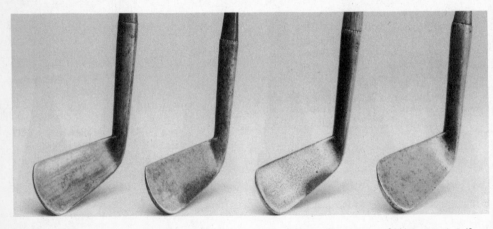

Lofting iron, blacksmith-made, dish face, featherball era club, mid 19th century; General iron, partial stamp on head and shaft, ca. 1875; Lofting iron, replaced shaft and grip; General iron, with concave face, period replacement shaft, ca. 1860s. *Photo courtesy of Old Tom Morris Golf, L.L.C.*

plate on the head that allows the club to tilt when lining up shots, this unique oddity is worth about $100,000.

"There are rare times when the collector has to put his foot to the floor and go for something that might not be seen again," advises Ellis. "One must be patient, and not get too emotionally involved, especially at auctions. Yet there are those times when you simply must take advantage of the opportunity, pay the price even if it's a high one, otherwise you might never see that club again."

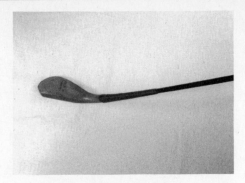

Long nose playclub by Alexander Munro
ca. 1835–40 with owners initials "W.M.K."
Photo courtesy of Will Roberto.

That "seizing of the moment" might even mean overpaying. As Ellis recalls, he paid $20,000 in 1992 for a W. G. Roy "President" Water Iron (an 1879 ring mashie that lifted balls out of water). "It was an unheard of sum at the time, but I didn't believe I'd ever find another water iron. Things do go crazy at auctions and that $20,000 is what it took."

That club is worth appreciably more today, but as Ellis reminds new collectors, "You can't win with every purchase. Everyone overpays. The average guy with a limited budget must simply buy stuff that gives him pleasure. So what if you overpay? If the club gives you enjoyment then it's worth it. Price isn't important. Even $20 steel shafted clubs, banjo putters from the 1990s, or putters with turquoise blue heads that remind you of big fin cars in the 1950s can be a delightful trip into golf history."

Discovering all sorts of bizarre, unique, and rare clubs is terrific fun. As Ellis says, "The hobby is a very fulfilling and fascinating journey." During this hunt, however, collectors must be aware that snakes and scam artists abound—that there's a thriving "industry of fakes." Feeling it's a "roll of the dice" to buy clubs on the Internet, Ellis warns collectors to be skeptical (about big-ticket items); to always ask themselves "What's wrong with this club?"

Understanding that collectors really want to believe they've discovered a treasure, he offers the following advice: (1) get photos of real clubs, examine the stamps on heads, and see if they match the proportions in the photographs, (2) when clubs are heavily rusted, "begin to wonder" if that was caused by different "aging" solutions, (3) inspect shafts, for fakers will burn or cook it to make the club look old, (4) "replica"

Longnose playclub with lemonwood shaft and holly head ca. 1865. This club belonged to Tom Morris Jr., 4-time winner of British Open. *Photo courtesy of Will Roberto.*

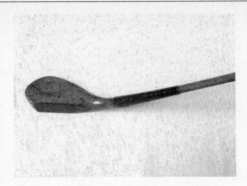

Long nose middle spoon by Tom Morris ca. 1865. Head made of thornwood. *Photo courtesy of Will Roberto.*

clubs are not objectionable, as long as they're marked as such, (5) "fraudulent clubs emit an air of uneasiness and discomfort," and (6) "good collectibles are not cheap."

Yet if novices are insistent on doing their own sleuthing, he cautions them: "If you're holding a club in your hand and don't know if it's real or not, keep walking. When too many things just don't feel right, when I don't know for sure, I just pass on the club. There's always another beautiful, captivating club. Life goes on."

♟ ♟ ♟

Some people have lots of money. They can go to auctions or work with dealers, and acquire the most vaunted clubs without any fear of overextending themselves financially.

Then there are the Will Robertos of the collecting world. These PhDs in golf club history snare rare prizes by relying on grit and guile, taking risks, and, above all, believing in the often-stated maxim that "knowledge is power."

"I don't have the financial resources of many top echelon collectors, so I must handle a lot of clubs, do my research, and get by in this pricey world with knowledge," says Roberto, standing in front of a dehumidified wall display that features nine horizontally-mounted (to prevent warping) antiquities. "I can't afford to compete with the Dick Esteys, legitimate millionaires. I must instead have information, know the clubmakers, keep up-to-date files complete with information about every known old club, and know where everything is. Jeff (Ellis) has more in-depth knowledge overall of the hobby. But I'm right up there when it comes to the earliest clubs, balls, and

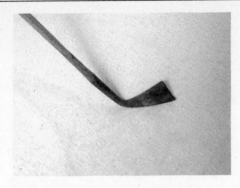

Blacksmith- or armorer-made spur toe iron
ca. 1600–50. *Photo courtesy of Will Roberto.*

Blacksmith- or armorer-made Child's heavy
square toe iron ca. 1750–80. *Photo courtesy
of Will Roberto.*

books." The fruits of his painstaking door-to-door searches in the British Isles, incessant cataloguing of auction sales, and networking with trustworthy dealers glorify his black barn wood walls (to give the fruitwood-headed clubs an attractive contrast) and illuminated cases.

Admiring an irregularly shaped clubhead with a rounded toe, an iron dating back to the 1820s–30s, Roberto notes, "I got this piece inexpensively because most people didn't realize it was as early as it was. You always have to be ready to step into a void when sure about a club's origins."

Enjoying his outmaneuvering competition at auctions and at other venues, Roberto continues, "You simply have to know your clubs before buying anything, who made them, how they were used and when. This club here [perched above the round toe iron] comes from the Phillip Mackenzie Ross [a golf architect] collection. People passed on this club at an auction. Not doing their homework, they thought it was a big oval-toed bunker item. But the patina is very even throughout. I was able to get it at a great price because unlike my auction rivals, I knew it's not a club where the toe was cut off. It's a blacksmith-made square toe iron that's worth $20,000 to $30,000."

Equally enthusiastic about early irons that grace his Wall of Fame, Roberto couples descriptions of every conquest with additional collecting tips.

"That spur toe iron on top is a first-generation iron with a rounded sweep into the hosel [early 17th century]. This club is very rare but many big-name collectors passed on it. Why? Maybe because the hosel was missing, it was offered at a fairly low price. I've taken a chance on a few damaged items. I felt I couldn't get hurt at the price I

Blacksmith- or armorer-made short face square toe iron ca. 1800–20. *Photo courtesy of Will Roberto.*

Blacksmith- or armorer-made track iron ca. 1780–90. *Photo courtesy of Will Roberto.*

paid, and you always have to keep that in mind. I was pretty sure I could turn around and quadruple my money. While it's not a perfect example of a blacksmith- or armorer-made club, I got this iron [that was used to cut through the gorse] at a fraction of what it's worth, $50,000."

Defying the ruling wisdom that collectible clubs must be in pristine condition, Roberto also appreciates his "impossible-to-find" blacksmith-made square toe iron (1700–50). "It's been reshafted, and I put the whipping on the club. Many people passed on it because it wasn't mint, but I'm buying the head, not the shaft. When you find an old club like this one you must go for it [worth about $50,000]." Casually moving away from an assortment of other crude-looking irons that are valued between $5,000 and $150,000 (that one is a very heavy "rut iron" with a short head), Roberto again underscores the importance of doing historical research.

"This long nose club could be the earliest [James] McEwan known to exist [circa 1780s] with no line under the 'c' on the club head—the first stamp McEwan used lacked an underlined 'c.' Because I did my homework (handling clubs in small Great Britain villages, visiting various golf society members, and keeping photographic records), I'm able to verify things no one else can. New collectors can follow that same formula. I paid $20,000 for this club, and it's worth over $100,000, even if it looked like someone's dog chewed on it."

Roberto owns dozens of other highly desirable clubs, including a $10,000 putter from John Patrick (1850s), one of two clubs stamped Strath and Beveridge (1871), and one with incredible provenance: a $40,000 to $50,000 putter made by Hugh Philp in the 1830s that was used by Willie Dunn against Willie Park.

Blacksmith- or armorer-made track iron
ca. 1800. *Photo courtesy of Will Roberto.*

But as Roberto shows off his 1850s brass driver made by Robert Forgan and a $1,000 brass spoon crafted by Tom Morris's brother John, he pays special attention to the item that's arguably his best "lightning in a bottle" purchase.

"Simply because someone didn't know what they had, I was able to get this blacksmith-made iron (1800–30) that wasn't too beautiful a piece. It was as rusted and corroded as anything I've ever seen, and I only paid $160 for it. The seller didn't have anything to compare it to, and there was no name on it. Plus it looked extremely shabby. But I knew what it was because of the size of the hosel (5³/₄ inches), the sweep of the neck. Once you look at a lot of clubs you can spot treasures like this that's worth over $20,000."

Holding one of his many loose-leaf binders that's used to store information about clubs (including the sales records of thousands of items to keep him abreast of current market trends), Roberto goes on to talk about such legendary clubmakers as Old Tom Morris, James Anderson rut or track irons (1850–75), a rare $3,000 to $5,000 iron produced by St. Andrews's Robert Wilson, a $3,000 rut iron made by Willie Park Sr., and a thornwood baffing spoon (valued around $20,000) with a small (John) Jackson stamp on the head.

Unable to toss around money like the heavyweight collectors, Roberto has acquired most of these clubs with his own brand of cunning and auction house gamesmanship. But collecting also brings its disappointments. No one always wins at this high-priced game. Convinced a rare prize is at hand, many collectors are all too willing to lose sight of reality (and their budgets which must be fixed before attending auctions). It's during these high-adrenaline sales duels that collectors make mistakes.

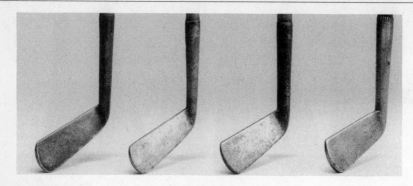

Cleek, slight concave face, replaced grip, 5″ hosel, good condition; Cleek, replaced grip, ca. 1880s; Cleek, blacksmith-made ca. 1865; Cleek, blacksmith-made, hickory shaft with whipping repairs, thick hosel with deep nicking, mid-19th c. *Photo courtesy of Old Tom Morris Golf, L.L.C.*

"No collector should feel this hobby is a free ride towards profits without any bumps in the road," cautions Roberto, soon referring to an Old Tom Morris stamped club that was acquired after a "bidding war" with the Japanese. "At the height of the market (early 1990s), I didn't want to let this go. I grossly overpaid ($13,000), for I just lost it at an auction. I didn't keep my cool, I just bid and bid. This club is only worth about $2,500 today. Collectors must know you don't always make a score. You will take some losses."

But still believing there are true bargains to be found—if collectors properly educate themselves—Roberto more cheerfully adds, "It's not the possession that's so critical, it's outtrumping someone, winning because of knowledge. Confirming things through research, tracing ownership, discovering who originally made the club, these are the things I used to need Jeff Ellis for. He was very good but I learned I could do it by myself when I started to go to Scotland, and get a real feel for the richness of the game. I got connected with the material, and ever since then I got more and more knowledgeable. That's the true satisfaction of collecting, knowing that knowledge can negate all the money in the world."

Along with his unvarnished passion for provocative Patent clubs, accomplished ball and book collector Jim Espinola is also worried that "a dark side is steadily creeping into the market."

"It's so easy to switch the components of clubs," says this fervent enthusiast, admitting that collecting true rarities can be as tricky as an Augusta National dogleg.

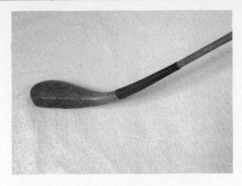

Bowmaker's long nose playclub ca. 1750.
Photo courtesy of Will Roberto.

"To really know what you're buying, you've got to serve a sort of apprenticeship, where you actually get dirt on your hands from the old suede grips, which shred with age. You can't just depend on books and all the price guides which have their own agendas. Instead you have to fondle the stuff, smell it, and get dust on your hands. Only then will you be able to distinguish fakes from real old clubs."

Taking the pains to develop an internationally renowned "eye"—a veritable sixth sense for discovering "the really creative stuff"—Espinola is surrounded by the weirdest—and most valuable—patent clubs in his New England home. Unceremoniously stuffing them into a wooden bin, stocked with "cheapies" and a 1715 blacksmith iron worth about $100,000, he lovingly reaches for a Holmac T-frame Rudder Putter with a "sighting bar," or aiming device, and says, "I love strange, the oddest pieces I can find."

That love affair seems to give this consummate and frenetic collector boundless joy.

Grabbing another one of his treasured marvels, he raves, "This is just wonderful, the first Allan Lard 'Whistler' (a two-piece perforated steel shaft iron valued at $15,000 to $20,000) in absolutely beautiful mint condition (patented in 1914, this club is described by Jeffery Ellis as "being made from four inverted U-shaped lengthwise ribs attached to a small, tubular steel core"). I feel going after mint condition clubs is the only and most profitable way to collect."

Underscoring that strategic (and costly) approach, Espinola next displays a Willie Dunn Jr. Triple Face club with an adjustable perforated hosel. Explaining that the angle of the face can be changed to convert this oddity into a putter, 3-wood, 4-wood,

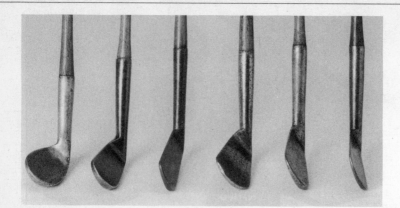

Robert Condie rut niblick with fern mark and stamped Slazenger shaft ca. 1890s; Willie Park, Jr. mashie ca. 1890s; blacksmith cleek ca. 1850, 5.1" hosel with deep saw tooth nicking; blacksmith bunker iron ca. 1850; blacksmith general iron ca. 1850 with period replaced shaft; blacksmith general iron ca. 1850, with nice patina. *Photo courtesy of Old Tom Morris Golf, L.L.C.*

W. Park Iron, with complete oval Park stamp, seldom seen; Rut Iron, blacksmith-made, circular head, all original, early 19th century; Square toe child's iron, mid-19th century or earlier; General or Bunker iron, blacksmith made, fine, ca. 1860. *Photo courtesy of Old Tom Morris Golf, L.L.C.*

and 7-iron, he exclaims, "There are only two of these known to exist. If you're going to collect forget the ordinary, be serious, and only go after the great stuff that gives you a sense of having uncovered true gems."

Suddenly moving into a whole different time period, this ardent, big-time money player turns into the golf historian, saying, "This is a blacksmith-made rut iron from 1840. It's pretty freaking heavy. Blacksmiths took pride in their work, you can't even see the seams; they're very shallow. The wood is just in impeccable condition, plus the face is just beautiful, almost pristine. You don't see too many blacksmith-made clubs, and if you do, don't hesitate. Buy them."

But Espinola soon returns to his favored Patent clubs, first holding a 1914 Jack White "Civic" Putter (the head is thoroughly punched with holes) that "never worked" (even though it was said to be effective because "the air could flow through it"). This club, Espinola insists, could be relatively easy to find (valued at $3,000 to $5,000), but far more rare is his Jack White "Deadun" backspin water iron (named for the 1904 British Open champ) with a perforated or drilled face.

In his million-dollar assortment of clubs that were "absolute mechanical busts," never delivering on their stated promises, Espinola has several double and single "water-fall" irons (or deeply grooved backspin irons), roller putters, convex-faced irons, and negative loft or concave-faced putters. Anything that's weird or remarkably bizarre has seemingly would up in his home. Clubs worth only $30 to $100, like a 1930s Wright & Ditson putter, are also crammed into his box of goodies. In that sense Espinola is a real democrat.

But reemphasizing his true aristocratic tastes, a fixation on rarities that has him constantly searching the international market for "Holy Grails," Espinola dispenses one final dose of wisdom.

"This club (an Old Tom Morris long-nosed driver from 1870) is totally original, including the grip, and that's the essence of collecting, finding the most exciting mint pieces that reflect a lot of history. Nothing I have has been refinished. My Old Tom Morris approach putter (used from 40 yards off the green) is also all-original and significant. You don't typically see any of this stuff on the Internet or in the open market—it's usually traded between private parties. Collectors who really want to have a meaningful collection must really try to buy the rarest stuff possible, even if that means only buying one or very few items each year. All the rest of that ordinary stuff just makes pretty wall hangings."

♀ ♀ ♀

Stirred by the testosterone-fueled action at auctions, Dick Estey regularly finds himself eyeing a long-sought golf club and "getting sweaty palms."

"My arms are getting wet, I'm starting to get fidgety, and all of a sudden I'm bidding, even if it's against guys with all the money in the world," confesses Estey, who has often "put pedal to the metal" to acquire one of the greatest long nose collections on the planet. "Beginners should be patient. They shouldn't get caught up in the action and forget their budgets. But once you have some knowledge, you have to go for things that may never come up again in your lifetime. Otherwise you've missed out on that one opportunity. They're gone."

Thrilled by the competition at these high-spirited sales, Estey has substituted the auction circuit for the senior amateur golf tour that once saw him jousting against the world's best. Today the collecting of balls, clubs, and ceramics is his way of probing history, and he's especially proud of two $300,000-plus acquisitions.

"I really stepped it up to buy a Simon Cossar long nose, for I really wanted to have the only Cossar in the world that's in private hands," insists Estey. "I also have a long nose crafted by Andrew Dickson, and that too is the only one in the world. It cost me $350,000 and that's okay. Those prices are worth it to me because I enjoy the clubs, and that should be a measuring stick for everyone who collects. I might even have overpaid for some items. You don't always win. Yet if you think you'll enjoy the item, go for it. Even if you have to overcome getting very sweaty."

The prices of golf collectibles fluctuate. The following values are estimates offered by various experts:
MM—Mullock & Madeley
WR—Will Roberto
JE—Jeffery Ellis
GLP—Golf Links to the Past

- An older Carrick ca. 1865, with the larger "Carrick" stamp and "X" trademark sheepskin grip with slight repair, in *The Clubmaker's Art,* p. 109, **$2,000, JE**

- This is the actual Willie Park Jr. Patent lofter pictured in *The Clubmaker's Art* pp. 239–40. Club has concave face, shaft stamp, and sheepskin grip. Patented 1889. Your chance to own the first iron ever patented and, of those, the one best documented! **$2,000, JE**

- Tom Morris long nose golden beechwood driver, 1880 stamped to the head, Slazenger & Sons, New York, original shaft, stunning club, 44$^{1}/_{2}$", **$2,100–2,200, MM**

- R. Forgan late long nose scare neck putter in stained persimmon, showing crisscross cut face lines, horn sole insert, **$500–600, MM**

- "The Bogee" slim alloy-headed putter featuring rectangular hosel (one faint crack), **$90–110, MM**

- Early left-hand metal curved face chole (a game played in Flanders) club fitted with sturdy ash shaft, ca. 1900, **$1,300–1,500, MM**

- Patent Perwit round-faced hollow backed steel head blade putter showing Mitre brand cleek mark, **$800–900, MM**

- Smith's Pat wing-toed anti-shank mashie with the Stag cleek mark of the St. Andrews Golf Co. fitted with good full-length leather grip but some pitting, **$60–70, MM**

- Early Forgan long nose putter in dark-stained beechwood, oversized name to the crown with elegant flowing lines, 1865, **$2,500–2,800, MM**

- R. Forgan transitional long nose bulged face driver in golden beechwood leather face insert, **$550–700, MM**

- Early Anderson Anstruther metal blade putter with 4.5" hosel and McEwan stamped to the original hickory shaft measuring 36" overall and fitted with a modern replacement hide grip, ca. 1895, **$90–110, MM**

- Topspin blade metal putter with heavy wide top flange bringing the centre of gravity above the ball to create the effect of topspin, head stamped with the Bear cleek mark and J. Stoker Darlington, shaft fitted with original rubberized grip, **$90, MM**

- A. H. Scott patented forked spliced driver in light stained holly two grain cracks in head, **$115–140, MM**

- Superb Forgan offset flanged blade putter in stainless steel and stamped "Forgan St. Andrews Gold Medal—Flanged Golf" together with Forgan shaft stamp below the replaced modern grip, **$80–90, MM**

- A very shallow rectangular metal blade putter with oval hosel and shaft, the head stamped Jas. Sherlock Hunstanton showing his circular Oxford cleek mark, original shaft stamped "Sherlock Selected" below the Whitcombe grip, **$125–150, MM**

- Bobby Jones's golf clubs, forged hickory-shafted clubs, a complete reproduction of the clubs Bobby Jones actually carried during his remarkable 1930 "Grand Slam." Handcrafted by Heritage Golf in St. Andrews, Scotland, each set of fourteen clubs is fully playable, individually numbered and accompanied by a letter of authenticity. Each set is one of only 1,930 available. **$3,650, GLP**

- George Nicoll Clubs and Bag, designed by Scottish clubmaker George Nicoll of Leven, fully playable reproductions. Each hickory-shafted club is handmade just like the original 1920s Nicoll clubs. This set of Gems (one of Nicoll's most popular brands) includes a brassie (driver), five irons, and a putter all in a leather and canvas bag, **$1,500, GLP**

- J. Anderson's child's putter, made of beech, all original, rare to find children's clubs, **$2,500–3,000, WR**

- Spur toe iron, ca. 1650–1750, very rare, about 8 known, **$265,000, WR**

- Square toe iron, ca. 1680–1820, 30 to 40 known, on first generation top edge of hosel rounds into hosel, on 2nd generation top edge has crease line where top edge meets hosel, **$35,000 to 150,000, WR**

- Round Toe, ca. 1750, rare, **$15,000 to 30,000, WR**

- Oval Bunker iron, ca. 1790–1830, rare, **$15,000–35,000, WR**

- Pre-1800 unmarked wood, very rare, cost range **$100,000–350,000, WR**

- McEwan wood with thistle, 1780–1820, very rare, **$200,000 plus, WR**

- McEwan wood without thistle, various stamps, 1790–1820, rare, **$30,000 plus, WR**

- Woods from A. Munro, R. Kirk, T. Morris, and other early clubmakers, 1830–50, rare, **$10,000, WR**

- Woods from T. Morris, R. Forgan, A. Patrick, Willie Park Sr., Willie Park Jr., Willie Dunn, J. Dunn, J. Jackson, H. Philp, and other named makers, 1850–80, **$2,500–50,000, WR**

- Woods from T. Dunn, L. Sandison, R. Simpson, Forgan, Willie Park Sr., 1860–90, **$1,000–5,000, WR**

- J. Beveridge putter, some expert restoration, scarce, **$750–1,250, WR**

- R. Forgan thornwood head putter, large letter stamp in very good all-original condition, stamp used 1856–63, fewer than 30 clubs exist with this stamp, **$5,000–6,000, WR**

- R. Forgan long spoon with large letter stamp, elegantly shaped club is missing a chip, ca. 1863–65, **$4,000–5,000, WR**

- J. Jackson golden thornwood head putter with lead weight to sole, ca. 1870, scarce, **$8,000–10,000, WR**

- McEwan thornwood head spoon, feather ball-era club, near mint, **$3,000–5,000, WR**

- McEwan thornwood head putter, original condition with slight crack to head, ca. 1850, **$800–1,000, WR**

- T. Morris large beech head putter, neck whipping replaced, refinished, **$1,000–1,200 WR**

- T. Morris thornwood head playclub, dark stain, ca. 1867 (date when Morris started using darker stain), **$10,000–13,000, WR**

- W. Park thornwood head putter original condition, ca. 1880s, scarce, **$2,500–3,500 WR**

- A. Patrick beech head putter, original condition, ca. 1880s, **$2,000–2,500 WR**

- A. Patrick thornwood head putter with the seldom seen St. Andrews bend, added lead weight to sole, ca. 1870, in original condition, **$3,000–4,000, WR**

- H. Philp golden thornwood head putter, good condition, **$5,000–6,000, WR**

- J. Wilson thornwood head putter, original condition, **$3,500–4,500, WR**

- Lofting iron, blacksmith-made, dish face, feather ball era, mid-19th century, **$1,500–2,000, WR**

- General iron, concave face, 1860s, **$1,500–2,000, WR**

- Willie Park Patent Driving Cleek, ca. 1900, Park's punch mark under name, **$350–500, WR**

- Brown's Slotted Water Iron, ca. 1903 with four oval slots, musselback, in good condition, rare, **$2,500–3,000, WR**

- Sharpe's Patent dual face mashie, patented by Thomas Sharpe in 1906, only iron known to cataloguer bearing the Sharpe Patent stamp, **$1,500–2,500, WR**

- Simplex club, ca. 1900, patented by Francis Brewster, good condition, **$2,000–3,000, WR**

- Cochrane's super mammoth putter made by J. P. Cochrane, face measures $2^{3}/_{8}''$ × $5^{3}/_{8}''$ with a 6" hosel, putter is the most rare of the mammoth clubs, **$3,000–5,000, WR**

- Super Giant Joe Kirkwood Waffle Iron by A. G. Spalding, face measures $5 \times 5^{1}/_{2}''$, extraordinarily heavy, last such club sold at auction went for **$13,000,** wood shaft iron with a head larger than this one was made expressly for trick shot artist Joe Kirkwood, **$5,000–10,000, WR**

- Goodrich All-One uncommon patent adjustable iron, ca. 1914, **$2,000–2,500 WR**

- Spalding Cran Cleek, **$400–500, WR**

- A. G. Spalding and Bros. oversize center shafted mallet putter with brass face and sole, lead back weight, **$400–500, WR**

- Walter Hagen concave sand wedge, **$250–300 WR**

- Spalding waterfall iron, ca. 1920, **$350–450, WR**

- Walter Travis wood mallet putter, **$400–500, WR**

- Unusual niblick with diamond back and pointed toe, patent date 1922, clean original condition, **$250–300, WR**

- Kroydon spade mashie with mini-waffle pattern, **$75–100, WR**

- Cardinal Giant Niblick by H & B, **$800–1,200, WR**

- Ogilvie Patent Niblick, **$150–250, WR**

- Mills Aluminum Fairway Club, **$200–250, WR**

- Forgan aluminum splice neck putter, **$350–400, WR**

- Willie Park Jr. Rut Iron, late 1880s, **$1,000–1,250, WR**

- Blacksmith-made lofting iron, mid-19th century, **$1,250–1,500, WR**

- Blacksmith-made general iron, mid-19th century, **$1,000–1,500, WR**

- Three early unnamed smooth face irons, **$300–500, WR**

- J. Gray iron restored by L. Auchterlonie, **$300–500, WR**

- Three Willie Park smooth face irons, two with shaft stamped "W. Park," the other with owner's initials, **$300–500, WR**

- R. Forgan transitional long nose play club with Prince of Wales plume stamp and stamped shaft, ca. 1890, ebony finish, very good condition, **$1,200–1,500, WR**

- J. Beveridge Shinnecock Hills splice neck driver, ca. 1890s, clear stamp, this well-known clubmaker partnered with David Strath in 1871, **$900–1,200, WR**

- Willie Park iron complete oval Park stamp, seldom seen, **$250–300, WR**

- Rut iron, blacksmith-made, circular head, nicking, 5$^{1}/_{2}$" hosel, all original, only a handful of these small circular head rut irons ever appear, early 19th century, **$8,000–10,000, WR**

- General or bunker Iron, blacksmith made, concave face, 5$^{1}/_{4}$" hosel, heavy stout shaft, fine, ca. 1860, **$3,000–4,000, WR**

- Cleek, ca. 1880s iron, slight concave face, 5" hosel, good condition, **$1,500–2,500, WR**

- Cleek, blacksmith-made, 4$^{3}/_{4}$" hosel, hickory shaft, ca. 1865, **$1,500–2,000, WR**

- W. Gibson & Co. rut niblick, Edinburgh, stamped "A&NC and Holdfast," dot punch face, hickory shaft, **$300–400, WR**

- Hagen concave sand wedge, **$400–600, WR**

- J. & D. Clark beech driver, hickory shaft, replaced grip, **$350–500, WR**

- Slazenger one-piece wood, shaft and head stamped, replaced grip, ca. 1895, **$2,000–2,500, WR**

- Wry neck-style putter, partial stamp "Willie N," letter of provenance, **$250–500, WR**

- Mac & Mac pointed back putter, shaft begins and terminates in square form, ca. 1920, letter of provenance, **$700–1,000, WR**

- McEwan brass putter, hosel with engraved ring, bold stamp, **$150–200, WR**

- Willie Park Jr. putter, lancewood shaft with stymie notch, excellent original condition, **$300–500, WR**

- Imperial Golf Co. aluminum cylinder putter, added lead weight, rare, **$1,000–1,500, WR**

- R. Ferguson putter, 1885, dark-stained beechwood head, **$1,000–1,500, WR**

- R. Forgan thornwood play club, ca. 1865 in unused condition, **$4,000–6,000, WR**

- McEwan thornwood head spoon, 1860 with dark finish, in unused condition, **$3,500–4,500, WR**

- Willie Park Sr. long nose play club, 1875, blonde finish, excellent stamp, very good, original condition, **$6,000–8,000, WR**

- Mungo Park play club, 1875, faint maker stamp, scarce if not rare, **$2,500–3,500, WR**

- Lofter, 1875, letter of provenance, **$400–600, WR**

- David McEwan putter by Condie, with "rose" cleek mark stamp, period reshaft, ca. 1895, **$200–300, WR**

- Willie Park Jr. brass putter, oval maker's stamp, shaft stamped, original condition, **$250–300, WR**

- Hendry & Bishop Giant Niblick, unusual and very scarce vintage club enabled escape from the deepest rough. This wooden-shafted club bears the famous maker's bishop's hat cleek mark. Its most dramatic feature is an extraordinarily large, 4^1/$_2$" long clubhead with distinctive bordered hyphen face scoring. Excellent to mint condition, with evidence of light, appropriate use. **$2,850, GLP**

- Walter Hagen sand iron with concave face, oversized flange, patented in 1928. The U.S.G.A. outlawed the club in 1931, but not before Bobby Jones carried and used the club during his 1930 Open Championship victory at Hoylake en route to capturing golf's Grand Slam, **$1,500, GLP**

- James Braid autograph "The Giant Niblick" with Wm. Gibson Kinghorn star mark and fitted with superb stiff shaft and original hide grip, **$180–190, MM**

- Scarce Slazenger deep face scare neck bulger brassie (dark-stained head), full brass sole plate and a very unusual over-length shaft measuring 44^1/$_2$" and stamped Slazenger below the original hide grip with thick underlisting, ca. 1895. Note the top 3" of the hide grip is missing, **$350–375, MM**

- Unusual brassie stamped "The A. J. Hildreth Co. Inc. Bridgeport Conn." In brown man-made material similar to vulcanite showing a small rear lead back weight with leather grip (shortened to 37^1/$_2$"). This club was produced to be indestructible and usable in all kinds of weather, **$80–95, MM**

- Bussey & Co. Pat. Steel Socket brass-headed putter with full length original Bussey Pat. stitched leather handle. A very collectible and much sought-after putter, **$350–375, MM**

- Scarce Wm. Park Musselburgh, famous Pat. compressed scare neck driver in hickory with original maker's shaft stamp and full-length hide grip. Note the head has had minor repair, **$350–375, MM**

- Rare full matching set of 10 x Patent "Mieville Lancier" Tsingli reed and lancewood dowel center clubs, with maker's stamp Bishop and Hendry Edinburgh, which comprises seven irons (Nos. 2–8), a No. 9 bent-neck putter, all with stainless steel polished heads, unusual 5^1/$_2$" hosels and stamped with the Pat. No. 436,625, together with two matching persimmon socket head woods (Nos. 2–3) both stamped to the head with the Bishop and Hendry Edinburgh straight line logo, **$1,700–1,850, MM**

- J. Sherlock persimmon socket head "Wooden Cleek" club. The dark-stained head has a similar loft to a 5-wood (20 degrees being the forerunner of today's modern "rescue club"), **$325, MM**

- James Braid stamped socket head spoon in dark-stained persimmon, fitted with period leather grip and underpadded for the left hand with triangular brass sole plate. It's more unusual to find a James Braid stamped wood ca. 1910, **$140, MM**

- Tom Morris long nose scare neck dark-stained beechwood grassed driver with curved face, 1875, shaft has been refitted, scarce, **$1,700–1,865, MM**

- Patent "one-piece" brassie in hickory wood with fiber face insert, retained by five plugs and filled with full aluminum sole plate, elegant slim head with sweeping high crown, **$800–930, MM**

- Late 19th-century rut iron with 5" hosel, sturdy stiff shaft and fitted with full-length hide grip, very elegant club, **$270–285, MM**

- Jack White autograph "palakona steel center split cane shaft" socket head spoon in very good condition and showing the famous Hardy Bros. Alnwick trademark (made famous by their split-cane fishing rods) below the full length leather grip, **$280, MM**

- Ben Sayers straight-faced, socket head driver in stained persimmon showing a clear wide center line with the maker's stamp mark and fitted with full-length leather grip and is in superb overall condition. Club carries the maker's X stamp mark to the sole indicating an extra stiff shaft, **$100–115, MM**

- Rare and very unusual Pat. Paisley mirror-site putter, Detroit showing stock No. 208. This aluminum putter has two mirrored sight lines in order to make the patent work. The True Temper Step-Down steel shaft retains the original cork and rubber grip and cap. A similar putter sold at Mullock Madeley online auction April 2003 and realized **$830, MM**

- F. H. Ayres "Championship Model–Super Brassie" socket head in stained persimmon fitted with half brass sole plate and later full-length Kinghorn Tacky leather grip. Note the super brassie refers to a stronger loft than a normal brassie making it almost a driver, **$75, MM**

- "The Pitcher" by Wm. Gibson Kinghorn showing a shallow wide sole head with straight top line, and fitted with original full-length leather grip, **$70, MM**

- Carrick cleek with slight concave face, 4^1/$_2$" hosel with heavy knurling, and partial Carrick cross stamp mark, club reshafted, ca. 1875, **$600–650, MM**

- Rare Payne Stewart–signed club head No. 1 iron autographed to face in felt tip pen and mounted in a picture display case fitted with special "Flexiglass." Official P.G.A. Tour mounted display, **$1,700–1,875, MM**

- Rare curved spliced neck driver in dark stain persimmon stamped to the head "A. N. Weir - Maker - Turnberry" and Pat. Reg No. 497,486 and fitted with a period leather grip. Note Alex Weir produced this club to bring the hands in line with the clubface in the hope of producing a straighter shot. **$700–750, MM**

- Unnamed Carruthers lofting iron with short hosel, original full-length hide grip, ca. 1890, **$100, MM**

- James Braid autograph sharp square cut off toe design niblick by Wm. Gibson for E. W. Taylor Whitley Bay and showing cross lines and dot face markings, ca. 1906. Fine club from this multiple Open Champion winner, **$90, MM**

- Range Finder "Bunny" compact D-shaped mallet head putter with an extravagant bowed shaft bearing the maker's stamp mark and fitted with a full-length leather grip. Note it shows the Bunny trademark but not the usual brass thro' insert to head, **$80–90, MM**

- Splice neck wood by R. Simpson with leather face insert stamped R. Forgan & Son, **$125–175, WR**

- William Park Jr. splice neck brassie with stamped shaft, **$400–500, WR**

- Spalding Kro-Flite Robert T. Jones signature model Calamity Jane putter, **$300–400, WR**

- Four woods; a brassie, Auchterlonie putter, and Winchester and R. Simpson drivers, **$300–400, WR**

- Playable set of five pre-1900 smooth face irons: a rut iron, a driving iron by Spalding, two Spalding irons, and a rut niblick, **$800–1,000, WR**

- D. Anderson putter, deeply cross-hatched face excepting a smooth toe rounded toward the rear, original stamped shaft, **$450–500, WR**

- Spalding special brass putter, **$40–50, WR**

- The Spalding niblick with smooth dished face, light nicks at sole, **$350–400, WR**

- Wright & Ditson niblick with dished smooth face, **$350–400, WR**

- Blacksmith-made cleek ca. 1870, 4³/₄" inch hosel with replacement grip, **$500–700, WR**

- An 1860s blacksmith cleek, 4³/₄" inch hosel, **$1,000–1,250, WR**

- Anderson general iron with a very faint stamp marking, slightly concave, **$250–300, WR**

- Willie Park Jr. mashie ca. 1890s, **$200–225, WR**

- Blacksmith cleek circa 1850, 5.1" hosel with deep sawtooth nicking, **$1,500–2,000, WR**

- Blacksmith bunker iron ca. 1850, thick 4³/₄" inch hosel with deep sawtooth nicking. Ash shaft has period repair, uncommon, **$1,300–1,500, WR**

- Blacksmith general iron ca. 1850, with nice patina and thick hosel, **$1,500–1,750, WR**

- Walter Hagen Sandy Andy wedge, aluminum head, lead back weight, coated steel shaft, **$20–25, WR**

- Thornwood head long nose putter ca. 1850 with bulging lead back weight, **$1250–1500, WR**

- R. Forgan blonde transitional bulger driver with original stamped shaft, **$500–600, WR**

- R. Forgan putter ca. 1855 with large letter stamp, **$1,750–2,000, WR**

- J. Anderson play club ca. 1870s with minor chip to toe, **$2,500–3,000, WR**

- R. Simpson long nose driver with golden head ca. 1880s, **$2,000–2,250, WR**

- G. Forrester play club in dark finish ca. 1870s, with an elegant thin neck, possibly a lady's club, all original, **$2,500–3,000, WR**

- M. Park playclub ca. 1875 with leather face repair, **$1,250–1,500, WR**

- T. Morris transitional putter with original stamped shaft and grip ca. 1895, **$800–1,000, WR**

- Lofter ca. 1860s, 4¹/₂" hosel with Tom Morris stamped shaft, **$600–800, WR**

- Five wedges including an R-90 and a Walter Hagen Sandy Andy, **$50–60, WR**

- Hardright driver, left-handed, head is made from condensite, the invention of J. W. Aylesworth, chief chemist to Thomas Edison for over 25 years, and has a threaded aluminum neck socket to accept a threaded shaft, very rare, in Jeffery B. Ellis's *The Clubmaker's Art,* **$2,695, JE**

- McEwan play club, ca. 1855, shapely head in superb original condition, wonderful play club, **$4,900, JE**

- Taplow driver, thick circular ivory "Hubbel" insert is laid in the face. Four black dowels and a red dowel in the center provide a fancy look to the face, in *The Clubmaker's Art*, **$165, JE**

- J.S. Caird scare neck brassie and lofting iron, the small-headed brassie is fitted with full brass sole plate, good maker's shaft stamp and shortened original hide grip, **$100–135, MM**

- James Braid light stained small-headed persimmon socket head brassie with full brass sole plate, rear lead backweight and retaining most of the original hide grip, **$100, MM**

4 A MORE RECENT VINTAGE
The Spirit of Invention

Square toe irons and equally rare long necks are only part of the club collecting world. The new collector lacking limitless funds can also savor the hunt for prized artifacts. In fact the budget-minded are arguably forced to be more resourceful and adventurous in tracking down relics—and might even have more fun in assembling a satisfying collection.

"The average guy doesn't have to pursue just 18th or 19th century clubs; the point of collecting is simply enjoyment," reasons Jeffery Ellis, the author of *The Golf Club: 400 Years of the Good, the Beautiful, and the Creative*, a work that describes several pieces that are within the economic grasp of "the average guy." Do you get pleasure out of owning a club? That's the key question collectors must ask themselves before they go out and purchase things. You collect for yourself, not to make statements to other people.

In that regard, steel shafted clubs (or more contemporary made items) can also be fun. They are not for investment. But they have their own appeal. You can relive an era with these clubs, for they have their own nostalgic value. Some 1970s clubs have nice logo detail, and there are even some clubs from the 1960s that mirror the spirit of that turbulent age. All clubs, no matter what their time frame, can bring enjoyment. It's certainly a joy-filled experience to thumb through Ellis's illuminating book.

Declaring that there are steel shaft clubs made during the mid–20th century and thereafter that possess significant creativity and genuine beauty as well as elements of nostalgia and history, Ellis adds, "The vast majority of steel shaft clubs are valued merely as used clubs once they hit the secondary market."

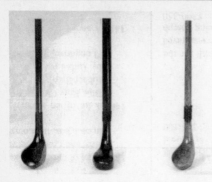

A. H. Scott (script) walking stick in the shape of a socket wood, lion and crown stamp; walking stick in the shape of a socket wood marked "special"; walking stick shaped like a putter. *Photo courtesy of Old Tom Morris Golf, L.L.C.*

Yet these clubs, he maintains, still have intrinsic value, and can be acquired at very affordable prices. Some of these clubs, if selected wisely (and if in top condition), can also become financially collectible in the future. As Ellis explains, "it is a club's place in history and innovative creativity—rather than 'instant collectibility'—that determine whether it will stand the test of time."

Another delightful "art" book, *The Golf Club*, pictures several clubs from the 1850s to the early 1900s that have retained their aura with enchanting results. A crescent iron with a British patent date of August 2, 1894, sold privately for $4,500. Even more attractive, a Montgomery (roller) putter from 1894 sold in 1994 for $5,000. A strange looking, center-shafted Centro Iron sold for $6,000 in 2001, while a 1904 Swan Neck Putter was auctioned in 1991 for a relatively modest $3,500.

These innovative pre–World War I clubs, with their inlays, center shafts, and club maker logos, certainly mirror golf's essential spirit—the quest for perfection that has man sipping from the fountain of invention in a desperate attempt to achieve lower golf scores.

But ingenuity didn't stop once the game's popularity soared in the 1900s, and manufacturers switched to steel shafts (even though golf's ruling bodies deemed them illegal), to compensate for the dwindling supply of hickory.

Paying tribute to this new era in clubmaking, when rubber-cored golf balls featured a hardened or vulcanized balata cover, Ellis describes several clubs that should be on every collector's wish list.

Clearly affordable, a Suitall putter with a distinctive raised point on the blade is a mere $2,500. A weird 1925 Duplex Metalwood suitable for left- and right-handed players is a "steal" at $1,500. For those with big dreams, and big checkbooks, there's the supergiant Cochrane Niblick with a face depth of $4^3/4''$. As Ellis notes, it's a whopping $14,000.

Always intent on spotlighting the creative genius that stirred club design, Ellis goes on to catalog woods from the 1940s and 1950s, adjustable irons, classic persimmons from the 1970s, and the modern-day graphite–titanium revolution. Though pricing is not discussed, as many of these clubs are still not in that "financially collectible" category, modern-era Carbonex 22 5-woods, DX Tourney woods, Wizard 600 putters, and Bee Line putters still have an inestimable beauty. Perhaps they will prove to be sound investments in the future, but in the meantime, Ellis writes about them as if they were pictorial and historical treasures. They are!

- Wright & Ditson, three pieces, the head, the shaft, and an intermediate piece that sockets into the head while also extending up and splicing to the shaft, patented in 1914, clean original, in *The Clubmaker's Art*, **$325, Ellis**

- Concave, clean original condition, **$475, Ellis**

- Swingrite Limber Golf Shaft, *extremely* flexible shaft is made from nine pieces, patented in the U.S. in 1931, pictured in *The Clubmaker's Art,* **$650, Ellis**

- William Gibson, Kinghorn, Smith's Model Niblick, antishank iron with lofted face, ca. 1897, in *The Clubmaker's Art*, **$250, Ellis**

- A. G. Spalding & Brothers, made in Great Britain, rare spring face iron, complete with a spring steel face riveted in place. The rivets and unique cross scoring on this face are original, face iron is filled with gutta-percha, in *The Clubmaker's Art,* **$1,100, Ellis**

- HB putter, Spalding, first produced in 1919, this putter was the originator of the famous MacGregor Tommy Armour putters made years later, **$450, Ellis**

- Spalding, Cran, face is inlaid with a wood block held in place by two screws in the back of the head, patented in 1897, sheepskin grip. Prime original example from 1897 (pictured in *The Clubmaker's Art*), **$1,250, Ellis**

- Otto Hackbarth, clean example of this putter made famous by Chick Evans when winning the 1916 U.S. Open and Amateur, **$850, Ellis**

- A. Fosbury, Tooting Bec, Smith-neck antishank putter, in *The Clubmaker's Art*, **$125, Ellis**

- Wilson concave face, face on this putter is curved heel-to-toe similar to the face of the Forgan MaxMo putter, weights in the toe and heel of the sole, underneath two brass plates, **$475, Ellis**

- BGI Bridgeport, ca. 1900, brass blade putter, with stamped shaft and sheepskin grip, near mint, **$200, Ellis**

- F. H. Winkworth Scott, patented in 1912, about the earliest steel-shafted club a collector has any chance of obtaining, in *The Clubmaker's Art,* **$765, Ellis**

- Ellis Glover's Adjustable Iron, ca. 1935, steel-shafted iron adjusts to nine different lofts, orig. black-coated shaft, **$250, Ellis**

- Crocker Streamliner Driver, ca. 1937, driver has a head shaped like a torpedo or bullet, original steel shaft, **$300, Ellis**

- Wilson Aim-Rite Putter, brass head has a nice flange with raised alignment bar, **$335, Ellis**

- Spalding Calamity Jane, bears the factory-stamped name of "Jack White," the 1904 British Open Champion, Robert Tyre Jones tried 16 different Jack White drivers before selecting the one he used to win the Grand Slam, **$750, Ellis**

- Thomas E. Wilson Driver, backweight and the wide strip across the crown are all made from the same piece of metal, ca. 1920s, in *The Clubmaker's Art*, **$295, Ellis**

- Mills Patent MSD, ca. 1900 long nose metalwood designed by Mills to replace irons, in *The Clubmaker's Art*, **$295, Ellis**

- David McEwan putter, ca. 1895, owner's initials "G. F." for Gertrude Fiske, **$150–250, WR**

- Scarce driver from Biarritz, France, ca. 1920, with "Ivorine" face insert, letter of provenance, **$150–250, WR**

- Two steel-shafted clubs, Gene Sarazen 22 oz. training club, Walter Hagen Sandy Andy, **$100–150, WR**

- Holdfast rut niblick for A & N.C.S. by Anderson, shaft stamped Army and Navy, **$200–300, WR**

- Morristown Rut Niblick, **$500–600, WR**

- BGI Rut Niblick, **$500–600, WR**

- Spalding concave rut niblick, **$500–600, WR**

- Spalding baseball mark brass putter, Slazenger star mark brass putter, **$300–350, WR**

- Ten smooth face Spalding irons, good condition, **$200–300, WR**

- Three woods, all brass face plates, **$200–250, WR**

- Osmond automaton caddie, all original, **$750–1,000, WR**

- Wicker golf bag, 33" high, all original, **$800–1,000, WR**

- Walter Hagen concave sand wedge, **$400–500, WR**

- Winton & Co. oversized niblick stamped "the last word in niblick," **$600–800, WR**

- Schenectady putter imported by Harry J. Lee for Cupples Co, St. Louis, **$175–225, WR**

- R. Forgan antishank lofter with ball backweight and original stamped shaft, very unusual, **$400–500, WR**

- Walter Hagen Sand Wedge, patented in 1928, this iron has a concave face and large sole. Bobby Jones used one of these when winning the 1930 British Open, **$525, Ellis**

5 THE PASSIONATE PAPER CHASE
Books

Once golf's Sam Spade locates a potential prize, he of course looks for any obvious damage: the ravages caused by time, sunlight, humidity, and improper handling.

But before really appraising the object's worth or integrity, this seasoned "book detective" fondles the material, then brings it up to his nose, and applies his near-legendary Smell Test.

"Before I visually inspect a book's binding, pages, and overall condition, I want to smell the book, determine if there are any signs of molding," explains antiquarian Dick Donovan, 68, an internationally respected sleuth who along with having keen olfactory gifts, has utilized his practiced "eye" to become known as "Mr. Condition."

"I want to feel the leather—some leather has a better tactile feel to it—and then I want to determine if it has a rich, luxuriant smell. If there are any traces of molds that's bad, very bad, for those molds will grow, and the book will be ruined. Molds can show up in any part of a book. It just depends on how a volume was stored. All too often when appraising libraries, or searching for a rare work, I have to cringe after discovering that books have been exposed to dampness [or] direct sunlight, or [have] not [been] stored in an upright position."

It's to be expected that this 35-year veteran of the rare golf book "hunt" would feel a certain pain when eyeing ruined or damaged classics. Still "incredibly excited" by the challenges of finding such extremely rare prizes as Mathison's poem *The Goff* (in either 1743, 1763, or 1793 editions), Robert Clark's presentation edition of *Golf: A Royal & Ancient Game* (1875), and Bernard Darwin's *The Golf Courses of the British Isles* (a

The Actis and Constitutionis of Scotland,
1566, by Robert Lepruick. First printed
matter to mention "golf." The 1457 edict
of King James bans golf. *Photo courtesy of
Will Roberto.*

Robert Clark's *Golf: A Royal Ancient Game,*
1875, first edition, in modern clamshell box.
*Photo courtesy of Old Tom Morris Golf,
L.L.C.*

1910 work by Charles Darwin's grandson), Donovan is driven by what he calls "the passion," a love for the game's written word.

"Clubs and balls are chief elements of the game, but books, pamphlets, the literature, that holds the ABC's of the game, gives you a sense of what golf is all about, and its fabulously rich history," insists Donovan, who maintains a personal collection of over 3,500 books. "Books are sustenance, they teach you all there is to know about courses, players, rules, golf's greatest personalities. They're essential primers offering a look at what makes golf so magical."

The meaning of Donovan's paean is clear. To successfully collect old golf books, newcomers to this "condition, condition, condition" pursuit must bring more than their checkbooks to the paper chase. They must realize that the true "blue-chip" classics are very scarce, and be in love with such timeless works as the "immortal" George Fullerton Carnegie's *Golfiana: or, Niceties Connected with the Game of Golf* (third edition, 1842, valued at more than $20,000), or any of Horace G. Hutchinson's early—and witty—1900s triumphs.

There are people who instruct Donovan and other advisers, retailers, or book experts to "put together a big collection for me no matter what the cost." But that hardly gives them a sense of the joys from collecting, the deep satisfaction of identifying a vaunted volume in excellent condition (i.e., handsome in appearance, no missing parts of the cover, no traces of sunning), and acquiring it at an advantageous price.

"When I meet with a potential client I want to find out if he has that passion, a reverence for books, if he's more than just an acquisitive trophy hunter," says Donovan, who buys books at auctions for clients, and also taps into networks of other enthusiasts to discover coveted works. "The 'buy me a collection' types who barge right in won't be buying the wrong material or won't be looking at financial disaster if they have me (or other reputable advisers like George Lewis or Golf Links to the Past President Ed Papczun) as a consultant. Without that help they could buy the wrong edition, buy an autographed copy that's not legitimate, or even books that aren't complete (missing plates, photographs, other images). When going it alone you must educate yourself and go slow."

An indispensable guide in that book "education" is *The Game of Golf and the Printed Word,* a remarkably comprehensive bibliography of golf literature first compiled by Donovan and Joseph Murdoch in the 1980s. Offering an encyclopedic array of pungent comments and "must read" tips, this reference bible, being revised at press time by Donovan, was projected to offer capsule descriptions of nearly 12,000 works. Besides celebrating such spirited, avidly pursued scarcities as Robert T. Jones and O. B. Keeler's *Down the Fairway: The Golf Life and Play of Robert T. Jones, Jr.,* this work separates golf literature into distinct categories (biographies, instructionals, etc.) and serves as a guide to "niche" collecting.

"Collectors with bigger budgets can choose to be 'completists,' go the route of acquiring everything," says Donovan, who is based in Endicott, NY. "Others might choose to focus on one category, collect everything in this one area, then move into another. In either case newcomers should talk to other collectors, join the Golf Collectors Society, attend auctions to get a sense of pricing, and go slow."

Steering clear of sounding self-serving, Donovan fails to mention the crucial importance of a newcomer's working with a trusted adviser. Experts in judging a book's condition (from completeness to the probability of needing an eventual repair) and pricing trends, veterans like Donovan, Papczun, and John Bonjenoor are personalized "insurance policies"—or security blankets.

They're evaluating scores of books every year, studying auction sales (along with catalogs), traveling to numerous book shows, and serving as a constraint against impetuous and testosterone- or ego-driven bidding at highly spirited auctions.

Admitting that his 1998 sale of Joseph Murdoch's $750,000 library of 1,218 objects attracted collecting's elite, the "heaviest hitters" in this big money game, Pacific Book Auction Galleries' senior auctioneer George Fox says, "People got very excited. Maybe collectors will find a better deal for a book when a sale doesn't have such panache, since when there are so many high-powered people, prices are naturally driven upwards. It might be a better buying strategy to go after books when a major library isn't offered, or the sale receives less hoopla."

Horace G. Hutchinson's, *British Golf Links*, 1897, first edition. *Photo courtesy of Old Tom Morris Golf, L.L.C.*

W. Park Jr.'s *The Game of Golf*, 1896, first edition. First book authored by a playing pro. *Photo courtesy of Old Tom Morris Golf, L.L.C.*

Yet if a book enthusiast is represented by an agent like Donovan—who strictly maintains, "I don't like price aberrations, I don't like being ahead of the market"—making costly mistakes becomes almost impossible. Along with providing a "comfort factor," such representation assures "educated" purchases (i.e., a 1st edition of Jones's *Down the Fairway* in dust jacket is valued at $3,000, while a rarer limited edition of this 1927 work sells for $12,000 to $15,000). Even more importantly, however, an agent works within fixed budgetary parameters, has a keen sense of what a book is worth, and prevents buyers from succumbing to "auction fever."

Confessing to making several mistakes as a beginner, collector James Espinola has realized that the initial pursuit of classic books demands a "special brand of sophistication and knowledge" that only a reputable adviser can provide.

"Now I can go after books on my own, I have the expertise," insists Espinola, "but in a field where condition is everything, beginners just don't understand what makes a book worth a specific sum. Buyers must know how many pages there are in a book. They must know how many end pages should be in a particular work. The condition of the borders and covers is important. Books can be in 'presentation' boxes, first editions, limited editions, have special bindings, and have slipcases. This is a very precise type of collecting, but beginners don't usually have sophistication when starting out.

"That's why working with a knowledgeable person is imperative," adds Espinola, who owns the "Holy Grail" of bookdom, Thomas Mathison's *The Goff. An Heroi-Comical Poem in Three Cantos . . . With an Appendix Containing two Poems in Praise of Goff and a Few Notes and Illustrations* (the 1793 edition is the rarest of these volumes,

Poemata Omnia by Arthur Johnston, physician to King Charles II ca. 1648, contains two poems in Latin with golfing references. *Photo courtesy of Will Roberto.*

Valerie Bumps McMahan's *The Golf Ball Kids and Little Caddy*, 1929, first edition, dust jacket. *Photo courtesy of Old Tom Morris Golf, L.L.C.*

the first book totally devoted to the game), and James Cundell's *Rules of the Thistle Golf Club* ("these rules help to show what members of newly instituted clubs, unfettered by past codes, considered to be the accepted laws of the game"). "Books are the hierarchy of collecting, and to fully appreciate this field's unique joys and certainly its complications, new collectors must network with other book lovers. That will help them increase their knowledge, which in this world means power."

How does one acquire that power? Just ask Eddie Papczun.

Adept at discovering signed Bobby Jones material, and other "blue-chip" books which have been consistently appreciating at 10 percent a year, Golf Links to the Past's Papczun is another antiquarian with detective-like talents.

Along with tracking down scarce volumes and tapping into collectors "who want to fly very low on the radar screen," this "library builder" also trumpets the "power of knowledge." Insisting that newcomers must "ground" themselves, or be dedicated to learning the ins and outs of the market, he wants his clients to have a basic understanding of what drives prices.

Departing from the orthodoxy that treats condition as the absolute determinant of values, Papczun stresses, "the number one factor is scarcity. If there is a book for sale that's in so-so condition, and only ten copies of that work are known to exist, that will significantly lower your threshold of pain when buying that book."

Take Harold H. Hilton and Garden G. Smith's 1912 book *The Royal & Ancient Game of Golf*, for example. There's a limited edition of their book that's signed by both men

Encyclopaedia Britannica ca. 1792. This is the first edition of this famous encyclopedia to list a definition of golf spelled as we use it today. Printed in Dublin, later and other editions in Edinburgh. *Photo courtesy of Will Roberto.*

(only 100 known copies). When this edition ($15,000 to $20,000 in pristine condition) comes onto the market, the buyer might not be crazy about its condition, but he must still realize how scarce the book is. Many collectors will buy that copy now, and hope to pick up a better copy later (with the caveat that an "exit strategy" for that copy is in place)."

Clearly an admirer of such rarities as Charles Blair MacDonald's *Scotland's Gift: Golf* (first edition, 1928) and H. B. Martin's *Fifty Years of American Golf*, Papczun believes that books, in stark contrast to antique clubs and balls, are far less vulnerable to huge, volatile price swings. To buttress his case for investing in golf's intellectual province, he recalls how the Japanese went on a ball and club spending orgy in the 1990s, only to see their home economy tank, and to have "all their stuff flowing back to the U.S. and UK at 30 cents to the dollar."

"The Japanese never pushed book prices to astronomical heights," adds Papczun. "Books are allowed to grow and appreciate on their own. The intellectual record of the game, these books just enjoy a gradual, very nice climb, instead of volatile, very quick spikes."

Supporting that very rosy view of book collecting, longtime enthusiast Phil Kostolnik traced the values of seven $300 to $1,000 volumes over the last twenty to twenty-five years, and concluded that their "11 percent growth rate outshone the Standard & Poor's 8 to 10 percent increase during that period." He also discovered that highly sought rarities "even appreciate at a much greater rate," since most of these treasures are hidden away, and seldom, if ever, are for sale.

Angliae Notitia: The Present State of England ca. 1682 contains first reference to David Gastier, Royal Clubmaker to Charles II. (See also pp. 223–24.) *Photo courtesy of Will Roberto.*

Yet despite these bullish expectations, which seemingly suggest that acquiring *any* scarce or highly desirable books will prove profitable, Papczun takes a more measured view. Urging collectors to study the Murdoch-Donovan bibliography, and to get a "feel for what's available in all price ranges," he stresses the importance of adopting "a clear collecting strategy." He urges beginners to focus on a niche which contains volumes that are priced within a predetermined budget.

"It's not easy to get everything that's printed on golf, so I tell beginners to fix a budget, select a specific area, such as history, architecture, instruction, and work with a trustworthy person. With the advent of eBay, people working all the angles, and the new increase in forged autographs, new collectors greatly need expert advice."

Book collecting has recently been plagued by sellers who restore high-priced volumes, and tout these works as "untouched originals." A classic like Sir Walter Grindley Simpson's *The Art of Golf* (1887) is notorious for having a leather spine that disintegrates, or peels off. It has to be respined, and that's perfectly acceptable (while Donovan feels "incredibly rare" books are worth repairing, he typically avoids buying those that are "untouchables" with missing pages or illustrations). But as the prices of books have climbed in recent years, unscrupulous sellers frequently fail to disclose that a rarity has been repaired.

"Realizing that restoration work will drive the value of a book down, people will all too often try to pass a volume off as a first edition without any kind of restorative work," rues Papczun. "A masterful restorer can do things without anyone knowing, like putting a new binding on a book. All sorts of tricks are used to make a quick buck."

Interior pages of *Angliae Notitia*. Photo courtesy of Will Roberto.

Alerting the uninitiated to a long list of "danger signs," Papczun continues, "Unsuspecting buyers must see that the endpapers are attached. They have to judge how the binding adheres to the spine, that there's not a lot of looseness, [or that there are no] pages breaking away from the spine.

"Then the actual condition of those pages must be considered. Are they marked up, dog-eared? Are there any signs of foxing, for the acidic nature of paper causes it to turn brown in areas. Buyers should also see if the edges are frayed, nicked, or banged up. If the cover has a gold inlay, is that inlay bright and shiny?"

The message here is clear. Book collecting is no longer "a gentleman's game" free of deception and intrigue. And anyone hoping to find "lightning in a bottle," or a $10 book that will magically be transformed into a $500 to $10,000 treasure, must have a very well-trained *eye*.

But even if that list of value-reducing flaws sounds menacing enough to frighten potential bookworms, Papczun insists on describing other "deadly sins."

"Sunlight is terrible for a book. You must see if there's been sunning to the spine, if the spine has been lightened or faded. Are the covers of a book bright? Does it have water spots, or any other kind of damage? The novice doesn't appreciate all of this, but these things greatly affect values. Most of these details can only be judged by an experienced broker."

Such expertise can also lead to acquiring profitable "sleepers," a limited edition (900 copies) like Alastair J. Johnston's *The Chronicles of Golf: 1457 to 1857*. Costing only

$100 when published in 1993, this exhaustive, lovingly compiled history of the game was certainly affordable a decade ago. Yet many brokers were immediately impressed by the work's sweeping majesty, its remarkably detailed content, and now this "historically significant" tome is valued between $1,500 to $1,750.

"I knew this book would jump in value," insists Donovan. It's very well-done, and a good antiquarian has that indefinable 'feel' for spotting sleepers."

The value of working with a book agent–turned–comforting aide-de-camp in these often murky waters is undeniable. Without such an agent, too much can go terribly wrong—overpaying for a book, acquiring a "lesser" edition, misjudging its condition, and failing to spot repairs. When investing in higher-priced books, the only strategy is to allow a Sherlock Holmes to do his sleuthing. Or else the many mysteries of scarcity and condition can cause a crime, one that entangles buyers in a financial bloodbath.

Though that collaborative approach offers a reassuring safety net, it's not the final word on collecting. There's also the charm of going it alone when tracking down inexpensive to moderately priced books. The buyers can avoid the fees and percentages charged by upper echelon Sherlocks, and turn themselves into curious, fun-loving Dr. Watsons.

As Phil Kostolnik recalls, "When I was a rookie I'd go into antique shops and just acquire relatively inexpensive items. I eventually networked with the experts. But I still enjoy showing up at a farmer's field, or rummaging through bookstores and flea markets by myself. You never know what you're going to find. Collecting is a challenge, adventure [into] the unknown, and maybe even [lead to] a profitable discovery. All that is rolled into one exciting chase."

To make that pursuit even more exhilarating, both financially and intellectually, PBA's George Fox recommends, "Talk to auctioneers. Get a perspective on the book, its provenance and history. Study auction catalogs. It's better to purchase fewer books and to acquire one in the greatest shape.

"It's also crucial to start off slowly. Start with $200 to $300 books. It's important to build your collection—and confidence—up. You can't start off going after *The Goff*. Get your feet wet. Finally, if you know an old golfer, one who's about to die, or his widow, that might be a (crafty) way to get a book or two that's worth buying."

While that "cemetery" strategy has its devotees, James Espinola looks at "death" in a different way. "To me condition is crucial, and a book is doomed, fatally flawed, if you can't read it. All of my books are near mint.

Assortment of 10 golf books. Photo from
Old Tom Morris Golf Catalog. *Photo
courtesy of Old Tom Morris Golf, L.L.C.*

"If it has a slipcase it's worth more. If it has pages missing it's worth considerably less. The same holds true if the spine is cracked, if there are molds, [or] foxing (brown spots from aging). When I bought *My Life of Tom Morris* (1909, by W. W. Tulloch) there were three copies in that sale. One was priced at £450, another £500, and I bought my virtually mint copy for £1,800. Why? Condition, condition, condition."

This absolutist view of condition is echoed by the world's foremost collector of rare golf books. After amassing the universally acknowledged largest and most comprehensive library (consisting of over 15,000 volumes), Alastair Johnston, the president and co-CEO of the International Management Group (IMG) says, "A book is something to be felt and touched. You must be able to look at it, and hold it, its heft and overall appearance is vital. If you buy a book in bad condition you will regret it. Only if a book has huge historical significance, and is extremely rare, would I consider buying it if it was missing pages, had a binding that was loose, or was defaced in some significant way."

A book collector for the last five decades, and also the author of *Vardon to Woods: A Pictorial History of Golfers in Advertising* (a collection of print advertisements that many of the finest golfers of the 20th century allowed themselves to be dragged into and some of them probably regretted soon after the checks were cashed), Johnston has a deep "reverence" for the written word. He feels treasured works from the past are an "inestimable joy," and has purposely expanded his house to suit this "museum-like collection" of the world's most legendary books.

"I have a lot of instructional books, yet I obviously haven't benefited from them, I'm a nineteen handicapper," he quips. "I'm also an aficionado of history, and most of my top five fun books would be biographies of eminent people I've known (IMG manages many of the game's leading figures, such as Tiger Woods, Arnold Palmer, and Mark O'Meara, along with dozens of other sports stars), histories of famous clubs, and books on course architecture. The beautiful Hilton and Smith book (*The Royal & Ancient Game of Golf*), the limited edition would be in that chosen group, and any of Herbert Warren Wind's works (such as *The Story of American Golf: Its Champions and Championships* or *Tips from the Top*)."

Long before becoming the world's preeminent bookman, Johnston had many conversations with the "bible's" author, the now-deceased Joe Murdoch. "Joe often told me, 'always pay the right price, don't pay too much for any book,'" recalls Johnston. "He felt books were like buses—they'll always be another one coming along."

But showing that collectors often have to act according to "gut feel," Johnston ignored Murdoch's reasoning, and bought many items his teacher would have passed on. "I bought a lot of stuff in the early days relatively inexpensively. I'm glad I did, for some of the rarer books I have I've never seen again. So collectors should know that another bus doesn't always come along. Sometimes you just have to take the risk, go for them, and hope the market catches up to you (pricewise)."

Yet Johnston also knows when to be cautious, adding, "Be very careful at auctions. It's very easy to get carried away at auctions, and to be left with the terrible feeling, 'Oh, my God, I paid too much for that book!' That happens if you get auction fever, if you let your ego cloud your better judgment, or allow your competitiveness to take over. You just don't want to ever say to yourself, 'I never would have paid that price if I bought the item in a bookstore.'

"Whatever happens at auctions, books are pure enjoyment. Place them on shelves, look, touch, and review them," insists Johnston. "Don't buy books and store them in boxes or basements. Keep them on shelves (not squeezed close together, for that won't allow them to "breathe"), so you can wander by them, and appreciate them. Detailing the history and spirit of the game, books are an immense pleasure, chronicles meant to be savored."

The prices of golf collectibles fluctuate. The following values are estimates offered by various experts:
PBA—Pacific Book Auction Galleries
WR—Will Roberto
GLP—Golf Links to the Past
MM—Mullock & Madeley
GC—Golf Classics

- Adams, Herbert. *The Body in the Bunker.* First American Edition. Philadephia: J. B. Lippincott, 1935. Chipping to jacket spine ends, rubbing to jacket corners, else very good, **$100–150, PBA**

- Adams, Herbert. *The Secret of Bogey House.* 1st Ed. 1924, *The Perfect Round.* 2nd Ed. 1929. *The Golf House Murder.* 1st Am. Ed. 1933. *Death on the First Tee.* 1st Ed. 1957. Together, 4 vols. Cloth, last in jacket. 1st & 3rd very good, 2nd with some shelf wear, various markings, and chipping and tape repairs to jacket, **$300–500, PBA**

- Allerton, Mark [William Ernest Cameron]. *The Girl on the Green.* Gilt-lettered reddish cloth. First Edition. London: Methuen, 1914. Mild soiling; else very good, **$100–150, PBA**

- André, R[ichard]. *Colonel Bogey's Sketch Book, Comprising an Eccentric Collection of Scribbles and Scratches found in disused lockers and swept up in the pavilion.* Illus. First Edition. London: Longmans, Green, 1897. Soiling and crackling to covers, rubbing to spine ends, else very good, **$1,500–2,500, PBA**

- Armour, Tommy. *How to Play Your Best Golf All the Time.* New York: Simon and Schuster. 1953 edition in dust jacket, along with six reels of instruction film, **$500–750, WR**

- Bailey, C.W. *The Brain and Golf: Some Hints for Golfers from Modern Mental Science.* Foreword by Charles Sherrington. Chapter on theory and practice by Bernard Darwin. Illus. Cloth. Second Edition. London: Mills & Boon, 1924. "Mr. Bailey was seized with the thought, very much alive today, that the subconscious execution of the swing would produce quicker and more satisfactory results than learning the physical aspect." **$80–120, PBA**

- Balfour, J. Stuart. *Golf, Containing List of Implements and their Uses, Glossary of Technical Terms and Latest Revised Rules of the Game.* Illus. Original decorative wrappers; custom-made chemise, and slipcase. First Edition. New York: American Sports Publishing, 1893. This is the first of Spalding's publications on golf, and the first booklet on the game published in America. Part of the Spalding Athletic Library, pages quite fragile & browned, extremely rare, **$500–800, PBA**

- Balfour, James. *Reminiscences of Golf on St. Andrews Links.* First Edition. Edinburgh: David Douglas, 1887. "One of the rarest of all golf items." The Balfours were a well-known golfing family, the most skillful of whom was James's son, Leslie Balfour-Melville, who won the British Amateur in 1895. The book relates tales of the old course during a time when there were relatively few golfers and is of great interest because it gives one of the few firsthand accounts of how the course was played in those early days. Fine condition, extremely scarce, **$3,000–5,000, PBA**

- Bateman, H. M. *Adventures at Golf.* Illus. throughout by Bateman. 11" x 8¹/₄" , pictorial boards, jacket. First Edition. London: Methuen, 1923. A collection of humorous golfing cartoons by the well-known *Punch* illustrator. Heavy chipping to jacket spine, still about very good, in scarce, bright jacket, **$300–500, PBA**

- Bauer, Aleck. *Hazards, Those Essential Elements in a Golf Course Without Which the Game Would be Tame and Uninteresting.* Illus. incl. folding course map. First Edition. Chicago: Toby Rubovits, 1913. A charming book devoted to golf hazards, **$2,000–3,000, PBA.**

- Baxter, John E. *Locker Room Ballards.* New York: D. Appleton & Co. New York 1st ed. 1923. Illustrations by James Montgomery Flagg. In original green and gilt pictorial cloth boards (some minor rubbing to top and tail of spine) otherwise internally good, **$185, MM**

- Beaman, S. G. Hulme. *The Adventures of Larry the Lamb: Golf (Toytown Rules).* First Edition. London: George Lapworth [ca. 1935]. Near fine, a children's fantasy of golf, **$100–150, PBA**

- Beldam, George W. *Great Golfers: Their Methods at a Glance.* Contributions by Harold Hilton, J. H. Taylor, James Braid, Alex Herd, and Harry Vardon. Illus. from 268 action photographs. Gilt-dec & lettered cloth. Second Edition. London: Macmillan, 1904. Beldam was one of the first advocates of teaching golf through photographs, book was beautifully produced with photographs of famous players. A bit of sunning to spine, else near fine, **$100–150, PBA**

- Bennett, Andrew. *The Book of St. Andrews Links, Containing Plan of Golf Courses, Descriptions of the Greens, Rules of the Game, By-Laws of the Links, Regulations for Starting, Golfing Rhymes, &c.* Frontispiece, folding course map printed in two colors. Original cloth-backed flexible cloth. 1 of 1000 copies. First Edition. St. Andrews & Edinburgh: J. & G. Innes & J. Menzies, 1898. Bennett's book, one of the few primary sources of information on the Royal & Ancient, provides the most definitive account of the evolutionary stages in the design, development, and growth of the courses. The book contains the first published color pull-out plan of the course, **$2,000–3,000, PBA**

- Boynton, Henry Walcott. *The Golfer's Rubáiyat.* Illus. First Edition. Chicago: [Herbert S. Stone], 1901. Wit & humor through seventy-eight poems. Charming contemporary original pen & ink drawing of a woman golfer to front free endpaper. Small pieces lacking from spine ends, chipping along front joint, else near very good, **$500–800, PBA**

- Braid, James. *Advanced Golf or Hints and Instruction for Progressive Players.* Illus. Gilt-lettered cloth. First Edition. London: Methuen, [1908]. A book of instruction, with two chapters of memoirs by the famous Scottish golf champion, **$150–250, PBA**

- Braid, J., J.A.T. Bramston, and H. G. Hutchinson. *A Book of Golf.* Ed. by E. F. Benson and Eustace H. Miles. Illus. from photographs by A. Gandy. Red dec. cloth. First Edition. London: Hurst & Blackett, 1903. Rubbing to spine ends and corners, else very good, **$150–250, PBA**

- Braid, James. *Golf Guide and How to Play Golf.* London: British Sports Pub, 1912. Later printing, illus., 162 pp, some wear, still very good, **$45, GC.**

- Braid, James, and Harry Vardon, *How to Play Golf.* New York: American Sports Pub, [n.d.]. Later printing, illus. wraps, 132 pp., **$45, GC**

- British Masters. *How to Improve Your Golf: Lessons by British Masters.* Contributions by Twine, Ray, Whitcombe, Padgham, Hodson, Alliss, and Havers. Illus. Jacket. First Edition. London: Hutchinson [ca. 1925]. Chipping to jacket spine ends, else very good, **$70–100, PBA**

- Brown, Innis, *Spalding Athletic Library No. 4B: How to Play Golf.* Contributions from Sol Metzger, Grantland Rice, and Jack Redmond. Illus. throughout from photographs, pictorial wrappers. First Edition. New York: American Sports Publishing, 1930. Fine. **$100–150, PBA**

- Browning, Robert H. K. *The Golfer's Catechism: A Vade Mecum to the Rules of Golf.* Illus. First Edition. London: H. O. Quinn, ca. 1935, Fine, an uncommon Browning title, **$100–150, PBA**

- Browning, Robert H. K. *Golfing in Southern England and on the Continent (Including the Channel Islands)*. Intro. by Browning. Illus. incl. map. First (11th) Edition. London: Southern Railway of England, 1931. Published to promote golf at the courses along the Southern Railway of England routes, very good, **$80–120, PBA**

- Bunner, H. C. *The Suburban Sage: Stray Notes and Comments on His Simple Life*. Illus. by C. J. Taylor. Pictorial wrappers. First Edition. New York: Keppler & Schwarzmann, 1896. Includes a chapter on "The Suburbanite and his Golf." Rubbing to spine else very good, **$70–100, PBA**

- B[illson], C. J. and P. S.W[ard]. *Horace on the Links, with Notes from Horace Hutchinson's Writings*. Foreword by Horace Hutchinson. Gilt-lettered green cloth. First Edition. London: Swan Sonnenschein, 1903. An amusing yet poetic look at golf. Soiling, else very good, **$200–300, PBA**

- *Burke Hole-In-One Club Yearbook 1925*. Newark, OH: Burke Golf Co., 1925. Illus. wraps, illus., 63 pp., lists of members, short articles on holes-in-one (dodos), poetry, cartoons, etc., **$85, GC**

- Campbell, Alexander. *A Journey from Edinburgh through Parts of North Britain: Containing Remarks on Scotish* [sic] *Landscape; and Observations on Rural Economy, Natural History, Manufactures, Trade, and Commerce* . . . 2 vols. [ii], xxiv, 408; viii, 380, [16] pp. Illus. with 44 single- and duo-tone aquatint plates. 11¼" x 8½", modern First Edition. London: T. N. Longman and O. Rees; Vernor & Hood, 1802. Contains descriptions of St. Andrews, Perth, and other Scottish locales, about fine, with beautiful aquatint plates, **$400–500, PBA**

- Campbell, Major Guy. *Golf for Beginners*. Forewords by J. L. Low & Cecil K. Hutchinson. Illus. Pictorial cloth. First Edition. London: C. Arthur Pearson, 1922. Campbell descended from one of the most famous golf families. Campbell distinguished himself as a player, official, course architect and writer, and in this book passes along his ideas of the fundamentals of the game, faint staining to spine, else very good, **$100–150, PBA**

- Carnegie, George Fullerton. *Golfiana; or, Niceties Connected with the Game of Golf. Dedicated, with Respect, to the Members of All Golfing Clubs, and to those of St. Andrews and North Berwick in Particular*. 16 pp. Period paneled calf, gilt-lettered spine. Third Edition. Edinburgh: William Blackwood and Alexander Hill, 1842. The second publication (after *The Goff*) entirely devoted to golf, this is another book of poetry originally privately printed in Leith in early 1833 as one long poem by the young George Carnegie (1800–1843); there is only one known copy of the first edition. This copy inscribed and signed by the author on the leaf preceding the title. Scuffing to spine, else very good, **$12,000–18,000, PBA**

- Chambers, Charles E. S. Golfing: *A Handbook to the Royal and Ancient Game, with List of Clubs, Rules, &c. Also Golfing Sketches and Poems*. Illus. by Ranald M. Alexander, with frontispiece, chromolithograph port. of Tom Morris. Pictorial red cloth. First Edition. Edinburgh: W. and R. Chambers, 1887. A touch of sunning to spine; else near fine & very rare, **$1500–2500, PBA**

- Clapcott, C. B. *The Rules of Golf of the Ten Oldest Golf Clubs from 1754 to 1848, Together with the Rules of the Royal & Ancient Golf Club of St. Andrews for the Years 1858, 1875, 1888*. Gilt-lettered cloth. 1 of 500 copies. First Edition. Edinburgh: Golf Monthly [1935]. C. B. Clapcott was an enthusiastic golf historian and book collector. This book, according to Murdoch, "represents a definitive study of the early rules and the first attempt to trace the evolution of golf rules." Before 1830, there were only six printed rules of golf. Light bumping to upper corners, else near fine, **$600–900, PBA**

- Clark, Robert. *Golf: A Royal & Ancient Game*. Illus., incl. twelve extra photographic illustrations for this large paper presentation edition, gilt-lettered spine. One of a limited number of Presentation Copies. First Edition. London: Macmillan, 1875. This copy contains the obituary of Young Tom Morris (pp. 281-284), who died on Christmas Day, 1875. Clark was an Edinburgh printer and an avid golfer, and this compilation of important golf writings up to the 1870s includes poems (including Mathison's *The Goff* and Carnegie's "Golfiana"), and Acts of Parliament, etc. Murdoch opines that "This book is one of the masterpieces of golf literature. It is also one of the most important contributions to the library of golf and one of the most handsomely produced of all golf books." Rubbing to spine ends, a couple of nicks along joints, else extremely good and scarce, **$5,000–8,000, PBA**

- Colt, H. S. and C. H. Alison. *Some Essays on Golf Course Architecture*. Contributions by A. MacKenzie, Horace G. Hutchinson, John L. Low, et al. Illus. from photographs. Original quarter cloth and boards, jacket. First Edition. London: Country Life & George Newnes, 1920. H. S. Colt was the first nonprofessional golfer to work with course design and employ formal renderings. Mild chipping to jacket spine, else very good and quite scarce, an important and valuable contribution to the field of golf course architecture, **$2,000–3,000, PBA**

- Cornish, Geoffrey S. and Ronald E. Whitten. *The Golf Course*. Foreword by Robert Trent Jones. Photographs by Brian D. Morgan. Illus. 11" x 8¼" jacket. First Edition. New York: Rutledge Press, [1981]. Warmly inscribed and signed by Cornish to Joseph. About fine, **$150–250, PBA**

- Cotton, Henry. *Golf: Being a short treatise for the use of young people who aspire to proficiency in the Royal and Ancient game*. Foreword by Bernard Darwin. Illus. from photographs. Jacket. First Edition. London: Eyre & Spottiswoode, 1931. Cotton's first book. Warmly inscribed and signed by Cotton to Sydney Bell on the frontispiece and title page, dated 1931, chips & tears to extremities, else good only, but uncommon in jacket, **$200–300, PBA**

• Cotton, Henry. *This Game of Golf.* Foreword by Bernard Darwin. Illus. incl. frontispiece, 10" x 7^1/$_2$" jacket. First Edition. London: Country Life, [1948]. Mild rubbing to jacket corners & chipping to jacket spine ends, else extremely good. **$100–150, PBA**

• Crombie, Charles. *The Rules of Golf Illustrated.* Illus. with twenty-four humorous color lithograph plates by Crombie. Oblong, 11^1/$_4$" x 17^1/$_2$" cloth-backed green boards lettered in red. First Edition. London: Perrier, [ca. 1905]. Crombie illustrated this wonderful book with whimsical characters in nursery-rhyme style medieval clothes caught in impossible situations. Hinges cracked, else good only outside, but clean and bright internally, **$1,000–1,500, PBA**

• Cundell, James. *Rules of the Thistle Golf Club; with Some Historical Notices Relative to the Progress of the Game of Golf in Scotland.* [4], 50, [1] pp. Period blind-tooled purple calf, gilt-roll borders, gilt-tooled, and lettered spine. First Edition. Edinburgh: James Ballantyne, 1824. This is one of only six books of printed rules published prior to 1830. These rules help to show what members of newly instituted clubs, unfettered by past codes, considered to be the accepted laws of the game. Rubbing and scuffing to spine & extremities, else very good, in a lovely contemporary binding, **$10,000–15,000, PBA**

• Curtiss, Fredrick and John Heard. *Country Club 1882–1932.* Brookline, MA: Privately printed, 1932, illus., 212 pp, **$495, GC**

• Dalrymple, W. *The Golfers' Referee.* Pictorial red cloth. First Edition. Edinburgh and London: W. H. White-Simpkin, Marshall, Hamilton, and Kent, [1897]. A small book on the rules of golf by the well-known Scottish golfer and writer. Mild soiling, a touch of sunning to spine, else very good, **$300–500, PBA**

• Darwin, Bernard. *British Golf.* Illus. incl. color plates. Jacket. First Edition. London: Collins, 1946. Rubbing to jacket, spine, ends, and corners, else very good, **$80–120, PBA**

• Darwin, Bernard. *British Sport and Games.* Printed wrappers. First Edition. London: British Council, [1940]. Naturally, Darwin leaves plenty of room for discussion on golf. Fine, **$70–100, PBA**

• Darwin, Bernard. *Every Idle Dream.* Illus. by Elinor Darwin. Jacket. First Edition. London: Collins, 1948. Chipping to jacket spine ends, initials inked to front panel, else very good in good jacket, **$100–150, PBA**

- Darwin, Bernard. *The Game's Afoot! An Anthology of Sports, Games, and the Open Air*. Gilt-lettered green cloth. First Edition. London: Sidgwick & Jackson, [1926]. Contributions by the game's best, including Hutchinson, Simpson, Low, and Darwin. Rubbing to spine ends and extremities, else very good, **$100–150, PBA**

- Darwin, Bernard. *The Golf Courses of the British Isles*. Illus. with sixty-four color plates by Harry Rountree; 9" x 6 ³/₄", gilt-lettered green cloth, First Edition. London: Duckworth, [1910]. Darwin's famous book covering the courses of Scotland, En-gland, and Ireland, front hinge cracking at title page, else extremely good, **$800–1,200, PBA**

- Darwin, Bernard. *A Golfer's Gallery of Old Masters*. Intro. by Bernard Darwin. Illus. with eighteen mounted color plates of paintings depicting golf or golf relatives (Dutch Kolf, Het Kolven, Jeu de Mail) in different forms, from the 16th to the 19th centuries. First Trade Edition. London: Country Life, [ca. 1920]. An important compendium of Old Master and 19th century paintings of golf in play and golf equipment. Tears to joints at spine ends, rubbing to corners, else very good, with beautiful, bright mounted plates, **$1,500–2,500, PBA**

- Darwin, Bernard. *Out of the Rough*. Green cloth. First Edition. London: Chapman & Hall, [ca. 1932]. Another collection of Darwin's columns and articles. Sunning and white spots to spine, else about very good, **$100–150, PBA**

- Darwin, Bernard. *Golfing By-Paths*. Jacket. First Edition. London: Country Life, 1946. Jacket heavily chipped and with upper half of jacket spine lacking, else good, **$70–100, PBA**

- Darwin, Bernard. *Rubs of the Green*. Jacket. First Edition. London: Chapman & Hall, [1936]. Chipping to jacket spine ends, darkening to spine, foxing, else very good, **$400–700, PBA**

- Darwin, Bernard. Five 1st ed titles incl. *Every Idle Dream* c–w dust jacket, *Golf Between Two Wars* (F), *Golfing By Paths* (Covers faded), *The World That Fred Made* (spine faded), *Life is Sweet Brother* (F), and *Candid Caddies*, some internal foxing, **$50–60, PBA**

- Demaret, Jimmy. *My Partner, Ben Hogan*, New York: McGraw-Hill, 1954. First edition. Signed copy, **$850, GLP**

- Dobereiner, Peter. *The Game with the Hole in It*. [1970] *For the Love of Golf: The Best of Dobereiner*. Signed. [1981]. *Down the Nineteenth Fairway: A Golfing Anthology*. [1982]. *The Book of Golf Disasters*. [1983]. Together, four vols. Jackets. First Editions. London: various dates. About fine, **$150–250, PBA**

- Donovan, Richard E. and Joseph S. F. Murdoch. *The Game of Golf and the Printed Word 1566–1985*. Intro. by Herbert Warren Wind. Gilt-dec. and lettered green morocco, a.e.g., slipcase. No. 6 of 20 presentation copies. First Edition. Endicott, NY: Castalio Press, 1988. Signed by Donovan, Murdoch, and Wind on the limitation page, fine, **$400–600, PBA**

- Duncan, George. *Golf at the Gallop*. 1951 first edition signed by the author, **$75–100, WR**

- Dunn, Seymour. *Golf Fundamentals*. Illus. gilt-lettered dark blue cloth. First Edition. Lake Placid, NY: Seymour Dunn, 1922. Contains a unique folding golf specification chart in rear which shows the characteristics of a golf club best adapted to the physical build of the golfer. Rubbing to spine ends, else very good, **$200–300, PBA**

- Edgar, J. Douglas. *Standardized Golf Instruction*. 1934 first wrappers edition, pivotal instructional, **$200–250, WR**

- Fairlie, Walter Edwin. *The Old Golf Course of St. Andrews: Plans, with Names of Holes and Bunkers*. Two copies. Illus. with plans printed in red & black. 7" x 3¹⁄₄", First and Second Editions. St. Andews: W. C. Henderson and Son, [1908 & 1920]. This was the first of many similar books and booklets to be published over the years that was planned and designed to help the golfer find his or her way around the Old Course with the least amount of trouble and strokes, **$200–300, PBA**

- Farnie, H. B. *The Golfer's Manual, Being an Historical and Descriptive Account of the National Game of Scotland, With an Appendix by "A Keen Hand."* xii, [ii], 96 pp. Frontispiece, lithograph port. of Allan Robertson. Original gilt-lettered & stamped red cloth, a.e.g. First Edition. Cupar: Whitehead, and Orr, 1857. The first edition was the first book of prose devoted entirely to the game of golf, and also the first book of instruction. Chipping along spine cloth, front hinge cracked through, else good and very scarce, **$3,000–5,000, PBA**

- Farnie, H. B. *The Golfer's Manual, Being an Historical and Descriptive Account of the National Game of Scotland by "A Keen Hand."* Originally Published in 1857. Intro. by Bernard Darwin. Illus. with wood engravings by John O'Connor. Gilt-lettered spine, jacket, slipcase. No. 325 of 750 copies. London: Dropmore Press, 1947. A limited edition reprint of the first book of prose written on golf and the first of golf instruction. Near fine, **$300–500, PBA**

- Flint, Violet [Col. J. E. Thompson]. *A Golfing Idyll: or, The Skipper's Round with the Deil on the links of St. Andrews*. Gilt-lettered stiff wrappers bound-in to period quarter red calf & cloth, gilt-lettered spine. Second Edition. St. Andrews: W. C. Henderson, 1893. Joints cracked, else fine in near very good binding, **$500–800 PBA**

- Forgan, Robert. *The Golfer's Handbook, including History of the Game, Hints to Beginners, the Feats of Champion Golfers, Lists of Leading Clubs and their Office-Bearers, &c.* Illus. with steel plates and woodcuts. First Edition. Cupar: John Innes, 1881. Includes instruction, history, outstanding golf feats and other golfiana. It also includes 'Rules,' the local rules for the Old Course at St. Andrews, a 'Glossary of Technical Terms' and a list of 'Clubs in Great Britain,' very good & extremely rare, **$2,500–4,000, PBA**

- Fox, G. D. *The Golfer's Pocket Tip Book.* Illus. from photographs of Jack White playing. 5¾" x 3½", gilt-lettered red cloth jacket. First American Edition. New York: James Pott, [ca. 1915]. Soiling & chipping to uncommon jacket, else near fine, **$100–150, PBA**

- Garden City Golf Club and Martin, H. B. *Golden Anniversary: The Garden City Golf Club.* Foreword by George Hubbell. No. 386 of 600 copies. Fulkerson and Thacher, 1949. *Seventy-Fifth Anniversary: The Garden City Golf Club.* No. 234 of 1000 copies. 1974. Together, 2 vols. Rubbing to corners of 1st, stains to lower cloth of both, else very good, **$150–250, PBA**

- Glynes, Webster. "The Maiden. A Golfing Epic, dedicated to Dr. W. Laidlaw Purves, Founder of the St. George's Golf Club, Sandwich." 19 pp. Original gilt-lettered flexible red cloth. First Edition. England: Privately Printed, ca. 1893. According to Murdoch this is a very little (and very rare) book of poetry. Soiling, hinges weak, very good, **$300–500, PBA**

- George, Robb. *Historical Gossip About Golf and Golfers, by a Golfer.* [6], 58 pp. Bound-in to quarter morocco and cloth, gilt-lettered spine. First Edition. Edinburgh: John Hughes, 1863. The first anthology of golf, this little volume contains an absorbing history of the Bruntsfield Links, descriptions of Dutch "Kolf" and French "Jeu de Mail," the now famous sketch of "Cock o' the Green," and a reprint of "The Golfer's Garland," one of the two poems added to the third edition of Mathison's *The Goff.* Fine, **$8,000–12,000, PBA**

- Grierson, James. *Delineations of Saint Andrews; Being a Particular Account of Every Thing Remarkable in the History and Present State of the City and Ruins, the University, and Other Interesting Objects of that Ancient Ecclesiastical Capital of Scotland . . .* Illus. with three copper-engraved views and a plan of the town. Morocco, gilt-lettered spine. First Edition. Edinburgh: Peter Hill, P. Bower, & Vernor, Hood, and Sharpe, 1807. An invaluable early work on the history of St. Andrews, the town where the first golf club began. Staining to lower half of plates & title page, **$2,000–3,000, PBA**

- Hagen, Walter. *The Walter Hagen Story, by the Haig.* Illus. Jacket. First Edition. New York: Simon & Schuster, 1956. Chipping to jacket spine ends, else very good and bright, **$100–150, PBA**

- Hagen, Walter. *Elements of the Golf Swing*. New York: Golf Illustrated, 1930. Illus. wraps, illus., **$265, GC.**

- Hagen, Walter. *The Walter Hagen Story*. New York: Simon and Schuster, 1957. 299 pp., very good in jacket, signed by Hagen, **$695, GC.**

- Hammerton, J. A. *The Rubáiyát of a Golfer*. Illus. from drawings by D. L. Ghilchik, 7" x 5¼", cloth jacket. First Edition. London: Country Life, [1946]. A parody of the famous poem. Chipping to jacket spine ends, else very good, uncommon in jacket, **$100–150, PBA**

- Haultain, Arnold. *The Mystery of Golf*. Foreword by Herbert Warren Wind. Wrappers. First Wrapper Edition. Cambridge: Applewood Books, 1986. Fine, **$40–70, PBA**

- Haultain, Arnold. *The Mystery of Golf*. 2nd edition revised and enlarged. New York: Macmillan, 1912. In original grey cloth pictorial boards (possibly first blank page missing, visible hinge) otherwise internally clean and sound; and Martin, H. B. *Golf Yarns—The Best Things about the Game of Golf* 1st edition 1913 published New York c–w frontispiece and other illustrations, in decorative paper hard back boards, very good, **$185, MM**

- Herd, Sandy. *My Golfing Life, Told to Clyde Foster*. Foreword by Earl Haig Illus. Cloth, gilt-lettered spine. First Edition. London: Chapman and Hall, 1923. The recollections of one of the great Scots. Herd won the 1902 Open against John Ball, using a Haskell. With lengthy signed inscription from Herd, near fine, with scarce letter and inscription, **$400–700, PBA**

- Hilton, Harold H. and Garden G. Smith. *The Royal & Ancient Game of Golf*. Illus. profusely, incl. three color plates and two photogravures; tissue guards. 12" x 9½", gilt-lettered full vellum, gilt-tooled pictorial lion emblem on front cover, a.e.g. No. 9 of 100 copies. First (Large Paper) Edition. London: London & Counties Press, 1912. Murdoch says: "This is one of the most magnificent books in the entire library of golf, comprehensive in content, very handsome in appearance and attractively illustrated." A fine copy of this rarity, **$4,000–6,000, PBA**

- Hogan, Ben. *Five Lessons: The Modern Fundamentals of Golf*. New York: A. S. Barnes, 1957, deluxe ed., ills, 127 pp, signed by Hogan, fine, **$500, GC**

- Hogan, Ben and Herbert Warren Wind. *Five Lessons: The Modern Fundamentals of Golf*. (Nevin Gibson's stamp to f.f.e.) [1957]. Barrat, Michael. *Golf with Tony Jacklin*. [1978]. Ballestros, Seve and Dudley Doust. *Seve: The Young Champion*. [1982]. Barkow, Al. *Gettin' to the Dance Floor: An Oral History of American Golf*. [1986]. Together, four vols. Illus. Jackets. First Editions. Various places: various dates. Short tear to jacket of 2nd, else very good to about fine, **$150–250, PBA**

- *Ben Hogan Flicker Book*. Extremely rare "Magic Eye" movie or flicker book features Hogan from set up through his full swing, very good condition, **$225, GLP**

- Hogan, Ben. *Here's Your Free Golf Lesson*. 1940 first edition (flicker book), **$150–200, WR**

- Hopkins, Frank. *Golf Holes They Talk About*. Illus. throughout by Hopkins. Oblong, 8¹/₂" x 12¹/₄", cloth-backed dec. boards, paper cover label. No. 135 of 880 copies printed by Redfield-Kendrick-Odell. First Edition. New York: privately printed, 1927. Signed by Hopkins on the limitation page. Rubbing to corners and a bit to spine ends, mild soiling, else very good, **$500–800, PBA**

- Hoskins, Mabel S. *Golf for Women, By a Woman Golfer*. Illus. from photographs. Gilt-lettered brick red cloth. First Edition. New York: Moffatt, Yard, 1916. Minor rubbing to spine ends and fading to spine, else extremely good, **$200–300, PBA**

- Houghton, George. Four paperbacks in Golf Addict Series, all first editions with dust jackets to include *Confessions of a Golf Addict*, *More Confessions of a Golf Addict*, *Golf Addicts through the Ages*, *Golf Addict Visits the USA*, and *The Golfer's ABC*, paperback, **$25-50, MM**

- Houghton, George. *An Addict's Guide to British Golf: A County-by-County Pictorial Directory*. [1959]. *The Full Confessions of a Golf Addict*. *Golf Addicts Galore*. [1968]. *How to be a Golf Addict*. [1971], Together four vols. Illus. Jackets First Editions. London: various dates. Good to very good, **$150–250, PBA**

- Houghton, George. *Golf Addict Visits the USA*. Wraps. 1st Ed. [1955]. *Golf Addicts Through the Ages*. 1st Ed. [1956]. *Golf on My Pillow*. Wraps. Later Ed. [1960]. [Title in Japanese]. DJ. 1st Japanese Ed. [1966]. *The Full Confessions of a Golf Addict, Believe it or Not—That's Golf!* 1st Ed. [1974]. *Golf Addicts to the Fore!* Together, 7 vols. Very good overall, **$150–250, PBA**

- Houghton, George. *Confessions of a Golf Addict*. 1st Am. Ed. [1959]. Gill, Howard, ed. *Fun in the Rough*. [1957]. Huston, Mervyn, ed. *Great Golf Humour*. [1977]. Huston. Huston, Mervyn, ed. *Golf and Murphy's Law*. Inscr. and signed by Huston to Murdoch. [1981]. Together, four vols. Illus. Jackets. First Editions. Very good overall, **$150–250, PBA**

- Hughes, W. E. *Chronicles of Blackheath Golfers*. Illus. with numerous plates, incl. First Edition. London: Chapman and Hall, 1897. Blackheath is the oldest golf club in England, and this chronicle is the first published history of any club, consisting of extracts from the minute books and records of the clubs, along with portraits of members. Rubbing to spine ends and a bit to corners, foxing to endpapers, else a very good copy of this scarce and desirable book, **$2,000–3,000, PBA**

- Hunter, Robert. *The Links*. Illus. from photographs. 8³/₄" x 6", green dec. cloth, jacket. First Edition. New York: Scribners, 1926. This is one of the early American books on golf architecture, and contains numerous fine illustrations of famous U.S. golf course holes. Chipping and tears to jacket, piece lacking from lower front panel corner, else fine in scarce jacket, **$500–800, PBA**

- Hutchinson, Horace G. *Fifty Years of Golf*. London: Country Life, 1919, cloth, illus., 229 pp., still very good or better, **$350, GC**

- Hutchinson, Horace G. *The Badminton Library: Golf*. 1890 small paper deluxe edition, **$850–1,000, WR**

- Hutchinson, Horace G. *After Dinner Golf*. Intro. by Joe Murdoch. Illus. by R. André. 6³/₄" x 9¹/₄", gilt-lettered dark green morocco, a.e.g., slipcase. No. 12 of 400 copies. [London]: Ellesborough Press, 1982. Hutchinson was an accomplished golfer who won the first two official British Amateur Championships in 1886 and 1887, and he was also a writer of considerable skill, fine, **$100–150, PBA**

- Hutchinson, Horace G. *Aspects of Golf*. First Edition. Bristol: J. W. Arrowsmith, 1900. Chipping and peeling to spine, soiling, else good, **$300–500, PBA**

- Hutchinson, Horace G. *Bert Edward, the Golf Caddie*. Gilt-lettered dec. cloth. First Edition. London: John Murray, 1903. Hutchinson's fiction attempt, a story in which a caddie becomes an Open Champion. Pink stains to lower cover extremities, soiling, rubbing to spine ends, else good. **$300–500, PBA**

- Hutchinson, Horace G. *The Book of Golf and Golfers*. Contributions by Amy Pascoe, H. H. Hilton, J. H. Taylor, H. J. Whigham, and Sutton and Sons. Gilt-lettered red cloth. First Edition. London: Longmans, Green, 1899. "Like many of the books that Mr. Hutchinson had a hand in, this is a complete review of the game, from a history of its development to a chapter on how to make a golf club, for those so bent." Near fine, **$300–500, PBA**

- Hutchinson, Horace G. *British Golf Links: A Short Account of the Leading Golf Links of the United Kingdom*. Illus. from photographs. 12³/₄" x 9¹/₄", gilt-lettered pictorial cloth. First Trade Edition. London: J. S. Virtue, 1897. An account of fifty-four British golf courses, including Pau, Biaritz, and Cannes, this is one of the more elaborate books of the period. A bit of rubbing to spine ends and corners, else near fine, **$1,000–1,500, PBA**

- Hutchinson, Horace G. *Fifty Years of Golf*. Illus. Green cloth, gilt-lettered spine. First Edition. London: Country Life, [1919]. Extremely good, **$300–500, PBA**

- Hutchinson, Horace G. *Golf*. Illus. by Thomas Hodge & Harry Furniss. 9¼" x 7½", 3–4 blue morocco & gilt-lettered orange cloth, gilt-lettered spine, No. 200 of 250 Large Paper copies. First Edition. London: Longmans, Green, 1892. The Badminton Library issued twenty-four volumes on twenty-two different sports, for use by the general public who knew little or nothing about sports. Hutchinson was a wise choice by the editor to author the volume on golf, as he was already becoming one of the most prolific and knowledgeable golf writers in history. Scuffing to spine ends, corners and joints, hinges cracked, still very good, **$700–1,000, PBA**

- Hutchinson, Horace G. *Golf: A Complete History of the Game, together with Directions for Selection of Implements, the Rules, and a Glossary of Golf Terms*. 5¾" x 4¼", silver-stamped green cloth. Revised Edition. Philadelphia: Penn Publishing, 1901. Chipping to spine ends, else very good, **$80–120, PBA**

- Hutchinson, Horace G. *Hints on the Game of Golf*. Illus. from diagrams. Pictorial light green cloth. Sixth Edition. Edinburgh: William Blackwood and Sons, 1886. Fading and soiling to cloth, else about very good, **$200–300, PBA**

- Hutchinson, Horace G. *The Lost Golfer*. Gilt-lettered green cloth. First Edition. London: John Murray, [1930]. Another book of fiction by Mr. Hutchinson, this one a detective novel. Sunning to spine, otherwise about very good to rare, **$1,200–1,800, PBA**

- Hyslop, Theo. *Mental Handicaps in Golf*. Baltimore: Williams & Wilkins, 1927, fine, **$85, GC.**

- J.A.C.K. [J. McCullogh]. *Golf in the Year 2000 or, What We Are Coming To*. Original printed wrappers, rebacked. First Edition. London: T. Fisher Unwin, 1892. A science fiction tale of the year 2000, with bizarre accounts of international golf tournaments, color photographs, patent balls, tubular railways under the Atlantic, and women as members of Parliament (!). Crudely rebacked, tears to wrappers at front and rear joints, worthy of rebinding as this is extremely scarce in original wrappers, **$300–500, PBA**

- Jenkins, Dan. *Dead Solid Perfect*. [1974]. Innes, Michael. *An Awkward Lie*. [1972]. Jones, Bob. *Gulls on the Golf Course*. Signed. [1975], *Sherlock Holmes, the Golfer* [1981], *Sherlock Holmes Saved Golf*. Signed. [1986]. Together, five vols. Last two in wrappers, others cloth in jackets. Mostly First Editions. Very good or better, **$150–250, PBA**

- Jerome, Owen. *Golf Club Murder*. Ed Clode, New York, 1929, **$65, GC.**

- Jones, Charles. (ed.) *Hoyle's Games Improved, Being Practical Treatises on Whist, Quadrille, Piquet, Chess . . . and Goff or Golf . . . .* viii, 290, + [2] ad pp. Illus. incl. folding plate of billiard tables. Period calf, morocco spine label. New Edition. London: J. F. & C. Rivington, et al., 1790. This was the first edition in which the game of golf appeared. In the whole book there are but 2½ pages on golf, "The favourite Summer Amusement in Scotland . . ." The section describes feathery balls, various irons, general course layouts, and one paragraph of rules. Rubbing to joints and spine ends, else very good, **$300–500, PBA**

- Jones, Robert T. *Bobby Jones on Golf.* Foreword by Grantland Rice. Illus from photographs. 12" x 9", pictorial wrappers. First Edition. New York: One Time Publications, 1929–30. Front wrapper detached, rear lacking, stains to front wrapper, spine wrappers perished, else fair, **$100–150, PBA**

- Jones, Robert T. *Golf Is My Game.* Illus. Jacket. First Edition. Garden City, NY: Doubleday, 1960. Inscribed and signed by Jones to Joe Murdoch on the front free endpaper, 2" piece of jacket lacking from spine head, else very good, a great association copy! **$1,500–2,500, PBA**

- Jones, Robert T. and O. B. Keeler. *Down the Fairway: The Golf Life and Play of Robert T. Jones, Jr.* Foreword by Grantland Rice. Illus. Jacket. Blue Ribbon (Fifth) Edition. New York: Blue Ribbon Books, [1931]. Jacket heavily chipped, incl. loss of jacket spine head, short tears & creases, else good and still bright, **$100–150, PBA**

- Jones, Robert T. *Down the Fairway.* 75th Anniversary Limited Edition, Bobby Jones's autobiography, limited to 100 copies, hand-crafted books sewn in Irish linen thread, pub. 2002, **$2,500, Golf Links to the Past**

- Jones, Robert T. and Clifford Roberts. *The Masters Tournament.* Illus. from photographs. Foreword by Bobby Jones and Clifford Roberts. 9¾" x 14", gilt-lettered padded green calf. First Edition. [Augusta, GA: Augusta National Golf Club, 1952]. Scuffing to spine foot and a bit to head & corners, else extremely good and quite rare, **$700–1,000, PBA**

- Keeler, O. B. *The Autobiography of an Average Golfer.* Jacket. First Edition. New York: Greenberg, 1925. Keeler was described by Murdoch as "Bobby Jones's Boswell." Keeler saw Jones win all thirteen of his major championships and traveled more than 120,000 miles of golfing trails with his cohort. Pieces of jacket lacking from spine and upper front panel, flaps clipped, rubbing to vol. spine head, else very good in good but scarce jacket, **$200–300, PBA**

- Keeler, O. B. *The Boy's Life of Bobby Jones.* Illus. Gilt-lettered green cloth, partial jacket. First Edition. New York: Harper, 1931. Extremely good, **$250–400, PBA**

- Keeler, O. B. *The Bobby Jones Story.* An "inside look" at the legend who at one point won thirteen of twenty-one majors **$200, GLP**

- Kerr, Reverend John. *The Golf Book of East Lothian.* 1896 limited large paper edition (250 copies) in modern box, **$2,750–3,000, WR**

- Lang, Andrew et al. *A Batch of Golfing Papers.* Ed. by R. Barclay. Illus. by John Duncan. Original printed wrappers. First Edition. London: Simpkin, Marshall, et al., [1892]. Lang was a Scottish poet and storyteller (his Fairy Book series was a favorite among Victorian children), and considered by some to be the poet laureate of golf. Tape to spine and along front joint, else about very good, **$200–300, PBA**

- Lardner, George. *Little Blue Book No. 535: How to Play Golf.* 64 pages, first edition, published in Kansas by a Socialist organization, ca. 1927, very rare, **$100–125, WR**

- Leach, Henry. *The Happy Golfer.* Gilt-lettered green cloth. First Edition. London: Macmillan, 1914. Mr. Leach wrote a number of charming essays on the intriguing subject of golf. Slight darkening to spine, short tear to upper edge of rear cover, else extremely good, **$400–700, PBA**

- Locke, Bobby. *How to Improve Your Putting.* Pamphlet, 1949. *The Basis of My Game.* ca. 1949. *Bobby Locke on Golf.* [1953].

- Longhurst, Henry. *Only on Sundays.* 2nd Ed. [1964]. With Geoffrey Cousins. *The Ryder Cup 1965.* [1965]. *Never on Weekdays.* [1968]. *The Essential Henry Longhurst: The Best of his Writing in Golf Illustrated.* [1988]. Together, four vols. Jackets. Last three are First Editons. London: various dates, very good, **$150–250, PBA**

- Loring, Philip Quincy. *Rhymes of a Duffer.* Title page vignette. Printed stiff green wrappers bound with string. Printed by Coe-Printwell. First Edition. Portland, ME: Loring, Short & Harmon, 1914, fine, **$200–300, PBA**

- Macdonald, Charles Blair. *Scotland's Gift: Golf.* Illus. incl. tipped-in color frontispiece by Henry C. Frick. Vellum and gilt-stamped red boards, morocco spine label, No. 46 of 260 copies. First Edition. New York: Scribners, 1928. Macdonald was a pioneer of golf in America, and he laid out the courses at the Chicago Golf Club, the National on Long Island, and Mid-Ocean at Bermuda. Signed by Macdonald, **$2,000–3,000, PBA**

- MacKenzie, Dr. Alister. *Golf Architecture: Economy in Course Construction and Green-Keeping.* Intro. by H. S. Colt. Illus. from photographs. Green cloth. First Edition. London: Simpkin, Marshall, Hamilton, Kent, [1920]. Dr. MacKenzie, one of the first great golf course architects, advocated the integration of natural features and terrain into the creation of a course. The book contains four short essays on golf course design. Near fine, **$800–1,200, PBA**

- MacKenzie, Dr. Alister. *Dr. Mackenzie's Golf Architecture*. Intro. by Robert Trent Jones. Commentary by Peter Thomson and Michael Wolveridge. Compiled and arranged by H. R. Grant. Illus. Gilt-lettered green cloth. "Review Copy" of 700 copies printed by the Perrymill Press. Worcestershire: Grant Books, 1993. As new, **$100–150, PBA**

- Maclennan, R. J. *Golf at Gleneagles*. Illus. profusely from photographs, many tinted in green, with color lithograph folding map. Original pictorial boards. First Edition. Glasgow: McCorquodale, [1921]. This book gives the history and background of the great courses at Gleneagles, Scotland. A bit of chipping to spine, else very good and rare, **$300–500, PBA**

- Marshall, Robert. *The Haunted Major*. Illus. by Harry Furniss. Pictorial cloth. Early Edition. London: Alexander Moring, [ca. 1902]. One of the classic British golf fiction stories. It is a thinly disguised novel of St. Andrews and the well-known figures there of the time. Stain to spine and front cover, else good, **$70–100, PBA**

- Martin, H. B. *Fifty Years of American Golf*. Foreword by Grantland Rice. Illus. Gilt-lettered red cloth, No. 160 of 355 copies. First Edition. New York: Dodd, Mead, 1936. Signed by Martin on the limitation page, dated Oct. 1936, and warmly inscribed by him to A. C. Wheeler, fine, **$1,000–1,500, PBA**

- Martin, H. B. *What's Wrong with Your Game*. Illus. Jacket. First Edition. New York: Dodd, Mead, 1930. Signed by Martin on the front, free endpaper. ". . . instructional in nature, each page containing a golf tip illustrated in the author's simple but direct style." Fine in very good, uncommon jacket, **$200–300, PBA**

- Mathieson, Donald Mackay. *The Golfer's Handbook*. (*Golfer's Handbook*) Fourteen vols., comprising the years 1909 (11th Ed.), 1910, 1911, 1912, 1913, 1914, 1915, 1919, 1921, 1922, 1924, 1925, and 1926 (28th Ed.). Illus. profusely. 5¼ x 4, red cloth lettered & black. Edinburgh: Scottish Newspaper Publishing, 1909. *The Golfer's Handbook* series runs from 1899 through the present. "A giant book of golfing statistics and information . . . ." Some hinges cracked, overall very good or better, **$2,500–4,000, PBA**

- Mathison, Thomas. *The Goff. An Heroi-Comical Poem in Three Cantos . . . with an Appendix, Containing Two Poems in Praise of Goff, and a few Notes and Illustrations*. [8], 32 pp. Bound in 19th-century gilt-lettered cloth. Third Edition. Edinburgh: Peter Hill, 1793. Of *The Goff*, Murdoch writes (p. 15, *The Library of Golf*), "Standing alone in a century of silence, the first book entirely devoted to golf was published in 1743, more than twenty years after Glotta and ninety years before another book would appear. It, too, is poetry, and is one of the classics of golf literature. The ultimate that any collector can attain is to have one of its three editions in his library." The poem has 358 lines and tells, in mock heroic vein, of a match played between two golfers, Pygmalion (the author) and Castalio (Alexander Dunning, of Edinburgh), and includes the names of many prominent players of the day, although in the first and second editions the names are identified by initials only. According to Murdoch, "This last edition is the rarest of the three . . ." Very faint stain to lower gutter area of middle pages, else fine, **$20,000–30,000, PBA**

- Maughan, William Charles. *Picturesque Musselburgh and its Golf Links.* Illus. by R. Gemmell Hutchinson. Pictorial cloth jacket. First Edition. Paisley: Alexander Gardner, [1906]. Scarce in hardcover and even more so in jacket, this little volume tells all about the town of Musselburgh and its famous links and players, spine chipped and torn along joints, else fine in near very good jacket, **$800–1,200, PBA**

- McMahan, Valerie Bumps. *The Golf Ball Kid and Little Caddy.* 1929, first edition, **$600–700, WR**

- McPherson, J. Gordon. *Golf and Golfers Past and Present.* Intro. by A. J. Balfour. Frontispiece port. Original pictorial red cloth. First Edition. Edinburgh: William Blackwood & Sons, 1891. An important book of reminiscences of golf of the day, particularly in Perth, where McPherson was from. A bit of soiling, light fading to spine, else very good, **$800–1,000, PBA**

- Middlecoff, Cary. *Golf Doctor.* Foreword by Bob Hope. 1st Ed. [1950]. *Advanced Golf.* 3rd Ed. [1960]. Another copy. Japanese Ed., Dampstained. [1958]. *Master Guide to Better Golf.* Deluxe Ed. [1960]. *The Golf Swing.* 1st Ed. [1969]. Together, five vols. Illus. Jackets. Good to very good, **$150–250, PBA**

- Moffat, William D. and C.A.P. Ricornus. *The Goat Club Golf Book: The Rules of the Game as Played by the Ancient & Honourable Order of Goats.* Illus. First Edition. New York: Knapp, [1911]. Fine, **$200–300, PBA**

- Monks of St. Giles. *Reminiscences of the Monks of St. Giles.* 3 vols. Illus. 7³/4" x 5¹/2", 3–4 levant dark blue morocco & marbled boards, gilt-lettered and tooled spines, raised bands, first edition. [Scotland]: 1883–1911. The Monks of St. Giles was a self-described "quasi-literary club" founded in 1852. Among the poems on golf included in these volumes are the following: Five poems, entitled "Curling Song" (by various authors), "Fore!" by A. P. Aitken, "Gae Bring to me my Clubs" by Alexander Gilmour, "Luffness Links" by Gilmour, and "The Gude Gaun Game o' Curlin'" by J. A. Sidey. A fine set in handsome bindings, rare, **$2,000–3,000, PBA**

- Murdoch, Joseph S. F. *The First Golf Book Bibliography: A Rough Draft of the Complete Story of Golf.* Twenty-page stapled carbon typescript with holograph corrections and additions by Murdoch. N.p. [1985]. Very good condition to unique, **$700–1,000, PBA**

- Murdoch, Joseph S. F. *The Library of Golf 1743–1966: A Bibliography of Golf Books, Indexed Alphabetically, Chronologically, & by Subject Matter*. Gilt-stamped & lettered cloth, slipcase. First Edition. Detroit: Gale Research, 1968. Inscribed and signed by Murdoch. Contains numerous ink annotations in Murdoch's hand. Fine, unique copy. **$1,000–1,500, PBA**

- Murdoch, Joseph. *Library of Golf 1743–1966, A Bibliography of Golf Books Indexed Alphabetically, Chronologically and By Subject Matter*. Gale, Detroit, 1968, illus., 314 pp., fine in very good slipcase, **$550, GC**

- Murdoch, Joseph S. F. *Golfer's Log: My Favorite Golf Games and Pet Score Cards*. Spiral-bound flexible boards. New York: 1951–53. Bibliographer Joseph S. F. Murdoch's personal golfing log, fine, **$300–500, PBA**

- Nelson, Byron. *The Byron Nelson Story*. Illus. Gilt-ruled and blind-tooled calf, gilt-lettered spine, slipcase. No. 556 of 600 copies. First Edition. [Cincinnati: Old Golf Shop, 1980]. Signed by Nelson on the limitation page, fine, **$100–150, PBA**

- Nelson, Byron. *Pecora's Winning Golf with Byron Nelson*. Twelve pamphlets. First Editions. Philadelphia: Pecora Paint Co. [1951]. Stains to first and edges of others, else about very good, **$100–150, PBA**

- Nelson, Byron. *Winning Golf*. (Chipping, price clipped.) [1946]. *Shape Your Swing the Modern Way*. [1976]. Another copy. [1985]. Together, three vols. Illus. Cloth, first two in jackets. First two are First Editions. First very good, others fine, **$80–120, PBA**

- Nicholson, William. *An Almanac of Twelve Sports*. Verses by Rudyard Kipling. Illus. with twelve color plates by Nicholson, incl. a golfer. 12" x 10", cloth-backed pictorial boards. First American Edition. New York: R. H. Russell, 1900. A beautiful book of striking prints by Nicholson, including that of a golfer by the sea. Very good, usually found in much more fragile condition, **$300–500, PBA**

- Nicklaus, Jack & Ken Bowden. *Golf My Way*. Illus. 9¼" x 7", jacket. First Edition. New York: Simon & Schuster [1974]. Warmly inscribed and signed by Nicklaus to Joe Murdoch on the frontispiece port. Price clipped, else very good, **$200–300, PBA**

- Nicklaus, Jack and Ken Bowden. *On & Off the Fairway, a Pictorial Autobiography*. Illus. Jacket. First Edition. New York: Simon & Schuster, 1978. Warmly inscribed and signed by Nicklaus to Joe Murdoch on the front-free endpaper, very good, **$200–300, PBA**

- Norval, Ronald. *King of the Links: The Story of Bobby Locke*. Dust jacket. [ca. 1951]. Together, four vols. First Editions. Very good overall, **$150–250, PBA**

- Ouimet, Francis, *A Game of Golf: A Book of Reminiscences*. Intro. by Bernard Darwin. Illus. Gilt-lettered cloth, glassine, slipcase. No. 377 of 550 copies printed by the Riverside Press. First Edition. Boston: Houghton Mifflin, 1932. Signed by Ouimet on the limitation page. Ouimet emerged as a "player of the highest rank" in the 1913 Open, fine, **$1,000–1,500, PBA**

- Palmer, Arnold. *Arnold Palmer's Golf Book: "Hit It Hard!"* 2nd UK Ed. [1961]. *Portrait of a Professional Golfer*. 1st Ed. [1964]. *Arnold Palmer's Best 54 Golf Holes*. 1st Ed. [1977]. *Play Great Golf*. 1st UK Ed. [1988]. Together, four vols. Illus. Jackets, Very good or better, **$150–250, PBA**

- Park, Jr., William. *The Game of Golf*. Illus. Pictorial cloth. First Edition. London: Longmans, Green, 1896. This was the first book to be written by a golfing professional. Park was not only a player, but also owned a successful clubmaking business and was a golf course architect. The book reveals some of the secrets of his success. Minor foxing and soiling, else near fine, **$400–700, PBA**

- Pendleton, Alex. *Better Golf with Brains*. Charles E. Tuttle, Tokyo, 1952, 1st Japan ed., illus. wraps, illus., 62 pp., signed by Pendleton, **$75, GC**

- Peter, H. Thomas. *Reminiscences of Golf and Golfers*. 55 pp. gilt-lettered red cloth. First Edition. Edinburgh: James Thin, [1890]. The book gives an interesting look into the past and early history of the game, front hinge neatly cracked, else very good, **$5,000–7,000, PBA**

- Pinehurst Golf Course [Anon]. *The Game at Pinehurst, North Carolina, Upon the Finest Golf Courses in the South*. Illus. Gilt-lettered plaid wrappers. First Edition. [New York: privately printed, ca. 1920s]. Fine–rare, **$150–250, PBA**

- Pinehurst Golf Course [Anon]. *America's Winter Playground* ca. 1912, 62 pp. book includes photographs, **$60–70, WR**

- Price, Charles. *The World of Golf*. [1962]. *The American Golfer*. [1964]. *A Golf Story: Bobby Jones, Augusta National, and the Masters Tournament*. [1986]. Illus. jackets. First Editions. Very good overall, **$100–150, PBA**

- Rare Copy *The Golf Links of France* published 1939, Paris. c–w. Foreword by Bernard Darwin with pictorial paper covers, 16 pages with illustrations and issued by French National Railways with text in English. Center fold, **$185, MM**

- Reid, William. *Golfing Reminiscences: The Growth of the Game, 1887–1925*. Gilt-lettered blue cloth. First Edition. Edinburgh: J. & J. Gray, [1925]. Fading to spine, else about fine, **$400–600, PBA**

- Reynolds, Frank. *The Frank Reynolds Golf Book–Drawings from 'Punch.'* Intro. by Bernard Darwin. Illus. throughout with clever cartoons by Reynolds. First Edition. London: Methuen, [1932]. Chipping to jacket extremities, else near very good, **$200–300, PBA**

- Rice, Grantland & Clare Briggs. *The Duffer's Handbook of Golf.* Illus. 9³/₄" x 7³/₄", plaid cloth, pictorial cover and spine labels, original box with pictorial cover label. No. 110 of 500 copies. First Edition. New York: Macmillan, 1926. Signed on the limitation page by Rice & Briggs. A book of golf humor, **$600–900, PBA**

- *Royal & Ancient Golf Club of St. Andrews Decisions by the Rules of Golf Committee of the Royal and Ancient Golf Club, 1909–1910.* [1910]. *Decisions by the Rules of Golf Committee of the Royal and Ancient Golf Club, 1909–1919.* [1919]. *Decisions by the Rules of Golf Committee of the Royal and Ancient Golf Club, 1909–1924.* (Two copies.) [1924]. Together, six vols. Gilt-lettered blue cloth (first lettered in black). St. Andrews: W. C. Henderson & Son, **$400–700, PBA**

- *The Ryder Cup Team versus Bobby Jones Challenge Team.* United Service Organizations, Detroit Golf Club, Detroit, August 1941, illus. wraps, illus., 32 pp., **$800, GC.**

- Sanders, Doug. *Action on the First Tee.* Dallas: Taylor Pub., 1987. Illus. wraps, illus., signed and inscribed by Sanders, **$20, GC**

- Sarazen, Gene and Herbert Warren Wind. *Thirty Years of Golf.* Copy of Memorial Edition of Sarazen's autobiography, **$150, GLP**

- S. R. A. *The Links: An Auld Kirk Allegory.* 14 pp. Later wrappers. First Edition. Edinburgh: J. Gardner Hitt, [ca. 1895]. A poem in 4-line verse about golf in the old country, fine, **$500–800, PBA**

- Scottish Parliamentary Laws & Acts. *The Lawes and Actes of Parliament, Maid de King James the First, and his Successours Kinges of Scotland: Visied, collected and extracted furth of the Register.* Includes Acts from 1424–1597, with glossary. 10¹/₂" x 6³/₄", plain period calf. Edinburgh: Robert Walde-Grave, 1597. These early Scottish Acts of Parliament include the first mention of golf, tracing its history to the Acts of 1457, when "Golfe," along with "Fute-ball," were prohibited by King James II due to the endangerment they caused to the sport of archery. Very good; a book whose importance cannot be underestimated, **$1,000–1,500, PBA**

- Simpson, Harold. *The 7 Stages of Golf and Other Golf Stories in Picture and Verse.* Illus. with bright color plates by G. E. Shepheard. 13" x 9¹/₄", pictorial boards. First American Edition. Philadelphia: J.B. Lippincott, 1909. Rebacked and with corners replaced, chipping along extremities, still about very good and internally bright, with humorous pictorial accounts of golf's most frustrating moments, **$500–800, PBA**

- Smart, John. *A Round of the Links: Views of the Golf Greens of Scotland.* Twenty etched plates by George Aikman from watercolor drawings by John Smart; printed tissue guards. Large oblong folio, original gilt-lettered buckram. No. 28 of a limited edition. First Edition. [Edinburgh: privately printed], 1893. Signed by Smart. Soiling and faint spots to covers, handsome plates depicting the best-known Scottish golf links being played in typically bleak weather, **$8,000–12,000, PBA**

- Smith, Garden. *The World of Golf; The Isthmian Library.* Preface by Temple Chambers. Illus. from photographs, incl. frontispiece of St. Andrews. Gilt-lettered green cloth. First Edition. London: A. D. Innes, 1898, very fine, **$200–300, PBA**

- Snead, Sam. *Education of a Golfer.* Simon and Schuster: New York. 1962, 3rd printing, illus., 248 pp., jacket with large chip to front panel, inscribed and signed by Snead, **$75, GC**

- Snead, Sam. *Sam Snead on Golf.* [1961]. *Sam Snead Teaches You His Simple "Key" Approach to Golf.* [1975]. *Slammin' Sam: An Autobiography.* [1986]. *Pigeons, Marks, Hustlers, and Other Golf Bettors You Can Beat.* [1986]. Together, four vols. Jackets. First Editions. Very good or better, **$150–250, PBA**

- *Songs of the Azooks: Being a Collection of Verse and Worse Sung by That Ancient and Honorable Society of Golfs by One of 'Em.* Ormond Beach, FL: [privately printed], 1940, 56 pp., fine in jacket with same illus. of golfer as cloth, an oddity, **$125, GC.**

- Spalding's Athletic Library. Stoddart, L. B., ed. *Spalding's Official Golf Guide.* Illus. Original pictorial wrappers; custom-made chemise & half morocco clamshell box. Second Edition. New York: American Sports Publishing, 1895. Chipping to extremities, fragile, else fair to good, but rare, **$300–500, PBA**

- [Stone, Dr.] A Member. *The Duffers' Golf Club Papers,* to which is added, *A Day on the Ladies' Links.* Gilt-lettered blue morocco. First Edition. Montrose: Standard Office, 1891. Scuffing to extremities, else about very good, **$3,000–5,000, PBA**

- Strutt, Joseph. *Glig-Gamena Angel-Deod or The Sports and Pastimes of the People of England, Including the Rural and Domestic Recreations, May Games, Mummeries, Shows, Processions, Pageants, and Pompous Spectacles, from the Earliest Period to the Present Time.* [ii], xlix, [7], 357, [1] pp. Illus. with thirty-nine copper plates, gilt-tooled spine. Second Edition. London: T. Bensley, 1810. Mild rubbing and scratches to covers, fine copy of this famous tome, with lovely sepia-toned illustrations, **$500–800, PBA**

- Sutphen, W. G. Van T. *The Golfer's Alphabet.* Illus. throughout with plates by A. B. Frost. First Edition. New York: Harper, 1899. "A book of cleverly conceived couplets which convey a thought for each letter of the alphabet. . . ." Heavy rubbing and scratching to covers, else good, with humorous illustrations, **$300–500, PBA**

- Taylor, John H. *Golf, My Life's Work.* Intro. by Bernard Darwin. Frontispiece, port. Jacket. First Edition. London: Jonathan Cape, [1943]. An autobiography of one of England's greatest golfers. Chipping to jacket spine head, else very good, **$200–300, PBA**

- Taylor, J. H. *Taylor on Golf.* 1902 second edition, **$75-100, WR**

- Thomas, Jr., George C. *Golf Architecture in America: Its Strategy and Construction.* Illus. from photographs and charts, green-lettered green cloth, jacket. First Edition. Los Angeles: Times-Mirror Press, 1927. "One of the outstanding books on golf course architecture." Chipping to jacket spine head and corners, else fine to near fine, **$1,000–1,500, PBA**

- Tillinghast, A. W. *The Mutt and Other Golf Yarns.* First edition, 1925, red cloth, 105 pages, **$2,000, GLP**

- Tillinghast, A. W. *Cobble Valley Golf Yarns and Other Sketches.* Frontispiece. Gilt-lettered olive cloth. First Edition. Philadelphia: Philadelphia Printing, [1915]. Warmly inscribed and signed by Tillinghast to a friend for Christmas on the front-free endpaper: "Maybe, one night beside your new fireplace, in your new house, closely our new golf course, you may find an hour of entertainment in reading of these tales," very good, **$400–700, PBA**

- Tolley, Cyril J. H. *The Modern Golfer.* Illus. from photographs, incl. frontispiece, port. Green cloth, gilt-lettered spine. First Edition. London: W. Collins Sons, [1924]. Tolley was British Amateur Champion in 1920, Welsh Champion in 1921 and 1923, and the French Open Champion in 1924, very good, **$100–150, PBA**

- Travers, Jerome D. *Travers' Golf Book.* Illus. incl. tinted frontispiece. Gilt-lettered & dec. cloth, pictorial cover label. First Edition. New York: Macmillan, 1913. Travers played a large part in the development of golf in America. Rubbing to extremities, else very good, **$100–150. PBA**

- Travers, Jerome D. & Grantland Rice. *The Winning Shot.* Illus. Pictorial green and yellow cloth. First Edition. Garden City, NY: Doubleday, 1915. An account of Travers's early golfing triumphs, and one of the first books Rice contributed to, extremely good, **$100–150, PBA**

- Travers, Jerome D. and J. R. Crowell. *The Fifth Estate: 30 Years of Golf.* New York: Alfred A. Knopf, 1st edition, 1926, original pictorial cloth boards, internally clean and sound, **$150–200, MM**

- Travis, Walter J. *Practical Golf.* Gilt-lettered & dec. green cloth. First Edition. New York: Harper, 1901. Travis was an early American champion whose career began after age 30 and whose putting method won him the 1904 British Open Championship. Three small spots to front cover, else near fine and bright, **$150–250, PBA**

- Trevino, Lee. *I Can Help Your Game.* 1st UK Ed. [1972]. *Groove Your Golf Swing My Way.* 1st Ed. [1976]. *Super Mex: An Autobiography.* 1st UK Ed. [1983]. *The Snake in the Sandtrap.* 1st Ed. [1985]. Together, 4 vols. Illus. Jackets. Very good or better, **$150–250, PBA**

- Tulloch, W. W. *The Life of Tom Morris, with Glimpses of St. Andrews and its Golfing Celebrities.* Illus. from twenty-seven photographs. 8³/₄" x 5¹/₂", pictorial green cloth, gilt-lettered spine. First Edition. London: T. Werner Laurie, [ca. 1908]. A biography of Scotland's most famous golfer. Old Tom Morris set the record for the largest margin of victory ever when he won the 1862 British Open by thirteen strokes. Mild rubbing to spine ends, else near fine, **$700–1,000, PBA**

- Tulloch, W. W. *The Life of Tom Morris.* Limited edition, 1982, full leather edition, excellent condition, **$395, GLP**

- *Universal Golf Dictionary.* Universal Golf Co., Springfield, MA, 1934. Fine, **$150, GC**

- Vaile, P. A. *How to Drive.* Illus. Pictorial wrappers. Part of the Wilson Athletic Library. First Edition. Chicago: Thomas E. Wilson, [1919]. Very good, **$80–120, PBA**

- Vardon, Harry. *The Complete Golfer.* Sixty-five illustrations, incl. frontispiece, port. Gilt-lettered blue cloth. First Edition. London: Methuen, [1905]. "The first of several books by one of golf's great immortals, one who probably exerted as much influence on the game as any one man could." Foxing, else near fine, **$300–500, PBA**

- Vardon, Harry, Alexander Herd, George Duncan, Wilfred Reid, Lawrence Ayton, and Francis Ouimet. *Success at Golf.* Intro. by John Anderson. Illus. incl. frontispiece of Ouimet. Gilt-lettered green cloth. First American Edition. Boston: Little, Brown, 1914. Soiling to lower front cover extremities, else near fine, **$100–150, PBA**

- Victim [D.W.C. Falls]. *An A.B.C. of Golf, by a Victim.* Illus. throughout with humorous stone lithograph drawings of golf by Falls. 10¹/₂" x 8", pictorial burlap wrappers, custom-made quarter morocco clamshell box. First Edition. New York: Blanchard

Press, 1898. Burlap wrappers expertly laid-on to backing boards, else near fine, with charming illustrations, **$1,000–1,500, PBA**

- Webling, W. Hastings. *Fore! The Call of the Links*. Illus. throughout, incl. frontispiece port. Cloth-backed pictorial boards. First Edition. Boston & New York: H. M. Caldwell, [1909]. A book of golf poetry, illustrated with some charming sketches. Near fine, **$250–400, PBA**

- Wethered, H. N. *The Perfect Golfer*. Illus. Gilt-lettered green cloth, jacket. First Edition. London: Methuen, [1931]. Wethered puts forth his ideas of perfection in a golf course, stroke, and other subjects. Chipping to jacket spine head, else near fine in very good jacket, **$150–250, PBA**

- Who's Who. *Who's Who in Golf and Directory of Golf Clubs and Members*. Gilt-lettered red cloth. First Edition. London: Stanley Publishing, 1909. The first and only edition. An invaluable reference guide for turn-of-the-century golfers, known and unknown, and of golf clubs of the British Isles. Internally browned, still very good, **$300–500, PBA**

- Wilson, J. H. *The Golfers of a Past Era: A Series of Photographs After J. H. Wilson Taken at Prestwick Golf Club and the Open Championship during the Years 1884–1894*. Intro. by G. S. Cumming. Illus. with twenty tipped-in reproduction photographs of golfers in candid poses in gilt-lettered cloth portfolio. No. 61 of 1000 copies. First Edition. Ayrshire, Scotland: B. Marshall, [1977]. J. H. Wilson was a Prestwick golfer and an excellent photographer who made this important record of early golf at Prestwick Golf Club, which was founded in 1851. Fine, **$100–150, PBA**

- Wind, Herbert Warren. *The Story of American Golf: Its Champions and Championships*. Illus. Cloth, jacket, slipcase. First Edition. New York: Farrar, Straus & Giroux, 1948. Chipping to jacket spine head, else fine in very good jacket and slipcase, **$200–300, PBA**

- Wodehouse, P. G. *The Clicking of Cuthbert*. Cloth. First Edition. London: Herbert Jenkins, 1922. First edition with only eight previous titles listed on page facing the title. Very good, **$100–150, PBA**

- Wodehouse, P. G. *Divots*. [1927]. *Wodehouse on Golf*. [1940]. Together, two vols. Cloth. First American Editions. New York: Doubleday, Doran. Very good. **$100–150, PBA**

- Wodehouse, P. G. *Golf Without Tears*. Cloth. 1st Am. Ed. (soiling & stains, front hinge cracked through, fair.) [1924]. *The Clicking of Cuthbert*. (Autograph Edition) [1956]. *The Heart of a Goof*. (Autograph Edition), [1956]. Together, three vols. about fine, **$100–150, PBA**

- Wood, Harry B. *Golfing Curios and "The Like" With an appendix comprising a "Bibliography of Golf," etc.* Illus. with plates. 11¹/₂" x 8³/₄", quarter vellum and green cloth, gilt-lettered spine, 1 of 150 copies. First (Subscriber's) Edition. London: Sherratt & Hughes, 1910. The first to attempt to gather a listing of golfiana (books, balls, clubs, cups, medals, prizes, etc.) in book form. Mild soiling, else near fine, an extremely rare and important volume, **$1,000–1,500, PBA**

- A leaf from a Flemish Book of Hours, ca. 1490, one vignette depicts a group in period costume playing a game with implements similar to golf clubs, double glazed with reverse image of an anatomical man, **$5,000–7,000, WR**

6 THE SKILLFUL TOUCH
Pottery

Some treasure hunters use their noses to strike gold. Renowned for picking up the scent of scarce and even seemingly lost works, book hound Dick Donovan sniffs and sniffs until he finds the right stuff.

Others on the trail of must-have collectibles rely only on their instincts, the aesthetic appeal of some object of desire. Or they simply use their eyes, touch the piece, and reach for a checkbook.

Then there's the man with the Pepsodent smile, the art lover who along with having a deep reverence for the game is a bit of a pirate, Captain Kidd style.

In those halcyon days of golden pieces of eight from the Spanish Main, the skeptical would bite into coins to determine if they were authentic. Now most people don't risk their $10,000 smiles to test the value of items, yet Wayne Aaron has always gone against the tide of convention. Still religiously using "a trick" taught to him by an old pottery maker, this serious collector often depends on his teeth to unearth golf's most prized ceramics.

Laughing as this stratagem is divulged, Aaron explains, "After collecting pottery for thirty years, I've discovered this technique works very well, particularly when you want to determine if a repair has been concealed.

"Hold the piece up, and tap the top of the item's rim with your teeth," instructs this aficionado of American Belleek and Royal Doulton. Aaron is a member of the United States Golf Association's Museum Committee who's acquired over 400 rare ceramic pieces. "You will hear a funny sound if there is a concealed crack in the piece.

Schoenhut Tommy golfing figure. *Photo courtesy of Old Tom Morris Golf, L.L.C.*

Royal Doulton Series Ware plate 10¹/₄" illustrated by Chas. Crombie, "Every dog has his day." *Photo courtesy of Old Tom Morris Golf, L.L.C.*

There's a consistent, very sweet ring in a pristine piece, similar to the ring made by your finger when you tap crystal with your finger. But if the pottery has been repaired, there will be a dead, sick, and sour sound."

This is just one "self-preservation technique" Aaron has used while hunting for such celebrated rarities as pre-1900s Burslems (pieces made by Doulton before it was given the "Royal" designation by the British Crown), Weller "Italian-styled" Dickens Ware such as vases and cups (with a three-dimensional look), and massive Simon Peter Gerz beer steins with large pewter lids.

Besides having a terrific ardor for these aesthetically pleasing pieces (with hand-painted golfing scenes and dashing colors), Aaron has gone to school to ensure that he is purchasing coveted objects. Never just believing in the power of the checkbook, he's relentlessly visited pottery manufacturers in the U.S. and United Kingdom, examined scores of documents (sales receipts, company ledgers, etc.), read numerous history books and encyclopedias on the subject, and networked with fellow enthusiasts. This educational process has taken him to all parts of the globe, and has at times been frustrating. But even his "mistakes" have been instructive.

Recalling his foolish refusal to buy a copy of golf's "bible," the extremely rare and hotly pursued *The Goff,* Aaron first tries to mitigate this error by saying "I just didn't know destiny was smiling on me. Every collector will one day find lightning in a bottle. There's always a stroke of good fortune awaiting you. I just had to acquire more knowledge."

Putting a brave face on his actions of thirty years ago, he quickly explains, "Lightning in a bottle also works the other way. There's not a collector I know that if he had

Royal Doulton stein with humorous golfers drawn by H. M. Bateman. *Photo courtesy of Old Tom Morris Golf, L.L.C.*

Royal Doulton stein with humorous golfers drawn by H. M. Bateman. *Photo courtesy of Old Tom Morris Golf, L.L.C.*

more knowledge he wouldn't have passed on some very important item. I was offered *The Goff* for a mere $3,000. Three weeks later I saw it go for $21,000 at an auction in Scotland. Today it sells at a minimum for $60,000. When I was offered it I didn't know what I didn't know. Yet that was a wonderful motivation for me. I had to acquire more knowledge."

Ever since developing that expertise, Aaron has not been afraid to make some heady moves. Firmly believing the pottery market is relatively unchartered territory, and that its pricing is "spike-proof" (not vulnerable to the volatility seen in club collecting), he's pursued ceramic pieces (many of these functional water pitchers, three-handled loving cups, and serving sets were originally commissioned by golf clubs to serve as prizes) with a dollar-signed vigor that has stunned his friends—and competing bidders at auctions.

"Original, one-of-a-kind ceramics could be one of the least understood niches in collecting, and that's why many people think I'm crazy when I'm willing to set a world record for a piece," laughs Aaron, who advisers art lovers to get a "feel for the universe out there" by viewing the USGA's pottery collection in Far Hills, New Jersey.

"Six months to a year later my prices were exceeded, sometimes double what I bid for a piece of pottery, and these same skeptics wondered how I had the vision to know prices would rise. It's no mystery. Pottery is art that ultimately attracts every collector.

"I feel pottery is one of those collecting areas where really rare, one-of-a-kind pieces are still attractively priced. Many collectors just know about Ming vases. They don't know this world."

Kingsware tobacco humidor by Royal Doulton ca. 1930s. *Photo courtesy of Old Tom Morris Golf, L.L.C.*

Fine Kingsware jug by Royal Doulton ca. 1930s. *Photo courtesy of Old Tom Morris Golf, L.L.C.*

Aaron does. He's often taken advantage of auctioneers who either "completely mis-label, overlook items, or don't have the knowledge to know a piece's true value. By outwitting the experts with his singular brand of savvy and willingness to study pro-duction records at factories, he has assembled a museum-worthy collection of Lam-beth (a studio producing stoneware that was a 19th-century precursor to Royal Doulton); German-made Amphoria statuary (i.e., golfers and their caddies); gray pastel or cobalt-blue Gerz whiskey jugs; and a rainbow-colored array of objects from Lenox, America's watchword in pottery.

A true Lenox piece typically features the Shinnecock (Long Island, New York) club-house in the background along with a golfer who's about to strike a ball on this al-most mythical, linksland-styled course.

Players caught in the rough, or facing some other sort of perilous circumstance are also the staple of Royal Doulton (that honorific designation from the Crown appeared after 1902 with one flairful distinction). To realistically capture "gentlemanly golfers at their sporting best," the Royal Doulton vases and bowls, whether embellished with silver rosette or not, always depicted the game's ambassadors in flaming red jackets.

These works celebrate the game's allure of Man versus the elements or Mother Na-ture, showing golfers pitted against bunkers and other hazards, standing alone to face the consequences of their actions. In a sense it's Man at his best, pottery as the glo-rious storyteller.

Yet as Aaron explains, Doulton, Copeland Spode, and other brands with unques-tioned cachet ("there are also many lesser-known makers with real artistry and

Copeland Spode pitcher with green background and white golfing figures, 4¹/₂″h. *Photo courtesy of Old Tom Morris Golf, L.L.C.*

Copeland Spode pitcher 4¹/₂″h in cobalt blue on gray with white figures. *Photo courtesy of Old Tom Morris Golf, L.L.C.*

Copeland Late Spode Pitcher 6″h in cobalt blue ca. 1905. *Photo courtesy of Old Tom Morris Golf, L.L.C.*

Green Copeland Spode pitcher 7³/₄″h ca. 1910 marked Copeland Late Spode. *Photo courtesy of Old Tom Morris Golf, L.L.C.*

value," insists this potteryphile) feature "tight" type of paintings. While vaunted collectibles, they epitomize an "old school" conservatism with depictions that are "very realistic, or as photographically as possible."

In stark contrast, American Belleek is the "French Impressionism" or "loose" style of rare ceramics, showcasing what Aaron calls "emotionalism, creativity, and a beautiful subjectivism" that's bewitchingly free-spirited.

Particularly delighted by a Belleek piece with an assemblage of cavorting mermaids armed with golf clubs, Aaron eyes its rainbow array of colors, and notes, "Belleek is very, very rare. I waited thirty years to find this beauty. Done in the late 1800s and

Cigarette jar 4¹/₂"h marked Nippon. *Photo courtesy of Old Tom Morris Golf, L.L.C.*

Green glass decanter 8³/₄"h with sterling overlay depicting a period golfer. No stopper. *Photo courtesy of Old Tom Morris Golf, L.L.C.*

early 1900s, Belleek was produced in very limited quantities, and is essentially the "Holy Grail" of American made pieces.

"At the USGA headquarters there's a Belleek with several rabbits in a field running around playing golf. It's wonderful, charming, but so is my large one-handled tankard which depicts two mermaids and a caddie. The mermaids are quite risqué, as their bosoms are very accentuated. They're playing golf underwater, and the colors are so vivid, blue, yellow, and pink pastels. While I know this very rare treasure existed, the only way I got it was by doing research, and networking with people of common interest."

Aaron also speaks glowingly about his highly prized German-made rarities, Simon Peter Gerz stoneware (whiskey and water jugs in gray, blue, and other pastels), and Haber and Ruther's beer steins with red-jacketed golfers. Gerz's earlier (and large "statement-making") items, dating from 1880 to 1910, typically sell for $2,000 to $6,000. The hand-painted green and brown glazed Habers are valued at $1,500 to $2,000, while 1900–1915 Amphorias are $1,000 to $2,000.

If a comparison to Italian painters makes this rarified collecting niche a little more understandable, those German works are the equivalent of Botticellis, Giottos, and Donatellos.

The Michelangelo-like pinnacle is from Doulton's Burslem studio (late 1800s to 1900), very fine bone china that's still made in the same-named town (dating back to the early 1700s, meaning "Burgweard Elms") near Newcastle. Characterized by thin walls, and artistic hand coloring that's typically blue and white, these pieces, according to Aaron, "are not just baked, big chunks of clay. This is much more refined production. A process is used to arrive at a clear background, and there are delightful depictions of golfers on the course, men and women in period dress and clubhouses. These ornamental accessories (vases and bowls for the most part) are the expression of the pottery maker's art."

Rarely appearing at auctions or in private sales (maybe one piece every few years), Burslems are understandably expensive. Small vases and bowls are typically in the $5,000 range, while larger "objects of envy" are in the $30,000 range.

But new enthusiasts shouldn't be intimidated by these four- and five-figure price tags. In this arena, where quality pieces often go unnoticed or underappreciated, there are many fabulous $500 to $1,000 pieces waiting to be acquired by collectors.

"You don't have to spend a lot of money to enjoy this world, or to own a piece of beauty," insists Aaron, who fondles a Royal ten-inch plate decorated with Pilgrims to emphasize his point. "This very successful line of dinnerware called 'Series Ware' was made in the late 1920s, early '30s, and along with golfing themes, they feature old English sayings, or proverbs like, 'Do Me Wrong But Every Dog Will Have His Day.' They make a lovely backdrop in the home, and a plate is just $400 to $500."

While Doulton hand-painted vases from 1885 are valued at $12,000 to $20,000, attractive 1950s Lladro porcelain figurines are priced at $500, Noritake porcelain can be acquired for $400 to $600, and there's always the chance that a highly valuable piece can be found at a garage sale or flea market from an unsuspecting seller.

Snooping around those venues or in antique shops is usually a pleasure-filled hunt. But don't let the spirit of adventure cloud your better judgment. "There are still bargains out there, but only if you know how to really recognize them," cautions Aaron. "First know this universe, that a company like Copeland Spode made beautifully graduated milk pitchers in green and blue, or that U.S.-made Weller produced highly respected American art pottery (Dickens Ware). Learn to tell if a piece is sound, or if it's been repaired. This is key. Whether it's a Burslem, or any rare, one-of-a-kind item, if it has a chip on it, or been repaired, I'd go ahead and buy it. Not for $20,000, but for $10,000 to $12,000, and then I'd have it restored for $500 to $1,000."

That type of formula doesn't apply to "common" pieces. If a $500 item is chipped or cracked, buying it is foolish. Wait for a sounder piece in better condition, even if it costs a lot more money.

Collectors don't have to worry much about forgeries or fakes, as they're usually easy to recognize. For example, Gerzes are heavy, while knockoffs are very light, and easy to spot. The coloring and glazing are also very different in counterfeit items.

Royal Doulton Series Ware plate 7¹/₂˝h.
"He that always complains is never pitied"
*Photo courtesy of Old Tom Morris Golf,
L.L.C.*

Morrissian Ware plate 10¹/₂˝h. Proverbs
"Fine feathers make fine birds . . ." *Photo
courtesy of Old Tom Morris Golf, L.L.C.*

As for sellers who try to conceal repairs, Aaron says, "most of these attempts are easy to discover. Just get a little education, and hold up a light to an area that's suspected to be repaired or repainted. It just won't capture the glazing. In that light the original glazing would be shiny, while the repaired area isn't."

Cracks can easily be discerned by putting an item under a black light. That detection method is usually foolproof. But Aaron is still that shrewd old-timer who leaves nothing to chance.

If, for some reason questions remain about an object's integrity—and to assure yourself of a piece's worth—follow Aaron's lead. *Tap-tap-tap* that object with your teeth. Just be careful not to bite off a piece of history.

♀ ♀ ♀

It was a brutal, long, frustrating exercise in futility.

For fifteen years Ronnie Watts, the CEO of the world's largest golf equipment retail chain (Edwin Watts Golf stores, *www.edwinwatts.com*) was on a dispiriting, Odysseus-like journey.

"Whenever I had a free hour or two, wherever I was, I would hunt for that perfect object," recalls this poetry-in-a-pot aficionado. "A 100-year-old piece of pottery is a wonderful painting, a fascination, yet no matter how hard I searched, I never found anything in a chance visit to an antique store."

Royal Doulton plate 10¹/₄″ with a colorful scene entitled "The Nineteenth Hole." *Photo courtesy of Old Tom Morris Golf, L.L.C.*

Lenox half-liter stein with sterling rim with female golfer and caddy. *Photo courtesy of Old Tom Morris Golf, L.L.C.*

Watts was of course "luckier" in a private sale. When personal circumstances dictated, Wayne Aaron sold Watts most of his prized collection (340 ceramic pieces). Yet this purveyor of everyday balls and clubs that could easily be labeled "the tools of ignorance" by long-suffering golfers, still hoped to assemble that *pièce de résistance* of Doulton and Lenox that would be exhibited in Watts's new Orlando, Florida, museum—the Taj Mahal of golf collectibles. The hunt had to continue, no matter what the cost.

"The odds of finding something terrific are even slimmer when it comes to pottery, yet finally after fifteen years, I got very lucky," coos Watts. "The piece was real big, 20 inches across, 14 to 16 inches high, a flowerpot depicting Scottish golfers, kings, in red outfits that was made by Royal Doulton (ca. 1900). It's Morrisian ware, really jardinière (a large decorative stand or pot for plants). I paid $2,500 for it, and I'm thinking it's worth $7,000 to $8,000. What a treasure!"

Finding this piece, an early-20th-century Gerz (an authentic item is inscribed "Gesch" on the bottom, an abbreviation for "Gesetzlich Geschützt" meaning protected by law) or a porcelain mug by the O'Hara Dial Company (Waltham, MA) goes well beyond mere acquisitiveness. This is not "trophy" hunting. It's golf's version of conquering Mt. Everest.

"The true joy here is a sense of terrific individual accomplishment, meeting a challenge," says Watts. "You have found something beautiful *yourself*. There's a great deal of personal satisfaction in that—a feeling that you have done the impossible."

A collector of rare photographs, autographs, and "unbelievable" glassware, Watts knows beauty. His entire universe revolves around "enlightening" objects from golf's memorable past. Yet the center of that star-studded galaxy is ceramics.

Gerz jug 8″ ca. 1910, with golfers in relief, in good condition. *Photo courtesy of Old Tom Morris Golf, L.L.C.*

T.P.C.O. Co. shaving mug with Christy transfer print "Fairly Won," ca. 1907, very scarce; crystal inkwell with silver lid and mounted golfer, silvermaker's hallmark to lid, excellent condition. *Photo courtesy of Old Tom Morris Golf, L.L.C.*

"Belleek; Copeland Spode in cobalt blue, blue, and greens; Lenox C.A.C., I love all this stuff immensely," says Watts. "The Belleek I have is very rare, and I also enjoy Lambent which made interesting ceremonial pieces or trophies (these golf items appeared after 1900). My O'Haras are very large trophy-type items. I have about fifteen of these very special, attention-grabbing pieces with wonderful enameled decorations."

Though Watts laughingly admits "I like just about everything," he's still been a very careful shopper following a few basic ABCs.

"Don't mess with cheap stuff," warns Watts. "Invest instead in one major piece. Buying one $5,000 item is much better than getting five $1,000 vases, jugs, or bowls. That means forget Series ware (such as proverbs plates, or basically decorated white china). It's a big mistake to buy a $200 item. That will never go up in value.

"This is a hobby, not a way to make money. Yet you don't want to lose money, so the best strategy is to focus on odd-shaped, unique vases or whatever stands the best chance of going up in value. Something a little odd-looking is a good bet. Lenox pieces have also gone up substantially in recent years."

Watts goes on to say, "The new collector must also be mindful of scarcity. So many of the big-named pieces are impossible to find, Lenox has gotten new appreciation and value. These hand-painted items are far more readily available nowadays, and also very attractive. Go for the ones with pewter lids. You can find them with a little diligence (worth $1,000 a few years ago, now valued at $3,000)."

As for Watts's own unflagging research and persistence, he's gained in pursuit of another enchanting rarity. Appreciating the fine bone china that was crafted by Doulton in the late 1890s, he's going to further distinguish his Orlando museum with arguably the "crown jewel" of ceramics, an $80,000 piece of Burslem.

Once it's in a glass case and delighting visitors, Watts will feel that heady rush of overcoming obstacles. Yet his hunt will soon start again. In this world of exquisite, hand-painted designs, there are many Mt. Everests to climb—other gems that epitomize "the stuff dreams are made of."

The prices of golf collectibles fluctuate. The following values are estimates offered by various experts:
MM—Mullock & Madeley
WR—Will Roberto

- Royal Doulton series ware cereal bowl depicting golfing figures decorated with caption "Every Dog Has Its Day" and "Everyman his hour," Stamped with makers Lion, 1911, **$325–375, MM**

- Scarce Royal Troon G. C. Royal Doulton group ceramic plateware set comprising dinner plate, side plate, and cup and saucer, each decorated with the club crest and blue trim, **$65, MM**

- Dartmouth Pottery–style golfing tankard decorated with embossed figure of a golfer and the handle in the shape of a golf bag and clubs, **$80–90, MM**

- Royal Doulton bone china character jug "Golfer," **$110–130, MM**

- Royal Bradwell Arthur Woods Sporting Scenes golfing tankard decorated with color transfer golfing scene and the handle in the shape of a golfing trolley, golf bag, and clubs, plus Jim Beam decanter, dated 1971, **$90, MM**

- Two Early Delft blue and white tiles, 5½", ca. 1670 showing a single golfer—and a similar tile ca. 1760 showing two golfers—some surface chips and cracks to glaze to both tiles, **$140, MM**

- Two Wedgwood china plates with raised golfing figures, white on blue, **$50–75, WR**

- Three German ceramics, female golfer salt shaker, pipe stand, and bud vase, **$100–150, WR**

- Two ceramics comprised of 9" Royal Doulton Kingsware jug with stopper, ca. 1920, and 6" mug attributed to Ceramic Art Co. ca. 1900, **$2,000–2,500, WR**

- Gerz Jug, 8", ca. 1910, with golfers in relief, good condition, **$1,750–2,250, WR**

- Ceramic jug with three athletic scenes, one golf, ca. 1900, piece plays musical tune, **$150–250, WR**

- Royal Doulton Kingsware mug, 5¹/₂", ca. 1920, very good condition, **$300–400, WR**

- Royal Doulton Series Ware bowl, 9¹/₂", scalloped edge, very good, **$300–400, WR**

- Royal Doulton Series Ware plate, 10", ca. 1920, good condition, **$200–300, WR**

- Two ceramic plates consisting of Crown Ducal 9" together with Royal Doulton Series Ware plate, 8¹/₂" with slight crack, **$150–250, WR**

- Copeland Spode pitcher, 8" decorated with traditional golfing figures, **$1,000–1,500, WR**

- Pair of Ceramic plates, Schwarzburg (NY & Rudolstadt Pottery) ca. 1915, Grimwades (Stoke on Trent) ca. 1920, both near mint, **$650–750, WR**

- Amphora Pottery Works, ceramic caddie figure including club, ca. 1910, repair to neck, Royal Doulton Gibson Series Ware vase, ca. 1910, mint, **$900–1,200, WR**

- Pewter chocolate or ice cream mold, ca. 1900s, in form of male golfer, **$150–175, WR**

- Dunlop caddie figure 16" high advertising "We Play Dunlop," **$600–800, WR**

- Penfold man countertop figure 20" high, figure has original pipe, **$600–700, WR**

- Penfold man countertop figure 20" high, lacks pipe, **$300–400, WR**

- Schoenhut Tommy golfing figure, **$200–250, WR**

- Two golf ball liquor caddies: musical Golfers Decanter and The 19th Hole (Czechoslovakia) each with six glasses and a small decanter, **$150–200, WR**

- Penfold man 20" high, marked with "He Played a Penfold," **$600–800, WR**

- Royal Doulton Series Ware plate 10¹/₄", illustrated by Charles Crombie "Every dog has his day," **$200–250, WR**

- Amphora Pottery Works male golfer 13³/₄" ca. 1910, one crack, **$250–350, WR**

- Dickens Ware vase 9.4" by Weller Pottery 1900, male golfer scene ca. 1900, **$1000–1200, WR**

- Dickens Ware vase 8³/₄" by Weller Pottery 1900, female golfer scene, **$1,500–1,750, WR**

- Pottery pitcher 5.15" in light green with white applications in the manner of jasper ware, German, ca. 1910s, scarce, **$1,000–1,200, WR**

- Lenox half-liter stein 5³/₄" high with sterling rim with female golfer and caddie, **$1,500–2000, WR**

- Pair of Royal Doulton steins 5¹/₂" with humorous golfers drawn by H. M. Bateman, **$400–500, WR**

- Gray's Pottery cigarette box and a beer mug, **$150–175, WR**

- Morrisian Ware plate 10¹/₂" proverbs "Fine feathers make fine birds . . ." **$250–300, WR**

- Royal Doulton plate 10¹/₄" with a colorful scene entitled "The Nineteenth Hole," **$200–250, WR**

- Kingsware tobacco humidor 6" high by Royal Doulton ca. 1930s, **$800–900, WR**

- Kingsware jug 8³/₄" by Royal Doulton ca. 1930s, **$700–900, WR**

- Copeland Spode pitcher 4¹/₂" high with green background and white golfing figures, **$400–500, WR**

- Copeland Spode pitcher 4¹/₂" high in cobalt blue on gray with white figures, **$500–600, WR**

- Copeland Late Spode pitcher 6" high in cobalt blue ca. 1905, **$600–750, WR**

- Green Copeland Spode pitcher 7³/₄" ca. 1910, marked Copeland Late Spode, **$1,000–1,250, WR**

- Cigarette jar marked Nippon, **$400–500, WR**

7 BEWITCHING MOMENTS IN TIME
The Hunt for Rare Autographs

During the "Golden Age" of sports in the 1920s and 1930s, baseball stirred Americans' imagination by touting the muscular Bambino, the compelling, larger-than-life presence of Babe Ruth.

Boxing in the epochal Jazz Age had its own Sultan of Swat, the unbeatable and flamboyant Manassas Mauler, Jack Dempsey.

These two megawatt figures certainly dominated the headlines with their athletic prowess and exploits far from the field of battle. They were celebrities well-suited to the surging spirits of the Roaring Twenties, that time in U.S. history when sports personalities were adored for their testosterone escapades—matinee idols who were part rascals, part Olympian gladiators.

Golf was also graced with a radiant favorite son who was considered above reproach, a "Renaissance Man" still lionized for his courtly mannerisms, dignity, intellectual brilliance, and silky smooth swing. The winner of a remarkable thirteen major championships in eight years, who continues to transcend such other shining lights as Hagen, Hogan, and Sarazen, Robert Tyre Jones Jr. remains the King.

A tragic Lou Gehrig type of hero, this cofounder of Augusta National and the winner of golf's only recorded Grand Slam of all four major championships (1930), Jones never lost his humanity or good-natured wit while battling syringomyelia, a degenerate disease of the spinal column (a form of crippling ALS). Stories about his courage have become ingrained in American folklore, and mirroring Jones's indomitable spirit—which partly explains his unique golfing accomplishments—he's the Ruthian name in the collectible autograph, rare letters, and photo market.

Candid signed photo of Denny Shute and Leo Diegel, two stars of the 1920s and 1930s. $500. *Photo courtesy Mark Emerson.*

Handwritten letter from H. Vardon to Chick Evans. $2000. *Photo courtesy Mark Emerson.*

Whether it's a signed late 1920s Currier and Ives limited edition print picturing Jones on the 18th green at St. Andrews or an autographed photo of him, these items are the unrivaled gems in this increasingly popular collecting specialty. Currently appreciating at 8 to 10 percent annually, authentic signed Jones material, according to many experts, hasn't even reached its full investment potential. Though those rising prices are an invitation to forgers and other scam artists (whenever prices rise in any category, collectors must be wary of thieves), there's no disputing the fact that Jones's American icon stature has turned his personal letters and photos (studio portraits with his signature and that of the artist are the elite pieces) into money-in-the-bank annuities.

But far more important than transforming paper into gold, these highly personal items are a connection to golf's storied past, a time capsule link to Jones, as well as to other famed—and lesser known—players.

Besides venturing into golfers' intimate feelings about the game, courses, and financial struggles (many championship winners were treated like "dirt" in the 1920s and 1930s), signed missives are a vivid tapestry of the past, crackling with drama, hope, elation, and despondency.

Bobby Jones never scuffled for money, and his letters and photos are a portal to a world of privilege, pomp, and exclusive circumstance befitting the game's royal ambassador. Yet equally illustrative of another era, correspondence from "The Great Triumvirate"—Harry Vardon, James Braid, and J. H. Taylor (the winners of a combined 16 British Opens at the turn of the century, along with 7 second-place finishes)—depicts the game's darker side. They complain about their being barred from entering the landmark clubs, bemoan financial difficulties that force them to appear at exhibitions for a few shillings, and in general cite how they're treated worse than the groundskeepers or kitchen help.

"Letters are exciting since they're so personal, they really give you the essence of somebody," explains "Mr. Paper," 20-year collector Mark Emerson. "Players talk about their ups and downs, sex, racism, financial worries. I have a note from a guy who won five major championships, and he's begging someone to buy a club for $10. There's nothing like letters (handwritten pieces are far more valuable than typed specimens) for they transport you back into time, and reveal somebody's innermost feelings."

To underscore his ardor for edifying manuscripts, Emerson takes out a piece of Jones's personal stationery, and reads from a September 19, 1947, letter:

Dear Mr. Gaston: Mr. Clifford Roberts [Augusta National's iron-fisted cofounder] and I had quite a little conversation about the Augusta National during our trip to California from which I've just returned. . . . our food situation at this club is so well taken care of by our *colored* steward, we have decided that what the club needs in addition is only a combination bookkeeper, office manager.

Therefore we may consider conversations between us with reference to this matter at an end.

However I may be in position to offer you the same proposition under discussion with respect to a new club here in Atlanta. . . . We will have a director's meeting on Monday after which I will communicate with you again. Very truly yours, Robert T. Jones Jr.

Awed by Jones's ability to construct a "richly textured note," or one that touches a variety of subjects, Emerson says, "There's so much history here. The colored steward, Roberts, Augusta National, and there's Jones's gentlemanly way of telling the guy he can't give him a job. Then he turns around and says he may be able to help him in the future. That sticks with me. It's funny, it's so revealing, so well-crafted. That's what I love about handwritten notes. They're illuminating."

Along with its educational value, Emerson's thoughtful, extremely ambitious approach to gathering documents and photos signed by the famous—and obscure—has also been a fun-filled adventure. Determined to unearth more of these bewitching "slices of history," Emerson conducted his own letter campaign in the 1980s for five years, writing to players' relatives, golf clubs, and various manuscript societies. Sparing no expense in this magnificent paper chase, this retired restaurant chain owner also took out ads in magazines and newspapers to secure signed items (letters, photos, event programs, menus, etc.) that had attracted little interest for decades.

"Serious collecting takes a lot of hard work, research and persistence," says Emerson. "My reward was learning about these guys, being able to relive certain moments through letters and a (14" x 20") photo like the one I have of Jones and Sarazen standing in a studio the day after the 1932 U.S. Open. It was taken by the Ansel Adams of sports photography in the early 20th century—George Pietzcker—and his stamp on the photo makes this item worth at least $15,000." (Emerson paid $5,000 for it in the early 1990s.)

The inherent scarcity of stamped photos (any distinguishing historical marks add to provenance, thus boosting values) or personally revealing notes complicated Emerson's massive hunt. While today's megacelebrities like Woods, Nicklaus, and Mickelson are besieged for autographs, most players from golf's early past were never "important enough" to be asked, let alone hounded, for their signature.

That noble triumvirate was certainly unheralded. Even after dominating European golf from 1894 to 1914, they barely eked out a living by making balls and clubs. Perceived as common laborers, reduced to begging for work, this trio used colorful stationery decorated with their gold medals to promote themselves, and as Emerson insists, "to build their self-esteem." A limited number of their plaintive notes survive, yet the exquisitely detailed letterheads are in stark contrast to the Big Three's mournful messages.

There were other golfers that thwarted Emerson's "completist" goals simply because they were illiterate (like three-time U.S. Open winner Willie Anderson), or played for a very brief time. Autograph collecting includes numerous specialized categories within a niche, such as Emerson's acquiring a signature from every major winner, or subsequently, "winners of three majors."

No matter how often he was stymied, or tantalized by attractive material, Emerson remained loyal to his collecting objectives—and most importantly, to his budget. "Some of my biggest regrets now come from not buying something because I didn't have the money," he laments.

"You have to set it up so that you're crash-resistant," cautions Emerson. "It's simply imperative that you have a very good idea about what you specifically want to collect, how much money you want to devote to this, and at the same time be aware of why you're collecting."

Despite his reasoned approach that prompted him to carefully investigate the provenance of letters and to check dealers' bona fides, this "paper" specialist did make mistakes.

"Everyone does, collecting is a crapshoot at times," he laughs, sitting in a room surrounded by autographed musings in protective binders, heartfelt confessions on vir-

1912 signed photo of Open Champion Ted
Ray. $1500. *Photo courtesy Mark Emerson.*

Wilson Sporting Goods signed photo of
Arnold Palmer ca. 1955. $150. *Photo courtesy
Mark Emerson.*

Signed photo of Ben Hogan in his prime.
$500. *Photo courtesy Mark Emerson.*

Signed photo of 1898 U.S. Amateur
Champion Findlay Douglas. $750. *Photo
courtesy Mark Emerson.*

tually pristine papers, and other documents with large, strong signatures (the more readable, the better). "I got burned along the way. Sure I did. It will happen no matter how careful you are. Overpaying for material. Buying phony merchandise. You just have to learn from these mistakes."

Emerson's baptism may have been rough at times, particularly when he met the sharks and scam artists who naturally gravitate towards high-priced collectibles. Yet passionate about the aesthetics and literary appeal of these "art objects," he redoubled his efforts and turned missteps into valuable insights: buyers should familiarize themselves with the intricacies of valued signatures, and watch out for penciled signatures which can't be dated easily, as well as shaky, small handwriting or blurriness.

Realizing that the key attribute of any signature is its authenticity, Emerson met with numerous sellers at trade shows and auctions, and painstakingly evaluated "whether the guy's story was believable as to where the items were coming from." Confidence in a seller creates a "comfort level": a willingness to learn more about this bewitching world.

Networking in this manner is crucial to building a respectable collection. One must know where "the bodies are buried," or who has the choicest items, for private trades are a prime way to obtain material. Such links to like-minded enthusiasts are also important for emotional support. When Emerson first began his quest for admittedly esoteric rarities, autograph sleuthing was viewed as a bit weird, and his communications with "manuscript people" ushered him into a comforting—and sophisticated—fraternity.

Handsome signed studio photo of five-time
Open champion James Braid, taken in front
of the Walton Heath clubhouse. $1500.
Photo courtesy Mark Emerson.

Their rarified, even "scientific" discussions about a golfer's cursive style, the way a T is either slanted or crossed, and an item's provenance, might be compared to a geneticist's complex musings about DNA strands.

But this is a hobby devoted to minutiae. To strengthen his credibility and expertise among other collectors (and to also "refine his eye"), Emerson delved into books that have facsimile signatures of golfers. This helped him distinguish genuine pieces from those that were autographed by family members, "secretarial" (signed by an assistant), and outright forgeries. (The spiraling prices for Jones material has recently fueled a burst of counterfeiting. Beware of material signed with a "Bobby," for he disliked this popularly used nickname).

His acquiring a certifiable document, such as an elegant-looking menu from the first Ryder Cup "Complimentary Banquet" in 1927 in Worcester, Massachusetts (worth $7,500), puts him in the middle of that historical event, or "a fly on the wall" in the middle of the festivities. He feels that same adrenaline rush when eyeing a print (or 1903 photogravure valued at $15,000) of Old Tom Morris (the ball- and clubmaker) standing next to a famous painting of himself that's signed by him and artist George Reid in fountain pen (in pencil it would be worth less). "These items have a personality, a pulse," exudes Emerson, who's now writing articles for the prestigious Manuscript Society. "That menu takes me right into the dining room with these men. I know what wines they drank, the food they ate, it's alive."

Yet examining items, especially if they're in the four or five figures, can be intimidating—and a lonely, fear-inspiring experience. (Except for Emerson, and a few other experts with golf knowledge, signature "authenticators" just don't exist.) Be prepared. Studying these documents, and determining their importance to the game is certainly akin to taking a crash course in golf history.

One of the ABCs in this field of study is the seminal importance of legibility. To enjoy Walter Hagen's June 1924 thank-you letter (on Royal Liverpool stationery) to British golfers acknowledging their "sportsmanship and friendship [during the Open Championship] which has always been extended in abundance," the material must be readable. The clarity of an object is certainly enhanced when the signature appears on a clean white card, rather than on paper with a dark background. It's also vital that the autograph not intersect with the text, or as Emerson says, "That there is a lot of 'white space' around the autograph for attractive framing purposes."

Meant to be time capsules, signatures are also far more intriguing—and valuable—when they appear on exciting subject matter. A Walter Hagen letter, for example, describing his joy from playing "the little island, or the home of golf . . . I shall come next year to defend my title" is far more desirable than his mere signature on a note card or blank piece of paper, as a simple signature is obviously easier to forge than a letter or photo.

MacGregor PROFESSIONAL GOLF

BRUNSWICK SPORTS / 4861 SPRING GROVE AVENUE, CINCINNATI, OHIO 45232 / 541-3464

JACK NICKLAUS
P.O. BOX 4497
COLUMBUS, OHIO 43212

September 3, 1964

Rev. S. H. Lloyd
2558 Eagledale Drive
Indianapolis, Indiana 46222

Dear Rev. Lloyd:

      It was very thoughtful of you to take the time to write, and I hope you'll forgive the long delay in answering your letter.

      Here's the autographed picture you requested.

      Many thanks for writing. It is always a good feeling to receive such kind words, but they mean even more from an "ex-Buckeye."

        Sincerely,

        Jack Nicklaus

JN/cd
Encls.

1964 typed letter from Jack Nicklaus. $150.
Photo courtesy Mark Emerson.

117

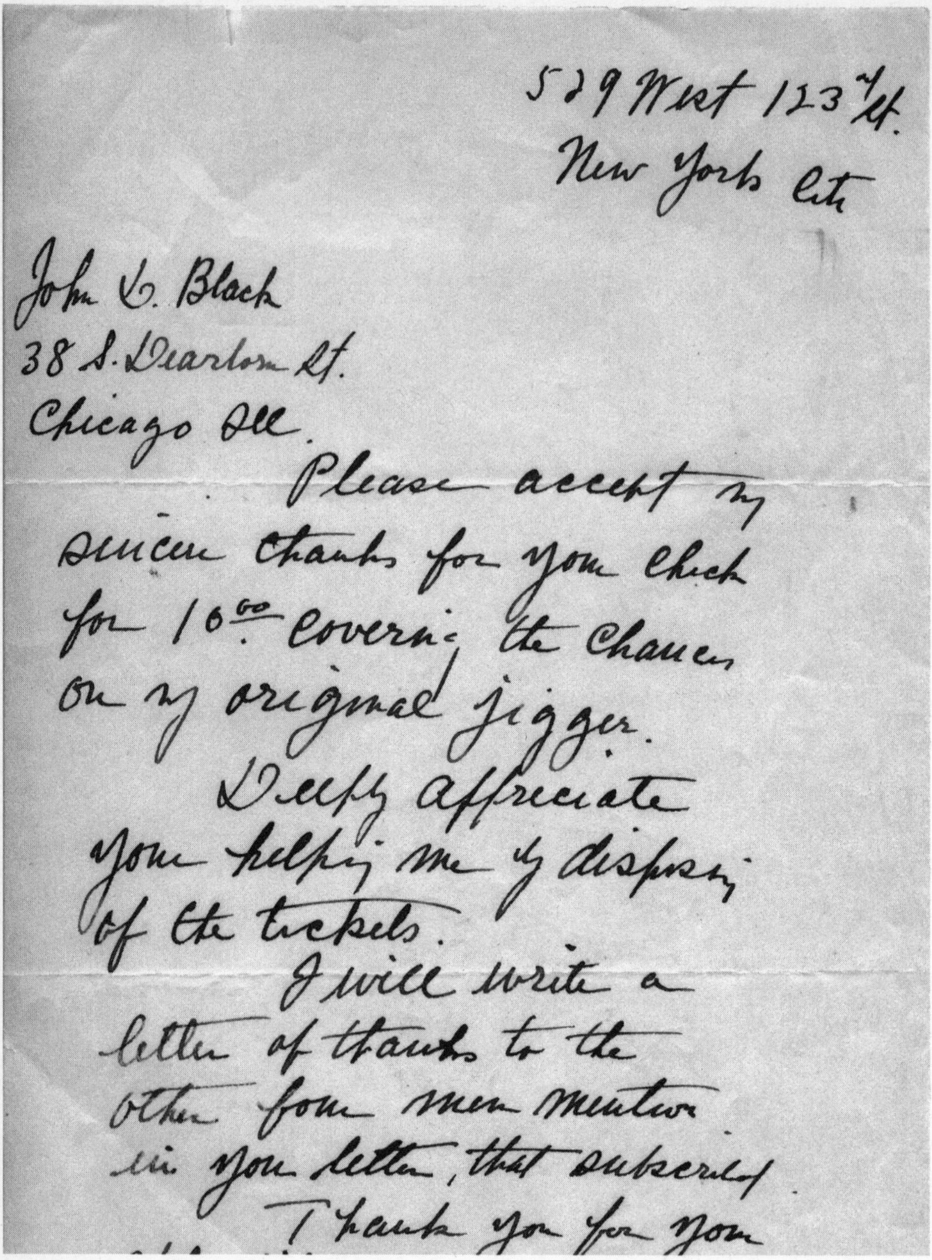

529 West 123rd St.
New York City

John G. Black
38 S. Dearlon St.
Chicago Ill.

Please accept my
sincere thanks for your check
for 10.00 covering the chances
on my original jigger.

Deeply appreciate
your helping me by disposing
of the tickets.

I will write a
letter of thanks to the
other four men mentioned
in your letter, that subscribed.

Thank you for your

1939 handwritten letter of Jerry Travers.
$1000. *Photo courtesy Mark Emerson.*

As Emerson emphasizes, "Content is very important. The more substantive the content, the more valuable a piece is—and the risk increases exponentially if it's just an autograph on a piece of paper. And content obviously includes to whom a letter is written, its 'association.'"

Unique subject matter also greatly impacts the value of photographs, which are best displayed by having professional archivists frame them. That signed, studio-stamped photo of Jones and Sarazen, or a 12" x 16" photo of Jones alongside Babe Didrikson Zaharias (dated 1936, with her looking at the King with a reverential smile, worth about $15,000), is far more appealing than a family snapshot of Robert T. If the image of those get-togethers—and again, association keenly affects the desirability of photos—is blurry, grainy, or in some other way flawed, the value of the image would predictably be diminished. Yet as a general rule, stamped-studio photographs are far more valuable than wire photos from United Press International and the Associated Press.

"Marked with a little stamp saying UPI or AP, there could be thousands of these (unsigned) photos, while a studio photo is either very limited, or one of a kind," explains Emerson. "A wire photo is typically a 'man on the street' type shot, while a studio picture is capturing a special event."

The value of a wire photo is increased if the original caption is attached to the back of it. Along with pinpointing or exactly dating the occasion, that caption makes the item more "historically relevant," and for some collectors, adds to the photo's overall provenance. When appraising wire photos, the general rules of condition apply, i.e., are there any tears, creases, stains, or signs of the photos being retouched?

Emerson has few concerns about buying these photos on eBay. Far more caution should be exercised in the pursuit of high-priced documents, as he stresses, "I want to see them close-up, handle them." If determined to buy on eBay, look up the transaction history of the seller, and see if there are complaints against him or her. Yet even though this collector of golf event tickets, programs, and contestant badges seems to be enthralled by the entire world of golfiana, he is strongly averse to acquiring second generation wire photos.

"It's absolutely far more desirable to collect first generation [a photo from the original negative] since they have much greater clarity," he emphasizes. "You must know the difference, for a second generation wire photo [which essentially involves making a negative from a first generation photo, then printing an image from that copied negative] is grainier. And while these distinctions are difficult to see, if you think a photo is second generation (it's also possible that photos can be third, fourth, or twentieth generation), save your money. These pieces (mere knockoffs) aren't worth very much."

Signed photo of the first U.S. PGA
Champion Jim Barnes. $1250. *Photo
courtesy Mark Emerson.*

ROBERT TYRE JONES, JR.
ATLANTA, GEORGIA

August
Fifteenth,
1 9 3 8

Dear Miss Curtis,

I am grateful indeed for your letter and wish very
much that I could possibly arrange my plans so that
I could be with you on September 4th. I am very
eager to meet the ladies of the British Team and
had planned hopefully on seeing at least one of
the two days of play. I am very sorry indeed that
other parts of my schedule have already taken such
definite form that it will not be possible for me
to come East any earlier.

I appreciate ever so much your thinking of me.
Please accept every assurance that it is with the
deepest regret that I am forced to decline.

Most cordially,

Robert Jones

Miss Margaret Curtis
Manchester
Massachusetts

1938 pristine typed letter from Bob Jones to
Margaret Curtis. $7500. *Photo courtesy
Mark Emerson.*

121

1924 typed letter on Royal Liverpool
stationery signed by Walter Hagen. $5000.
Photo courtesy Mark Emerson.

One additional word of caution. Golf photo collecting is a relatively recent phenomenon, a still-growing market where the pricing hasn't yet reached its full potential. There might be "bargains" in such virgin territory, but since this niche is just beginning to emerge, estimating the values of unsigned material can be very inexact and unpredictable.

One photo enthusiast argues, "Once it becomes impossible to find material in other niches, terrific photos will be discovered, and prices will soar just like everything else in the golf market."

In the meantime, however, Emerson recently sold a Robert T. Jones Jr. snapshot that was once part of a family album, expecting to net at least "a respectable four figures." The photo went for a "very disappointing" $250.

But Emerson is not concerned. He's a time traveler, convinced these paper artifacts are bringing his heroes back to life.

Admiring a hand-tooled, deep chocolate brown leather golf bag that spins its own brand of magic, he says, "This is the actual bag Walter Hagen used in the 1929 Ryder Cup. His name is embossed on the bag and those papers hanging from it are old railroad tickets. It's very luxurious looking. I know it's authentic, for a friend got me this photo that shows Hagen standing next to the bag. This bag is *him*. Now that's terrific provenance."

♀ ♀ ♀

A seminal figure in golf folklore, Hagen is also a favorite of Eddie Papczun, the founder and president of Golf Links to the Past.

Admitting that the flamboyant Hagen, who despite winning two U.S. Opens, and four British Opens is overshadowed by Robert Tyre Jones Jr., Papczun feels "We don't have the breadth of literature about him as we do about Jones. I'm still a big fan of him. Hagen changed the rich man image of the game. While Bobby was very unassuming, the pure gentleman, Hagen could perform at the highest levels, and still be the party boy. I think Hagen material (photos and signed letters) is undervalued. I think his prices will increase in the future."

Predicting that ex-caddie Francis Ouimet will enjoy a similar burst of collectible enthusiasm, he continues, "This wonderful player is at the center of a defining moment in American golf. He beat [Harry] Vardon and Ted Ray (two dominant Brits) in the 1913 U.S. Open playoff. The general public was so excited by that win, [golf was no longer seen as just a sedate pastime for gentleman], it put golf on the map."

Legendary moments, whether captured in documents or signed photos, is a Papczun specialty. Heading a company that's been handling rare golf memorabilia for the last nine years, Papczun has a unique talent for discovering artifacts and predicting their future worth. Much like Emerson, he too has that "eye," or experience to appraise and authenticate choice material—and this talent has paid handsome dividends. Reputed for selling hard-to-find items with unimpeachable provenance, Golf Links (*www.golflinkstothepast.com*) is licensed by the Jones estate to market photos and correspondence.

In possession of the "world's largest collection" of Jones rarities (the company keeps a private archive and a commercial inventory), Papczun is well-attuned to market trends. He knows what sells—and why.

"Bobby Jones's signature appeals to aficionados because they're beautiful, vintage flowing autographs," says this lover of the printed word. "The early Jones signature is much more desirable than the later signature that was seen while Jones was battling his disease. The Jones autograph goes through the most drastic changes of any golfer in history, and collectors must know how to distinguish the differences.

"In the heyday of his playing career we see the flowing, bold autograph. In the 1960s, towards the end of his life, he was signing his name with a pen attached to a large ball. That's how he could grip the pen. We see a disjointed, almost childlike signature. If he'd sign his full name there'd be a Robert, then a T, another space, the Jones, and then Jr. Signing anything was an effort, and it all looked like a signature of a very old person."

Papczun points out these distinctions to emphasize the doubled-edged sword realities of highly collectible autographs. Pursuing four- and five-figure "blue chips" is a seductive thrill ride, yet it's also dangerous. Forged and fraudulent Jones material is abundant.

June 8th

Dear Keith:—
Your letter as to your hobby was very interesting indeed and I only regret that I am unable to help in your collection of data about Babe Dedrichson Zaharias.

I had the opportunity of instructing Mildred (the name I prefer for her) and she was a very apt pupil. Besides that she is an extremely nice, sweet girl.

To my way of thinking she should have made a fortune, with her very unusual athletic talent, but was badly managed.

With best wishes

I am
Cordially
Tommy Armour

1945 handwritten letter from Tommy Armour discussing Babe Didrikson Zaharias. $1500. *Photo courtesy Mark Emerson.*

36 • GOLF/MAY 1963

Signed magazine photo of 1964 Open
Champion Tony Lema. $750. *Photo courtesy
of Mark Emerson.*

Hoping to deter these counterfeiters, and autograph dealers who unwittingly promote suspect material, Papczun notes that there are three variations of Jones's signatures. The most valuable type is the full Robert Tyre Jones Jr. Similar to the desirability of a full "Abraham Lincoln," as opposed to "A. Lincoln" or "Abe," the complete Jones signature has the most appeal.

Worth slightly less in this burgeoning market is the "Bob Jones" variety. This type of signed note was addressed to acquaintances, not to friends. These closer relationships were honored with a simple "Bob." Collectors will never find an authentic letter with a "Bobby" scrawled on it. Jones disliked this tag, and as Papczun says, "anytime someone is offered a 'Bobby Jones' autograph warning bells should go off."

Disregarding Papczun's expertise in this area, forgers are continually "testing" him, hoping to pull off fast ones. Papczun also feels that a lot of reputable autograph dealers "unknowingly" sell phony material. "Collectors must get the advice of authenticators," he cautions, "people who really know the Jones signature."

But Papczun is most worried about Internet sales. "Now you have a vehicle for people to sit in their house and knock off forgeries, put them on the Internet, and hide behind a veil. There's just not a lot of [authentic Jones] stuff floating around. The sheer numbers being offered out there should be a clear warning."

Insisting there's "never been a problem with Golf Links material," Papczun is also concerned about the rash of Tiger Woods forgeries. After touting the authenticity of a $1,500 Woods-signed pin flag on his Web site, Papczun says, "We pay a fee to get this stuff. We don't have to worry about fakes. Yet everyone recognizes Tiger's name, there's a lot of value in his autograph, and that's why thousands of items are forged. Just go to eBay and punch in "Tiger Woods." See how much stuff there is. His signature lends itself to be forged because he signs it very fast, it all flows in one direction, and that's why buyers have to be very vigilant."

As Papczun berates corrupt "knockoff artists," he couples his criticism with one key bit of advice. "Look for unique [photo] images, those rich associations like a Jones with Sarazen or Alister MacKenzie, that's what will retain value," he counsels, looking at one of his own prized photographs, an $1,850 hand-printed image (from the original glass negative) of Old Tom Morris (the British Open winner who's regarded as the "Patron Saint of Golf") that was taken in Scotland by famed golf course architect A. W. Tillinghast. "More than tapping into the past, this photo is wonderful aesthetically. It's folklore, unique historical association, strong looking, just a delightful moment in time."

Other important signposts in the search for signatures:

1. Beware of "once-in-a-lifetime" offerings on the Internet.

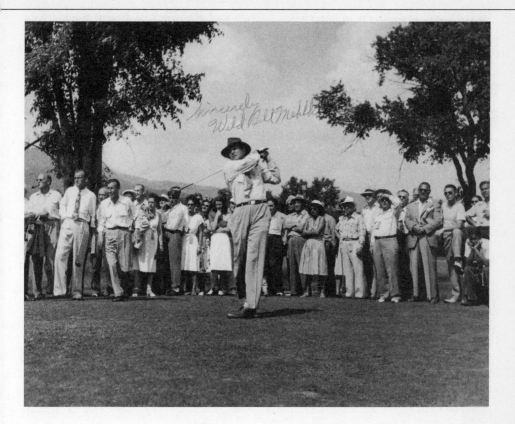

Signed action photo of 1927 U.S. Ryder Cup
player Wild Bill Melhorn. $500. *Photo
courtesy Mark Emerson.*

2. Check and double-check provenance and bills of sales if possible. Getting caught with
   items that have been stolen from libraries or museums can mean embarrassment and
   costly legal battles.

3. Network with other collectors and attend shows or auctions to get a feel for market
   trends.

4. Select a distinct collecting niche, and learn about personalities in that category. This
   makes the hunt more fascinating.

5. The most conservative—and wisest—strategy is buying the "big names" in autographs and photos since they'll be the easiest to liquidate.

6. Don't become involved in this market for profit. The first priority is always fun.

7. While choice photos are desirable, letters are the "absolute cream" in the autograph world, according to Philadelphia dealer Steven Raab.

8. Read journals, learn which dealers are reputable, and only work with golf autograph–photo specialists. As Raab advises, avoid autograph boutiques at airports, golfing resorts, and malls.

9. Be extremely wary of penciled signatures, and get lifetime, money-back guarantees from long-established companies.

10. Jones is "hot." So is Woods. That makes them favorite targets for forgers.

The prices of golf collectibles fluctuate. The following values are estimates offered by various experts:
MM—Mullock & Madeley
GLP—Golf Links to the Past
WR—Will Roberto
ME—Mark Emerson

- Rare sepia photograph of James Braid and A. Kirkaldy, with Braid preparing to tee off at first hole watched by his opponent Kirkaldy and two other players. 7$^{1}/_{4}$" x 13" **$275, MM**

- Walter Hagen autograph, Open champion 1922, 1924, 1928, and 1929, signed in ink "Sincerely, Walter Hagen," April 25, 1929, **$250–275, MM**

- Bobby Jones signed letter, framed, to *Golf* magazine editor Charles Price with swing photo, 1960, 26" x 29", **$5,800, GLP**

- Bobby Jones autographed copy of *Golf Is My Game*, second and final autobiography, **$2,800, GLP**

- Bobby Jones writes to Lincoln Werden (famed golf writer), authenticated 1959 letter, Jones mentions a historical anecdote about the Prince of Wales, **$2,500, GLP**

- Bobby Jones vintage autograph on a book page, **$2,400, GLP**

- Bobby Jones vintage autograph, bold dark ink autograph suitable for framing, **$2,500, GLP**

- Hogan, Nelson, and Nicklaus signed first day cover, surrounded by five first generation b/w photos honoring Bobby Jones, **$1,575, GLP**

- Babe Didrikson Zaharias handwritten letter, on personal letterhead—the first woman to challenge leftover Victorian notions of "women's place" in athletics, **$2,000, GLP**

- Bobby Jones autographed letter, 1965 letter to Canadian Golf Museum secretary, signed in full, **$3,000, GLP**

- Francis Ouimet handwritten letter, dated 5-24-47 on the Bruce Hotel, Carnoustie letterhead, writer to English golf legend Henry Cotton thanking him for "a sincere note of congratulations over the success of our Walker Cup Team." Ouimet was 1947 Walker Cup Team captain, **$2,500, GLP**

- J. H. Taylor handwritten and signed letter, on personal letterhead—along with Harry Vardon and James Braid, the "British Triumvirate" captured sixteen British Open titles in twenty years, **$1,000, GLP**

- Ben Hogan signed personal letter, **$415, GLP**

- Tiger Woods autographed sand save, Woods is seen blasting out of a trap, engraved plaque with description of the action, **$1,050, GLP**

- Jack Nicklaus 1978 autographed British Open photograph, event played at the Old Course at St. Andrews, limited edition of 78, **$750, GLP**

- Jack Nicklaus autographed photo, "A Study in Concentration," limited edition of 500, includes a ball actually struck by Nicklaus in 2002, **$650, GLP**

- Sam Snead framed autograph, with St. Andrews card, 8" x 10" photo and plate, **$400, GLP**

- Jimmy Demaret autographed 8" x 10" b/w photo, boldly signed by the three-time Masters champion, **$650, GLP**

- Ben Hogan vintage autograph, along with three other golfers, **$500, GLP**

- Jerome Travers autograph—won U.S. Open in 1915, by 1913 he had won U.S. Amateur four times, considered to be one of game's greatest amateurs, **$350, GLP**

- Jack Nicklaus autographed U.S. Open ticket packet, a complete collection of unused 1997 tickets signed boldly on the front by the Golden Bear, **$295, GLP**

- Lee Trevino autograph, **$20, GLP**

- Chi Chi Rodriguez autograph, **$10, GLP**

- Tiger Woods autographed 2000 U.S. Open Pin Flag, actual pin flag, and two photos from Pebble Beach event, **$1,200, GLP**

- Tiger Woods autographed "Fist Pump," 16" x 20" color photo with engraved plaque, **$1,050, GLP**

- Jack Nicklaus signed photo at the 1986 Masters, **$700, GLP**

- Sam Snead autographed Masters scorecard, **$400, GLP**

- Old Tom Morris framed photograph, print taken from original glass negative by A. W. Tillinghast, 1896, hand-printed limited edition, framed, **$1,850, GLP**

- Bobby Jones, Gene Sarazen, and Walter Hagen, 11" x 14" b/w, **$49, GLP**

- Old Tom Morris original first generation photograph, $6^{1}/_{2}$" x $8^{1}/_{2}$", albumen photograph rumored to be from Morris's personal belongings, excellent to mint, rare image, **$2,000, GLP**

- North Berwick Links, original first generation photograph, ca. 1880s, 8" x 10", **$365, GLP**

- Bobby Jones and Francis Ouimet, 11" x 14", b/w, **$49, GLP**

- Babe Ruth with golf clubs, 11" x 14", b/w, **$49, GLP**

- Bobby Jones and his Calamity Jane putter, 11" x 14", b/w, **$49, GLP**

- Bobby Jones 1930 ticker tape parade, **$49, GLP**

- Old Tom Morris—Keeper of the Greens, 11" x 14" b/w photo, **$49, GLP**

- The Caddy and friends: Jerry Lewis, Dean Martin, Sam Snead, Ben Hogan, and Byron Nelson, 11" x 14" b/w photo, **$49, GLP**

- Bobby Jones 1930 British Amateur Championship, 11" x 14" b/w photo, **$49, GLP**

- Ben Hogan vs. "The Monster," 11" x 14" photo of Ben Hogan holding the 1951 U.S. Open trophy that was won at the fear-inspiring Oakland Hills course after Hogan "brought the monster to its knees," **$49, GLP**

- Donald Ross and Ben Hogan, 11" x 14" b/w photo, **$49, GLP**

- Bobby Jones's 1930 Harvest, Jones with the four major championship trophies he won in 1930, 11" x 14" b/w photo, **$49, GLP**

- Two small photos of Bobby Jones for Spalding ca. 1940 and unsigned form letter explaining photos, **$75–100, WR**

- Autograph book containing thirty signatures including Bobby Jones (dated 1924), Gene Sarazen, J. H. Taylor, Bernard Darwin, Francis Ouimet, **$1,750–2,500, WR**

- Robert T. Jones signed photograph, 16½" by 14", signed in somewhat shaky hand, **$1,000–1,250, WR**

- Signed b/w photos of Bob Hope and heavyweight champ Joe Louis, **$200–300, WR**

- Signed b/w photo of Ben Hogan, 14" by 11", **$200–250, WR**

- James Braid newspaper photo signed by Braid, **$750–1,000, WR**

- Handwritten letter dated March 26, 1959, signed by J. H. Taylor, **$1,000–1,250, WR**

- Autograph book containing thirty-seven signatures including J. H. Taylor, Joe Kirkwood, and James Braid, **$400–600, WR**

- Jock Hutchinson, signed photo of 1921 Open Champion at St. Andrews, **$750, ME**

- Signed photo of Ben Hogan in his prime, **$500, ME**

- Signed album page of Johnny Golden, rarest autograph of all U.S. Ryder Cup players, **$500, ME**

- Robert Riger sketch of three-time Masters Champion Jimmy Demaret, signed, **$750, ME**

- Fountain pen autograph of Bobby Jones on early photo, ca. 1920, **$9,500, ME**

- Signed studio photo of five-time Open Champion James Braid, **$1,500, ME**

- Signed studio portrait of 1893 Open Champion Willie Auchterlonie, **$1,250, ME**

- Signed magazine photo of 1964 Open Champion Tony Lema, **$750, ME**

- Wilson Sporting Goods signed photo of Arnold Palmer, ca. 1955, **$150, ME**

- 1909 signed photo of U.S. Amateur Champion Walter Travis, **$1,500, ME**

- 1942 handwritten letter from Sam Snead on U.S. Navy stationery, **$750, ME**

- 1934 original customs document signed by Gene Sarazen, **$500, ME**

- Signed color photo of Payne Stewart, **$250, ME**

- 1924 typed letter on Royal Liverpool stationery signed by Walter Hagen, **$5,000, ME**

- 1938 pristine typed letter from Bob Jones to Margaret Curtis, **$7,500, ME**

- 1964 typed letter from Jack Nicklaus, signed, **$150, ME**

8 BADGES OF GLORY
Programs, Tickets, and Other Valuables

♀ ♀ ♀

It was one of those golden, serendipitous moments. Another instance that trumpeted the value of "doing your homework."

The power of knowledge was certainly reinforced when golf memorabilia enthusiast and auctioneer Lew Lipset saw a rather innocuous listing on eBay. This self-taught appraiser, with a passion for all things paper (pairing sheets, programs, postcards) might have dismissed this item, and shrugged, "Oh, just another U.S. Open (spectator) ticket. I have scores of tickets from the '60s."

Yet Lipset has religiously educated himself and taken the time to study golf's past. He knows the "lay of the land," those timeless "big moments" that seize our attention. Lipset is also steeped in the fine points of Internet buying, and that awareness came into play while watching his computer screen.

There it was, a Monday ticket to the 1962 U.S. Open playoff that Arnold Palmer lost to Jack Nicklaus. A rare find!

"I looked at that listing a few times, and finally realized it was a very scarce Monday ticket," beams Lipset, a decade-long admirer of the stylized graphics that grace major event tickets, badges, and programs. "From doing my research in the past, I knew Monday signals something special, a playoff. In any collecting niche, the slightest details are pivotal. You must take the time to do the homework. I don't think the seller knew the significance of Monday ticket, so I got it real cheap."

1926 U.S. Amateur Championship ticket. It is the earliest known to exist. $1500. *Photo courtesy of Mark Emerson.*

The 62-year-old Lipset, a devotee of Masters, Ryder Cup, and U.S. Open artifacts, is a grade-A student. By connecting with "Paper King" Mark Emerson, other collectors and dealers, and poring over books, he's become extremely qualified to explain the arcana of collecting paper items that were long banished to the scrap bin.

In his rather esoteric world of P.G.A. money clips (worth up to $500), Masters series or patron tickets, and early Ryder Cup memorabilia, the acknowledged cachet collectible is dated contestant badges.

Increasingly difficult to obtain, these metal, celluloid, or even paper relics, as Lipset emphasizes, rank highest on the desirability pyramid for "they, along with the player, went around the course."

That personal link, or association with an event contestant, endows badges with a unique aura. They are at the scene of the action, the talisman that allows entry into the Kingdom, and are therefore "kissed by time."

A silver and soft blue badge, such as the 3-inch by 4-inch piece of cardboard that's survived from the 1898 Women's Championship (indicative of its excellent condition, the string is still attached) might not be aesthetically comparable to a work of fine art. Yet this is not just "another piece of paper," insists Emerson.

"The badge (valued at $4,000) would have been tied to a ladies dress, so it really harks back to a long distant time," says its proud owner. "While not fancy looking, it is incredibly rare [there were only sixteen contestants in the event], and special."

Price **6**^{D.}

The
Open Golf Championship
CARNOUSTIE
1953

Order of Play

FRIDAY, 10th JULY

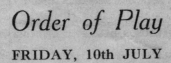

BURNS & HARRIS, LTD., DUNDEE

Final round pairing sheet for the 1953
British Open, when Ben Hogan competed
in and won his only British Open. $200.
Photo courtesy of Mark Emerson.

1959 U.S. Amateur Championship badge.
Jack Nicklaus wins his first major
championship. $400. *Photo courtesy of
Mark Emerson.*

Adding to the scarcity of most contestant badges, most players threw these items away the day after the tournament. They had no intrinsic worth, and if they were preserved, they stayed with a player's family. In either case, contestant badges, particularly from "Majors," are a rarity of rarities, keepsakes that are meant for only the most adventurous hunters.

"Sure you have to be lucky, savvy, and totally dedicated to finding one," admits Emerson, the owner of nearly 350 badges from prestige events, who has tried to establish those "association" links by writing to the players (or if deceased, to their estates) that wore them. "But the fascinating aspect of a badge, tangible or intangible, is the fact that it was on somebody's body for that event. Take my Bobby Jones badge (the one he wore during the 1929 U.S. Open is worth about $10,000). He wore it for four days. That to me is special. It's a very close connection."

Affirming that link is keenly challenging. Only a mere handful of badges have players' names on them, and the typical collector doesn't have the resources or time to engage in a relentless writing campaign such as Emerson's. It would be exhausting to trace the descendants of most bygone players, and the few dealers of these items can't be depended upon to authenticate their provenance.

To overcome those "identification" hurdles, a resourceful collector can follow Emerson's advice. Referring to prized Masters badges, he says, "Get the pairing sheets [another paper collectible detailing who played on a certain day, which increase in value according to the significance of the event and their age—the prime items are $500 to $1,000], see the number on them, and associate that number to the one on the badge.

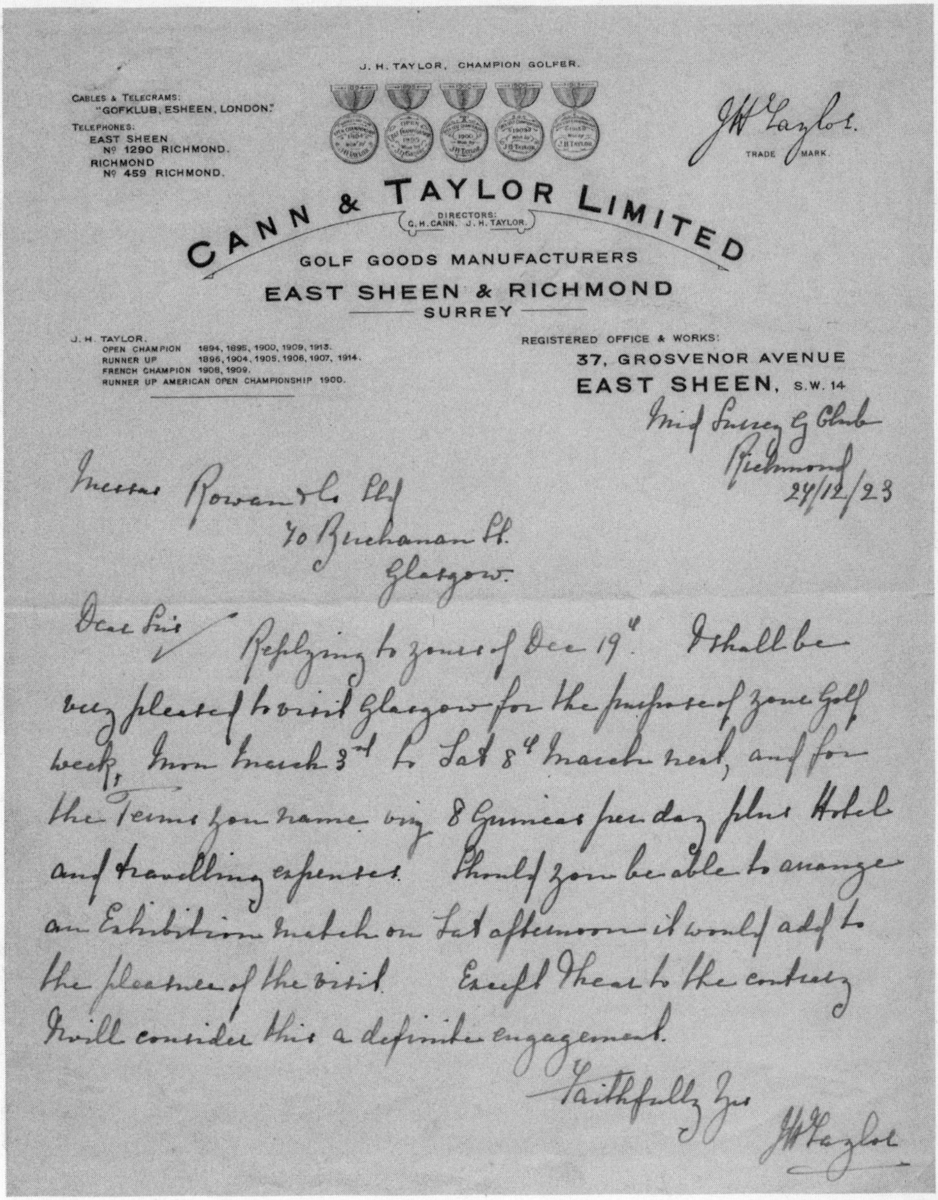

J. H. TAYLOR, CHAMPION GOLFER.

CANN & TAYLOR LIMITED

DIRECTORS:
G. H. CANN. J. H. TAYLOR.

GOLF GOODS MANUFACTURERS

EAST SHEEN & RICHMOND
SURREY

CABLES & TELEGRAMS:
"GOFKLUB, ESHEEN, LONDON."
TELEPHONES:
EAST SHEEN
Nº 1290 RICHMOND.
RICHMOND
Nº 459 RICHMOND.

J. H. TAYLOR.
OPEN CHAMPION 1894, 1895, 1900, 1909, 1913.
RUNNER UP 1896, 1904, 1905, 1906, 1907, 1914.
FRENCH CHAMPION 1908, 1909.
RUNNER UP AMERICAN OPEN CHAMPIONSHIP 1900.

REGISTERED OFFICE & WORKS:
37, GROSVENOR AVENUE
EAST SHEEN, S.W. 14

Mid Surrey G Club
Richmond
27/12/23

Messrs Rowan & Co Ltd
70 Buchanan St.
Glasgow.

Dear Sirs

Replying to yours of Dec 19th. I shall be very pleased to visit Glasgow for the purpose of your Golf week, from March 3rd to Sat 8th March next, and for the Terms you name viz 8 Guineas per day plus Hotel and travelling expenses. Should you be able to arrange an Exhibition match on Sat afternoon it would add to the pleasure of the visit. Except I hear to the contrary I will consider this a definite engagement.

Faithfully Yours

J H Taylor

1923 handwritten letter of J. H. Taylor on company stationery. $1000. *Photo courtesy of Mark Emerson.*

1953 U.S. Women's Open program. It is the
first one sponsored by the USGA. $200.
Photo courtesy of Mark Emerson.

That's how I connected seven Masters badges to actual contestants (a collection eventually sold to Lipset)."

This technique is also used to establish a historical link to caddy badges which flex their own muscular values. A 1³/₄ inch, 1930 U.S.G.A. Open red and yellow caddy badge used at Interlachen Country Club west of Minneapolis featured on Lipset's Web site *(www.oldjudge.com)* is valued at $1,500 mainly because of its excellent condition, bold graphics, age, and "association" with a notable event (at this Open, Bobby Jones won the third leg of his Grand Slam).

As Lipset stresses, "Badges worn by players are the pinnacle, along with tickets to fabled U.S. Opens. Yet a caddy badge is also hotly pursued since this is one more link to a player [particularly if that bag toter can be verifiably coupled to a marquee player, or if the event has historical significance]. Caddy badges are valuable because they too went around the course."

From that perspective, badges can be viewed as "battle trophies," the souvenirs of war which rise and fall in value according to their proximity to the action. Among Masters memorabilia, for example, the hierarchy includes "Radio" (broadcaster) badges, along with those worn by photographers, spectators, clubhouse entrants, and various employees, such as groundskeepers and the catering staff. It must be remembered that the word "badge" is rather loosely applied, for many of these tokens are really paper tickets with strings or clasps, and not always made of metal. The condition of these items is crucial in appraising their worth (Is the clasp intact?) Determine if there is any chipping or filling on enamel badges. Old paper badges could be stained and are prone to fading and foxing. But even flawed badges, if decidedly rare, have won new appreciation in the market.

"Badges are a surging market," insists Emerson, who contributed to Roger E. Gilchrist's newly published *Guide to Golf Collectibles*. In that book Emerson states that "the popularity of the winning player often affects the value of a particular badge." Attesting to the power of big-name players, that guide lists a generic 1935 Masters badge (the year Gene Sarazen won) at $5,000, a 1963 (Nicklaus's first win at Augusta) at $750, and a 1951 (when Ben Hogan won his first Masters championship) at $1,500. Convinced these prices will rise, Emerson adds, "Call them what you want, badges, tickets, there's a finite number, so this is an area that's about to explode."

Indicative of this "badge craze," Lipset's Web site lists a rare green 1954 Masters Radio badge issued to NBC that sold for $400, a 1947 Radio Masters badge and ribbon that was issued to an Augusta station (this "extremely rare" item harks back to the event when Jimmy Demaret won his second of three green jackets, and sold for $600), and one of "the earliest badges known," a 1922 U.S.G.A. Amateur Championship piece which is gold with a green cloisonné circular banner inscribed "The Country Club" and "Brookline Mass" (valued at over $1,000).

CHAMPIONSHIP COMMITTEE.

W. NORMAN BOASE, C.B.E., CHAIRMAN.

R. K. BLAIR.	ROBERT HARRIS.	LT.-COL. A. N. LEE, D.S.O.
H. M. CAIRNES.	CAPT. ANGUS V. HAMBRO.	JOHN L. LOW.
BERNARD DARWIN.	WILLIAM A. HARVEY.	E. MARTIN SMITH.
W. HERBERT FOWLER.	HAROLD H. HILTON.	F. M. RICHARDSON.
ALLAN J. GRAHAM, C.B.E.	J. L. C. JENKINS.	J. GORDON SIMPSON.

OPEN GOLF CHAMPIONSHIP

QUALIFYING ROUNDS

(SOUTHERN SECTION)

TO BE PLAYED ON THE

OLD COURSE of THE SUNNINGDALE GOLF CLUB

At SUNNINGDALE

ON

Wednesday and Thursday, 16th and 17th June 1926.

PLAY COMMENCES AT 10 O'CLOCK PRECISELY.

Any Competitor playing with balls or clubs not in conformity with the directions laid down in the clause in the Rules of Golf on Form and Make of Golf Clubs and Balls shall be disqualified.

By Order of the Championship Committee of the Royal and Ancient Golf Club of St. Andrews.

HENRY GULLEN,
Secretary.

W. C. HENDERSON & SON, UNIVERSITY PRESS, ST. ANDREWS.

1926 British Open pairing sheet to qualifying at Sunningdale when Bob Jones shot 33-33-66, called at the time the first "perfect" round of golf. $1000. *Photo courtesy of Mark Emerson.*

Pairings and Starting Time
Sunday, April 13, 1997

A.M.	Caddie No.		1st Day	2nd Day	3rd Day	Total	Caddie No.		1st Day	2nd Day	3rd Day	Total
11:50	7	Corey Pavin..................	75	74	78	227	40	Clarence Rose..................	73	75	79	227
11:59	61	Frank Nobilo (New Zealand)........	76	72	74	222	70	Larry Mize..................	79	69	74	222
P.M.												
12:08	4	Jumbo Ozaki (Japan)..............	74	74	74	222	59	Ben Crenshaw..................	75	73	74	222
12:17	11	Lee Westwood (England)...........	77	71	73	221	87	Jack Nicklaus..................	77	70	74	221
12:26	3	Jim Furyk..................	74	75	72	221	66	Sam Torrance (Scotland)..........	75	73	73	221
12:35	82	Ian Woosnam (Wales)..............	77	68	75	220	69	Duffy Waldorf..................	74	75	72	221
12:44	83	Scott Hoch..................	79	68	73	220	17	Sandy Lyle (Scotland)............	73	73	74	220
12:53	76	Steve Elkington (Australia).......	76	72	72	220	46	Scott McCarron..................	77	71	72	220
1:02	80	Paul Azinger..................	69	73	77	219	74	Craig Stadler..................	77	72	71	220
1:11	6	Lee Janzen..................	72	73	74	219	8	John Huston..................	67	77	75	219
1:20	41	Willie Wood..................	72	76	71	219	79	Mark Calcavecchia..............	74	73	72	219
1:29	15	Bernhard Langer (Germany)........	72	72	74	218	68	Mark O'Meara..................	75	74	70	219
1:38	5	Per-Ulrik Johansson (Sweden)......	72	73	73	218	78	David Frost (South Africa)........	74	71	73	218
1:47	72	Vijay Singh (Fiji)...............	75	74	69	218	10	Stuart Appleby (Australia)........	72	76	70	218
1:56	84	Nick Price (Zimbabwe)............	71	71	75	217	52	Tom Lehman..................	73	76	69	218
2:05	56	Tommy Tolles..................	72	72	72	216	25	Fuzzy Zoeller..................	75	73	69	217
2:14	43	Jesper Parnevik (Sweden).........	73	72	71	216	37	Justin Leonard..................	76	69	71	216
2:23	33	Jose Maria Olazabal (Spain).......	71	70	74	215	18	Fred Funk..................	73	74	69	216
2:32	73	Fred Couples..................	72	69	73	214	85	Davis Love III..................	72	71	72	215
2:41	57	Colin Montgomerie (Scotland)......	72	67	74	213	48	Ernie Els (South Africa).........	73	70	71	214
2:50	60	Tom Watson..................	75	68	69	212	22	Jeff Sluman..................	74	67	72	213
2:59	29	Paul Stankowski..................	68	74	69	211	64	Tom Kite..................	77	69	66	212
3:08	71	Tiger Woods..................	70	66	65	201	77	Costantino Rocca (Italy).........	71	69	70	210

INVITEES WHO ARE PRESENT AND NOT PARTICIPATING

Bob Goalby
Herman Keiser

Byron Nelson
Gene Sarazen

Sam Snead
Art Wall

HONORARY NON-COMPETING INVITEES WHO ARE PRESENT

Stewart M. Alexander
Charles R. Coe
Dow Finsterwald

Marvin M. Giles, III
David Graham
Lou Graham

Hubert Green
John Harris
Dave Marr

Andy North
Jerry Pate
Fred S. Ridley

Bill Rogers
Ken Venturi
Charles R. Yates

AUTOGRAPH POLICY: For player safety and protection, there will be a **NO AUTOGRAPH POLICY** enforced on the golf courses for the practice and tournament days. Autograph signing will only be allowed on the parking lot side of the Clubhouse. It is expected that all parties (patrons, press, players, etc.) will comply.

1997 final round Masters pairing sheet when Tiger Woods won his first professional major by a record number of strokes. $10.
Photo courtesy of Mark Emerson.

"The attractiveness of a badge definitely affects its value," says Lipset, "but heritage is arguably more important. U.S. Open badges from the 1920s, the years that Bobby Jones won [1923, 1926, 1929 and 1930] can be worth 50 to 100 percent more than badges from years he didn't win."

Palmer and Nicklaus associations also drive values. Prices of 1960s badges are significantly higher when either of these two legends won an event (a Masters badge from 1964, a year Palmer won, is worth $600 according to Gilchrist, and dramatizing the impact of Arnie's winning in 1960, this Masters souvenir is valued at $750). In sharp contrast, a generic badge from 1967 (Gay Brewer's year) is priced by Gilchrist at $175, a 1969 (when George Archer was victorious) again at $175.

Though 1920s and 1930s U.S. Open player badges are extremely valuable, they're rarely offered for sale (in the 1920s, only a limited number of players participated in the national championship, thus the scarcity factor). As Lipset says, "When you [go] back to the 1930s, even the 1940s, people don't care what's on the badge, who wore them, caddies, the press, etc. They are that scarce."

Spectator tickets (some collectors call them badges) from 1960s Masters are also extremely desirable and rare. Whether for daily admission or for the entire event, these "Promised Land" ducats can sell for as high as $2,000 (primarily depending on their condition and the marquee name value of the winner).

"There's just not a lot of these in circulation," says Lipset. "The average price for a good year (when a recognizable player won) is more than $1,000. A '61 badge, the first year the Masters issued a series ticket (for the four days), goes for $2,000 (neither Palmer nor Nicklaus won). Keep in mind, if any ticket doesn't have a string, that would adversely affect the value. Or if something is written on it, this too would cheapen it. Next to player badges, series tickets are the most coveted, while tickets stamped 'complimentary' are worth much less since these were given away."

Lipset owns several delightful tickets, including a multicolored 1926 U.S. Open (Bobby Jones won this Scioto Country Club affair) valued at over $1,000, and a heart-shaped 1925 artifact from the U.S. Open in Worcester, MA. inscribed with "in the heart of it all" (only a handful of these $3,000-plus tickets are still extant). He feels these mementos are "gorgeous" enough to frame, but the revered "centerpiece" of his collection is a final round, shield-shaped ticket (valued at $8,000) to the 1935 Masters (eventual winner Gene Sarazen forced a playoff by holing a "magical" 4-wood for a double eagle).

"The rest of my collection features a 1941 ticket signed by Craig Wood and Ben Hogan (Wood won) radio and clubhouse badges. Radio marked pieces (valued at $1,000 or more) are very rare. There were just very few people covering the event in

1946 PGA Championship program. Ben
Hogan's first major championship win.
$1250. *Photo courtesy of Mark Emerson.*

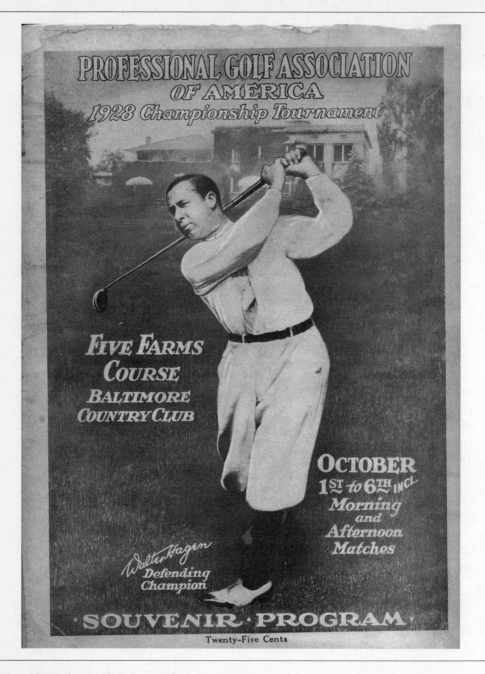

1928 PGA Championship program. Walter Hagen's last major championship on U.S. soil. $2000. *Photo courtesy of Mark Emerson.*

July 23, 1918, Red Cross exhibition tournament. $400. *Photo courtesy of Mark Emerson.*

the 1930s and '40s. It's amazing, in fact, that they were there, and like all Masters memorabilia, these badges are getting very expensive. It's now a fashionable niche because of Tiger Woods's celebrity power."

Ryder Cup materials (particularly the six matches before World War II) are another increasingly popular niche where prices are rising. Due to the competition's steadily soaring TV ratings—and well-publicized intensity—badges, tickets, and programs (valued at $5,000) are "a big growth sector," says Lipset, who's owned 1933 and 1935 tickets and a 1933 program with loose pages (it still sold for $1,400, showing that rarity often supersedes condition in price appraisals). "While P.G.A. Championship memorabilia is losing ground [financially, for this event has lost some of its luster over the years], due to the rising interest in the Ryder Cup, [its] memorabilia is in much greater demand."

What ultimately gives a 1927 Ryder Cup ticket (worth $3,000) or a 1953 British Open memento such luminosity among collectors? The "Fly on the Wall" factor.

"If you have [a] ticket or a pairing sheet to that final round day in '53 [when Hogan shot his fourth consecutive lower round, and clinched his only British title—he only entered one], you're essentially right there," explains Emerson, who keenly appreciates the "pedigree" of such sheets as those from Ben Hogan's 1953 year, the 1925 U.S. Open won by Willie MacFarlane, and Bobby Jones's qualifying round for the 1926 British Open at Sunningdale, when he shot a sixty-six "perfect round," as a British newspaper described it, "as perfect and chaste as Grecian statuary."

Trumpeting the glories of pairing sheets, Emerson continues, "You're witnessing history, you're part of the crowd. The names on a pairing sheet are like a menu [like the one he owns from the 1927 Ryder Cup dinner]. You just have to pretend you're a fly on the wall."

Adamant about preserving the purity of a pairing sheet, Emerson passionately adds, "My earliest pairing sheet is from the 1924 British Open (worth between $1,000 and $1,250) and putting an autograph on that defaces it. It's a who's who of the best, a piece of paper that transports me back to that day. It must remain pristine."

Emerson feels programs are still undervalued, and this opportunity to profit, along with his taste for pleasing artwork, has prompted Lipset to collect them.

"With programs there aren't as many variables. . . . Some people feel they're marred if signed, but if autographed by the event winner, I feel that greatly adds to the value.

"My U.S. Open programs, 1930, '31, '34, '35, '36, '38 through '41, they're on average worth $1,000. My 1931 Ryder Cup is [*sic*] worth over $2,000 (bought on eBay) could be my most valuable. You won't find a 1930 too easily, so if one has loose pages; it's one of those rarity-condition tradeoffs. You might have to go for it. Even if a program is missing pages it might be worth buying if the price reflects the damage."

Unlike rare autographs, programs aren't a target for forgers. Their values just don't justify all the work that would be necessary to counterfeit these books. That makes Internet surfing far less worrisome for the "addicted" golfiana enthusiast like Lipset, who says, "There are still some [program] bargains out there. You just have to follow what's for sale, and what people are paying. Places like eBay are a tool. You can see and learn where the market is, and headed."

Ever the A student, Lipset returns to his computer screen, confident he will soon "steal" another prize. Even if he doesn't, one thing is for certain. Sorting through the various offerings will be fun, another pleasurable journey back into time.

The prices of golf collectibles fluctuate. The following values are estimates offered by various experts:
WR—Will Roberto
ME—Mark Emerson

- Eleven programs including the 1984 U.S. Women's Open and the 1979 U.S. Open, **$300–400, WR**

- Seven items including *Baltusrol 100 Years*, *Baltusrol 90 Years in the Mainstream of American Golf*, a 93rd U.S. Open Official Annual by Rolex, and four programs concerning Baltusrol, **$300–400, WR**

- Scarce program from the 1961 Women's Open Championship, **$75–100, WR**

- Metal "B" Class caddie badge from the St. Louis Country Club ca. 1930s, **$100–125, WR**

- Blue and silver enameled Player badge marked 118th Open Championship, **$300–350, WR**

- U.S. Open badge Inverness 1979 for a contestant's wife, **$70–80, WR**

- Twenty-six cigarette cards, Walter Hagen from Wills Famous Golfers, and others, **$150–200, WR**

- Two U.S. Open items: ticket and program from the 83rd at Oakmont, **$175–200, WR**

- Complete set of Famous Golfers by Wills ca. 1930, **$650–700, WR**

- Seven unused artist-drawn blotters, 3.8" x 9", all with color golf illustrations, 1927–32, **$80–90, WR**

- All-tournament badge to 1997 U.S. Amateur Championship, Tiger Woods's record-setting third U.S. Amateur win in a row, **$50, ME**

- Final round ticket to 1994 U.S. Amateur Championship, the day Tiger Woods won his first major championship. **$75, ME**

- 1930 U.S. Amateur Championship ticket, Bob Jones completing the grand Grand Slam, **$2,000, ME**

- 1959 U.S. Amateur Championship badge, Jack Nicklaus wins his first major championship, **$400, ME**

- 1923 U.S. Women's Amateur Championship program, earliest known, **$2,500, ME**

- 1990 Solheim Cup program, first one, **$125, ME**

- 1946 U.S. Women's Open program, recognized as first professional Women's Open program, it had local sponsors. **$1,000, ME**

- 1922 Walker Cup program, first match, **$2,500, ME**

- Final round ticket to 1994 U.S. Amateur Championship, the day Tiger Woods won his first major championship, **$75, ME**

- 1926 U.S. Amateur Championship ticket, earliest known to exist, **$1,500, ME**

- 1930 U.S. Amateur Championship ticket, Bob Jones completing the Grand Slam, **$2,000, ME**

- 1961 U.S. Amateur Championship, Jack Nicklaus wins his second major at Pebble Beach, **$200, ME**

- 1946 U.S. Women's Open program, recognized as first professional Women's Open program, **$1,000, ME**

- 1986 final round Masters pairing sheet from Jack Nicklaus's record-setting sixth win at the Masters, **$20, ME**

- 1926 British Open pairing sheet at Sunningdale when Bob Jones shot 33-33-66, called at the time the first "perfect" round of golf, **$1,000, ME**

- 2000 U.S. Open program from Pebble Beach when Tiger Woods won his first U.S. Open, **$20, ME**

- 1928 P.G.A. Championship program, Walter Hagen's last major championship on U.S. soil. **$2,000, ME**

- 1946 P.G.A. Championship program, Ben Hogan's first major championship win, **$1,250, ME**

- 1900 ticket to Harry Vardon exhibition, oldest known dated golf ticket, **$2,500, ME**

- 1907 ticket to J. H. Taylor and Arnaud Massy exhibition, **$750, ME**

- 1997 final round Masters pairing sheet when Tiger Woods won his first professional major by a record number of strokes, **$10, ME**

- 1986 final round Masters pairing sheet from Jack Nicklaus's record-setting sixth win at the Masters, **$20, ME**

- 1960 U.S. Open pairing sheet when Arnold Palmer stormed back to win his only U.S. Open, **$50, ME**

- 1953 British Open final round pairing sheet when Ben Hogan competed in and won his only British Open, **$200, ME**

- 2002 U.S. Open program from Bethpage when Tiger Woods won his second U.S. Open, **$10, ME**

- Signed photo of 1898 U.S. Amateur Champion Findlay Douglas, **$750, ME**

- Signed photo of 1900 U.S. Amateur Champion Walter Travis, **$1,500, ME**

- Signed photo of three-time major champion Payne Stewart, **$250, ME**

- Signed photo of first Masters Champion Horton Smith, **$1,000, ME**

- Signed photo of Vijay Singh, **$25, ME**

- Signed photo of 1912 British Open Champion Ted Ray, **$1,000, ME**

- Signed photo of Arnold Palmer, **$100, ME**

9 THE REWARDS OF VICTORY
Historical Medals

Nothing stopped the immortal Haig. Not even a willow tree that "miraculously" sprouted overnight.

Sounding much like a heroic tale straight out of Greek mythology, this saga begins on the 17th hole at the Inwood Country Club in Far Rockaway, New York, during the 1921 Professional Golfers Championship.

Rather than driving his ball straight down the fairway, the great Walter Hagen discovered that it made much more tactical sense to approach the heavily-bunkered 17th green by playing from the adjacent 18th hole. From there he'd have an unobstructed approach shot to the 17th, so Hagen wisely planned to take this alternate route to the green even if it meant violating tradition.

He did exactly that during the first round of play. But his resourcefulness greatly irritated Inwood's stodgy club members.

Congregating in the clubhouse grill after, the always flamboyant and controversial Hagen "outwitted" the 17th's penal design. Angered club officials met with Inwood's groundskeepers and devised their own counterattack.

To foil Hagen's stratagem, they sent a crew into the woods that evening, and had them uproot a 15-foot high weeping willow tree. They then "planted" that tree between the 17th and 18th fairways to close the gap in the tree line. Now, they reasoned, Hagen would be forced to take the conventional path down the menacing 17th fairway.

Arriving at the 17th tee the following morning, Hagen looked down the fairway and quipped, "I never saw such a fast growing tree in my life."

1 Oil painting of Old Tom Morris, ca. 1904. *Photo courtesy of the Joseph R. Tiscornia collection.*

2 1690s oil painting showing children playing golf. *Photo courtesy of the Joseph R. Tiscornia collection.*

3 1566 Acts of the Scottish Parliament. *Photo courtesy of the Joseph R. Tiscornia collection.*

4 Clubs from the 1700s. *Photo courtesy of the Joseph R. Tiscornia collection.*

5 Clubs made by Hugh Philp. *Photo courtesy of the Joseph R. Tiscornia collection.*

6

7

8

9

10

11

6 Three silver medals from the early 1800s. *Photo courtesy of the Joseph R. Tiscornia collection.*

7 Willie Fernie's 1883 (British) Open championship gold medal. *Photo courtesy of the Joseph R. Tiscornia collection.*

8 Wooden boxwood ball from the 1500s. *Photo courtesy of the Joseph R. Tiscornia collection.*

9 Feather balls from the late 1700s and early 1800s. *Photo courtesy of the Joseph R. Tiscornia collection.*

10 Early rubber-cored golf balls, ca. early 1900s. *Photo courtesy of the Joseph R. Tiscornia collection.*

11 Clubs made by three different members of the Patrick family. *Photo courtesy of the Joseph R. Tiscornia collection.*

12

13

14

15

16

17

12 View of the sixteenth hole at Cypress
Point, with golfer Alister MacKenzie.
Linen card, 1930s, $75. *Photo courtesy of
Lew Lipset.*

13 Turnberry lighthouse and golf course,
1910, $25. *Photo courtesy of Lew Lipset.*

14 "The Evening Cruise" Royal & Ancient
Golf Club House. *Photo courtesy of Lew
Lipset.*

15 Coral Gables Golf Club and Gene
Sarazen, 1920–30, $50–75. *Photo courtesy
of Lew Lipset.*

16 "Ethnic" card captioned "The Life Saving
Crew at 10th Hole—No. 3 Course.
Pinehurst, N.C." Albertype, 1920,
$75–100. *Photo courtesy of Lew Lipset.*

17 Augusta National Golf Club, looking up
the eighteenth fairway, ca. mid to late
1930s. *Photo courtesy of Lew Lipset.*

18

19

20

21

22

23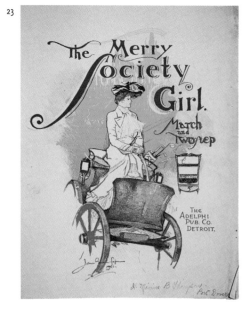

18 Postcard captioned "Golf House, Montrose." *Photo courtesy of Lew Lipset.*

19 Postcard captioned "Sunningdale Golf Links from Knigs Hill, Surrey," features airship flying overhead, ca. 1910–20, $30–40. *Photo courtesy of Lew Lipset.*

20 "Rags Rabbit" comic book cover, 1950s. *Photo courtesy of Michael Hurdzan.*

21 "Honor Caddy" image: Bing Crosby—Bob Hope—Golf. These personalities are closely identified with golf, so the cost of this would be $150–200. *Photo courtesy of Michael Hurdzan.*

22 Freddie Tait, a British champion killed in Boer War, ca. 1900, by W. Rolland. London, ca. 1892, plaster. *Photo courtesy of Will Roberto.*

23 "The Merry Society Girl" Although it is from 1901 and very colorful, the only golf-related items featured are the clubs in the car. $150–200. *Photo courtesy of Michael Hurdzan.*

24

25

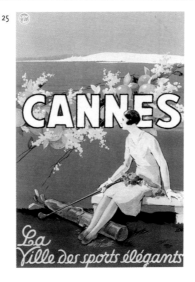

26

27

24 Poster advertising Hyères, in the south of France, by Rodger Broder ca. 1930s, matted and framed. $2000–2500. *Photo courtesy of Old Tom Morris Golf, L.L.C.*

25 Poster advertising Cannes. *Photo courtesy of Old Tom Morris Golf, L.L.C.*

26 Poster advertising the Danbury Fair of October 1930, with illustration captioned "A Mental Hazard," matted and framed. $500–750. *Photo courtesy of Old Tom Morris Golf, L.L.C.*

27 From left to right:
A Dunlop caddie figure advertising "We play Dunlop," lacking bag strap, $600–800.

A Penfold Man advertising "He Played a Penfold," $600–800.

A Penfold Man, with original pipe, advertising "He Played a Penfold." $600–700.

A Penfold Man, featuring some restoration, $300–400.
Photo courtesy of Old Tom Morris Golf, L.L.C.

28

29

30

31

32

28 Cover of *Scribner's* "Fiction Number" magazine, ca. 1895, framed. $400–500. *Photo courtesy of Old Tom Morris Golf, L.L.C.*

29 A Dickensware vase with male golfer scene, by Weller pottery, ca. 1900. $1500–1750. *Photo courtesy of Old Tom Morris Golf, L.L.C.*

30 A pottery pitcher in light green with white applications in the manner of Jasper Ware, marked "2295." Germany, ca. 1900. Scarce. $1000–1200. *Photo courtesy of Old Tom Morris Golf, L.L.C.*

31 A Dickensware vase with male golfer scene, with an unusual brown glaze rim, by Weller pottery, 1900. $1500–1750. *Photo courtesy of Old Tom Morris Golf, L.L.C.*

32 A Dickensware vase with female golfer scene, by Weller pottery, ca. 1900. $1000–1200. *Photo courtesy of Old Tom Morris Golf, L.L.C.*

33 From left to right:
Hagen concave sand wedge, $400–600.

Slazenger one-piece wood, shaft and head stamped, grip replaced, horn affixed with two screws. This club hung at C.CA. of Farmington, Connecticut, and was owned by the first golf pro, Charles Henderson, ca. 1895, $2000–2500.

A wry neck-style putter, with a partial stamp reading "Willie N." Formerly owned by H. F. Whitney, Sr., USGA President, 1921. Letter of provenance. $250–500.

A Mac & Mac pointed back putter, shaft begins and terminates in square form, deep groove face, ca. 1920. Letter of provenance. $700–1000.
Photo courtesy of Old Tom Morris Golf, L.L.C.

34 An auction lot of two silver items, $800–1000.
Left: Leather card case with repoussed sterling cover of golfer, hallmark 1905.

Right: American vesta lighter with painted figure of golfer, ca. 1895
Photo courtesy of Old Tom Morris Golf, L.L.C.

35 A green Copeland Spode pitcher, ca. 1910, marked Copeland Late Spode. $1000–1250. *Photo courtesy of Old Tom Morris Golf, L.L.C.*

36 A W. J. Gourlay feather ball, ca. 1840, size 32. This is a very large feather ball with equatorial ring mark (perhaps owner's identifying mark), with original paint, in generally quite good condition. $10,000–12,000. *Photo courtesy of Old Tom Morris Golf, L.L.C.*

37 A T. Alexander feather ball ca. 1790–1800. This oversize ball is typical of the late 1700s. A fine example. $15,000–20,000. *Photo courtesy of Old Tom Morris Golf, L.L.C.*

38

39

40

41

42

43

38 An Eclipse gutty (made from 1877–92).
$300–500. *Photo courtesy of Old Tom Morris Golf, L.L.C.*

39 A Haskell golf ball, remade, with minor paint loss. $700–1000. *Photo courtesy of Old Tom Morris Golf, L.L.C.*

40 A Wonderball by John Wanamaker, N.Y., ca. 1920s. As new, in wrapper. Nice diamond pattern. $750–1000. *Photo courtesy of Old Tom Morris Golf, L.L.C.*

41 A Reach Eagle mesh golf ball, as new in box. $250–350. *Photo courtesy of Old Tom Morris Golf, L.L.C.*

42 A Springvale Falcon wrapped bramble. Fine. $350–500. *Photo courtesy of Old Tom Morris Golf, L.L.C.*

43 Magnificent fountain pen autograph of Bob Jones, on early photo, ca. 1920. $9500. *Photo courtesy of Mark Emerson.*

English 18-karat gold medal, one of a pair.
ca. 1920s. $400–500. *Photo courtesy of Old
Tom Morris Golf, L.L.C.*

A Sterling silver vesta case with enameled
golf scene. Fine. $800–1000. *Photo courtesy
of Old Tom Morris Golf, L.L.C.*

Not knowing where to hit his ball, Hagen hesitated for a few moments. Then the golfing gods intervened.

Winds started to gust, knocking down the wires that held the weeping willow in place. Hagen again laughed, and proceeded to drive his ball into position on the 18th fairway. He'd soon hit his ball close to the pin, en route to winning the first of his five P.G.A. crowns.

It was a brilliant stroke of genius, as stunning as the diamond-studded gold medal that celebrated Hagen's masterful play.

"Decorated with a large diamond and the P.G.A. emblem, this was one gaudy S.O.B.," exclaims Bob Burkett, the longtime "keeper" of the "Willow Tree" medal. "The size of a half-dollar, it's absolutely beautiful. It was very dear to Hagen, and that's why medals are so appealing to me. They are an intimate, very personal connection with the golfer. I love medals because they're so alive with history.

"Hagen battled for this medal. It represents his overcoming the opposition, the course, and even the battles in his own head. He overcame so much adversity to achieve greatness during this very special event."

Medals also punctuate a fall from grace, the less golden aspects of the game. After reaching stratospheric heights, golfers hitting bad times have to scrape for money and sell their shining treasures. Lost medals are all too symbolic of a sad, dispiriting decline.

But even if careers go skidding into the rough, medals never lose their original luster. Whether pure gold, gold-washed, or sterling silver, such tokens as collector William

A small cut glass jar with removable sterling lid by Unger Brothers, ca. 1900. Jar shows wear, silver decorative lid very good. Uncommon form. $1100–1200. *Photo courtesy of Old Tom Morris Golf, L.L.C.*

One of a lot of four foreign bronze medals: Gulmarg (Cashmere, India), Liguanea, Luffness New and Walton Heath. $100–150. *Photo courtesy of Old Tom Morris Golf, L.L.C.*

Anderson's golf medal from the 1904 Olympics (the earliest known medal from this international competition) or his Club Maker's Medal that belonged to the immortal Old Tom Morris (club- and ballmakers competed for this award at St. Andrews), honor more than a singular moment in time. They represent that glorious sweep of achievements known as the game's heroic and thrill-filled past.

"More than beauty, a medal's history is what really affects its value," explains Burkett, the president of Old Sport Golf (a golf equipment retailer) who first started acquiring these celebratory gems in the early 1980s, and now has one of the world's largest collections, about 250 medals. "The charm of each medal is its telling a unique story. I don't know every story, but whether it's a Bobby Jones (1930) British Open medal, or my 1844 Royal Calcutta (India) piece with an Indian motif, a medal is more than an attachment with a player. That Calcutta medal with balls and a ribbon across it was won during the feather ball era, so a prize like that also offers a connection to an entire time period."

That powerful, even magnetic appeal exacts a heavy price. Once the "undiscovered" jewels of collecting, medals from important events and landmark golf clubs have soared in value (as they very rarely come on the market) now that scores of enthusiasts are charmed by them. Simple English medals with intricately worked engravings, $40 to $75 stuff in the 1980s, are now selling for $600 to $700, while that Willow Tree medal (which Burkett acquired for $9,000 in 1988) sold five years ago for $35,000 (and is now worth $40,000 to $50,000).

"When I first got into medals it was a fairyland, you could find anything at unbelievable prices because nobody was doing anything with them," recalls Burkett. "I made

A U.S. Amateur Championship medallion ca. 1890s by John Frick Co., New York. Appears identical to the gold USGA Amateur medals in Golf House, struck from the same die, but this is probably copper with a gold wash or plating. It is uninscribed, but might possibly have been given to a tournament dignitary. $2000–$2500. *Photo courtesy of Old Tom Morris Golf, L.L.C.*

One of a lot of two turn-of-the-century medals, bronze with golfing figure ca. 1900, large sterling medal with group scene. $250–300. *Photo courtesy of Old Tom Morris Golf, L.L.C.*

the big mistake of not educating myself enough, reading about the game, and so I stumbled around. I could have bought stuff that was really good and inexpensive, and I just didn't. Plus there wasn't the information around that there is today. If I had to do it all over again, I'd spend an extra $100, $200, $500, whatever, to get the better pieces. Always buy the best you can afford."

Even if Burkett did make mistakes (and unschooled collectors will invariably buy the wrong items at questionable prices), he ultimately turned himself into "a student of history." By putting a premium on medals with "a real past," or those mirroring "an individual battle that was fought and won" (rather than just focusing on an item's aesthetic appeal), he collected several exemplary pieces.

"Lineage, legacy, to me that's key," says Burkett, as he lovingly admires a $5,000 gold medal with a red-enameled cross given to Hagen by the Red Cross for playing an exhibition match against Bobby Jones during World War II. "You have to learn how to separate the good stuff that's mixed in with the ordinary minutiae. The best way for a beginner to do that is to avoid eBay because some of the merchandise could be questionable, and to work with dealers. Let them know what your goals are, whether it's just to have a beautiful decorative display of stuff that's not necessarily valuable, or if you want to be a very serious collector."

One of a lot of two medium-sized pre-1900 British medals, woman's bronze award inscribed 1894 and gentleman's silver medal inscribed 1893. $300–350. *Photo courtesy of Old Tom Morris Golf, L.L.C.*

Blackheath Medal. *Photo courtesy of Old Sport Golf.*

Burkett is intensely serious. A frequent participant at auctions where the bidding becomes "one crazy testosterone battle," he's opened his checkbook to find "that one rarity which beautifully completes a collection," gives it an exclamation point, or a distinctive aura.

"Buying at auction is not really for beginners, they can get really hurt at these sales," he warns. "There was this auction I went to in 1993, '94, where I was willing to spend $6,000 to $8,000 for Jack Fleck's U.S. Open medal. I was really determined to buy it, but so were a few guys from the club who wanted it for display purposes, and this heart surgeon. That medal [otherwise known as the Jack Fluke, since Fleck didn't win any other majors] was thought to be worth $8,000 at the most, but I had to drop out at $9,000. It went for $27,000, 28, $29,000. The bidding became this ego contest. New collectors have to know that auction fights often spin out control."

There was still the "pain" of losing that Fleck medal. It was unique, and Burkett has also failed to acquire other desired items for various reasons. How has he dealt with the heartbreak?

"The collector has to be resilient, know that you do find things if you put in the work. I have. Lots of objects with meticulously hand-engraved, incised, and raised work. These are usually from the 1920s when the workmanship was stunning, with all sorts of elaborate designs. These are far different than the stuff from the 1930s and '40s, when the quality and material, reflecting the bad economy, just fell off the edge of the world."

One memento that will forever retain its distinctive brilliance is a ceremonial "match-safe" in three shades of gold dating back to 1919. A throwback to the days be-

One of a lot of two medals from Royal Clubs, Royal Western India G.C. coin silver (80%) dated 1897, and Royal Calcutta G.C. 10- Karat gold, ca. 1940s. $400–450. *Photo courtesy of Old Tom Morris Golf, L.L.C.*

A sterling silver Goodnow Choice Score Trophy medal from the Bob O'Link G.C., inscribed and dated 1919. Uncommon. Chicago area wartime award. $90–100. *Photo courtesy of Old Tom Morris Golf, L.L.C.*

fore cigarette lighters, when matches had to be carried in small, "sweat-proof" boxes, this one-of-a-kind delight was presented to Jones after the 1919 U.S. Amateur.

"It's just exquisite, beautifully inscribed 'From his fellow members of the Atlanta Athletic Club' to honor his second place finish in the event," recalls Burkett, obviously proud of owning this historical keepsake. "It's only the size of a book of matches, but with those three colors of gold, the piece is simply magnificent. A real joy!"

Besides treasuring other Jones rarities, including a Grecian pitcher that the "King" won at age 12 in the (Tennessee) Cherokee Invitational, Burkett especially likes a gold-plated membership card given to Hagen by the Golf Club of Detroit. A little bigger than a credit card, this ceremonial object gave Hagen a lifetime membership to this prestigious club. (Before Sir Haig demanded better treatment for fellow pros in the early 1920s, golfers were treated as virtual servants, barred from entering clubs). It's a very attractive, near-mint piece, but a medal's condition isn't crucial to Burkett.

"If there are two medals dating back to the same year, I'd of course prefer the one that's in better condition. Yet the occurrence of two identical medals is very rare [British Open medals after 1908 have all been standardized, and the same holds true for other prominent events]. So I'm not worried about condition. Rarity is my key concern."

That pursuit of the most select, hard-to-find medals has also steered Burkett away from "a crazy numbers game." He's only interested in the highest pedigreed pieces, the "exceptional stuff," even if that chase often means acquiring smaller medals that are "more subtle and less over-the-top splash."

XVI Club, silver with crossed clubs and golfer in relief ca. 1890. *Photo courtesy of Will Roberto.*

A history buff, Burkett will often look at his mementos to reacquaint himself with a certain time period—to flash back to his heroes' exploits. He's satisfied with the number of pieces in his collection. Yet continually thinking of the individual accomplishments that enhance the aura of major championship medals, he's still hopeful of adding one more prize to his renowned collection.

"It might be a bit much too expensive [*sic*] for me right now, but a very early U.S. Open medal would certainly help me forget that Macfarlane piece I didn't get. U.S. Open medals just don't come on the market too often. Yet that's the thing about these very personal, intimate items. Players dreamed about winning them, putting them on their shelves, and so do collectors."

♀ ♀ ♀

It's a room worthy of Captain Kidd, a den rich with lustrous golden booty.

After using guile and secret tricks to unearth these "tributes to greatness," the "Monster Man" has found many bewitching prizes that point to his collecting savvy. Relishing the gamesmanship of the hunt, this slangy, direct, and profane New Englander takes special delight from outwitting the market's heaviest hitters. Particularly when he can flaunt his stockpile of knowledge to nab another "monster."

"Just look at this solid gold medal, there are only five of these in private hands," boasts Jim Espinola triumphantly. "Worth about $75,000, this is Tony Manero's 1936 U.S. Open reward. He scored 282 to win (at Baltusrol), a record at that time, and this medal has to be considered one of the greatest of all time."

The Bucceleuch-Royal Perth Medal ca. 1838.
Golfers in tri-cornered hats and colonial-era
attire in bas-relief by famous sculptor E.
Wyon. *Photo courtesy of Will Roberto.*

Still flushed with the joy of obtaining this "piece of American history," the ebullient
Espinola soon reaches for another awe-inspiring artifact.

"This is unique, a wonderful piece from the very first Irish Open at the Royal Dublin
Golf Club in 1894," he explains, excitedly, looking at a medal that's been turned into
a brooch. "I've done my research. That's the only way you prosper in this world, and
how I know the winner (Andrew Kirkaldy) and his wife didn't get along. She
must've turned this ($30,000) piece into a brooch."

Before that Irish charm can be fully appreciated, the frenetic, fast-talking Espinola
displays another piece of intriguing "jewelry."

"It's small, about the size of a quarter, but just think of the provenance, its origins,
this (silver) medal that could've been worn as a belt decoration belonged to the Bobby
Jones of his era, John Henry Taylor (five-time British Open winner)," crows Espinola. "This is his 2nd place medal from the (British) Open in 1904. I have a picture
showing him wearing this. I have lots of medals, but few of them are as evocative of
another era as this one."

Espinola's entire golf collection, from ceramics to books and dozens of "Patent" clubs,
whisks him back into another, more innocent age. To take such a spirited run at history, Espinola has had to distinguish between reputable and dishonest dealers, study
the dynamics of auctions, and, above all, familiarize himself with those epochal accomplishments that make medals more than just expensive glitter.

"Do your homework, knowledge is the true name of this game," advises Espinola, as
he lovingly cradles another extraordinary object from his veritable gold mine.

Displaying a sparkling "Winter Prize" medal from the illustrious Thistle Golf Club (a golfing society founded in 1815, played on the links of Leith near Edinburgh, Scotland), along with a December 7, 1822, scorecard that shows the winning score, he says, "to really appreciate the historical value of this silver piece (decorated with two thistles) you have to know that golf was traditionally a winter game. It was played by the very rich who tended crops, sheep, and herds. In the winter they had time to play golf. *The Rules of the Thistle Golf Club* is one of the rarest books in the world, and this particular medal is also unbelievable. It's one of the earliest medals we know of that has a scorecard (valued at $30,000), so it's worth over $100,000."

Insisting that investing in only big-league items makes financial sense, Espinola strides past a silver U.S. Open plate awarded to Henry Cotton, and stops in front of a bookcase lined with "priceless" mementos. Smiling knowingly to himself, he reaches for a medal the size of a quarter, and says, "I have trophies all over the place. That Cotton trophy (two feet in diameter and presented to this legend for winning the 1948 Open) is probably worth $20,000. It doesn't pay to buy junk. Either buy the best or don't buy at all.

"But this medal (three different gold pieces which flip open to reveal three different maps) is priceless. I go for the monsters, items in impeccable condition, and there are only twelve of these in existence. Think about it! Ben Hogan gave this medal to Gene Sarazen in 1952, and it's probably the greatest piece of Masters memorabilia of all time. Look at this! After Hogan won the Masters in 1951, he started a Masters dinner, and gave a medal to twelve former champions [there were only twelve champions up until then]. I have Sarazen's, a truly historical medal, and that's what collectors should go after, timeless pieces, those with a real unique link to the past."

In Espinola's "throne room," where hand-carved sculptures and plates are "statements of history," there are thin slivers of gold like a dinner plate tag from a Ryder Cup affair, and an elegant looking fountain pen given to Gene Sarazen in 1941. Each item has its own grace, or attractive appeal, and that's to be expected in this setting dedicated to the game's leading lights. Espinola is a noncompromising "condition guy" (a scratched and dinged medal just isn't in his vocabulary); the purist convinced golf's legendary "ghosts" will feel at home among his picture-perfect possessions.

Yet this eminent collection is not just a gold and silver journey through history. It's also a revealing "window" into personalities, a look at men who gave the game its gusto, particularly Espinola's most "intimate" piece that establishes "a very powerful connection with both an event and a golfing god."

"When you talk about monsters, this amber and gold cigarette holder has to be included," says Espinola in a near-reverential tone. "Geez, this is special, very personal.

"Elegant and exquisite, it was given to Harry Vardon by the R & A (Royal & Ancient Golf Club of St. Andrews) after this great champion won the 1899 British Open. It's an appreciation piece that's incredibly precious."

Seduced by the cigarette holder's charms (beauty is a critical determinant in assessing value, along with age, wear, and origin), Espinola twirls the piece in his hand, and adds, "Vardon used this. I'm sure it was dear to him."

It's certainly enchanting to Espinola. He's typically the sharp-tongued, high-octane negotiator, wheeling and dealing by his computer screen. But now, while savoring this piece of Vardoniana, he's almost kittenish, the monster transformed.

That's the power of silver and gold pleasures. Along with being dazzling "story-tellers," they herald a player's triumphs, his turning adversity into glory—and in golf that's always a saga suggestive of Beauty and the Beast.

The prices of golf collectibles fluctuate. The following values are estimates offered by various experts:
OS—Bob Burkett's Old Sport Golf
MM—Mullock & Madeley
WR—Will Roberto

- Two silver golf club medals both silver hallmarked and presented by Stover Golf Club, comprising silver and enamel star and inlaid Beauchief Golf Sheffield. Sterling silver Medal from Penang Golf Club, Scotland, hand-engraved with two crossed long nose styled clubs, dated 1906, **$900, OS**

- Silver medal 2¹/₂" diameter, elaborate cast border with thistles, engraved with two golfers and caddy, one seems to be Old Tom Morris, from Worlington and Newmarket Golf Club, 1894, **$1,850, OS**

- Cased Royal Blackheath Golf Club silver medal with original ribbon clasp and case, oval shaped 1³/₄" high with raised crest of club, 1923, **difficult to price due to rarity, OS**

- Gold medal from the Ardsley Club (NY), 14-karat President's Cup 1917, half-dollar sized, sharply detailed golfer in swing surrounded by wreaths with crossed clubs, very early, rare medal, **$2,000, OS**

- Gold Medal from Pinehurst Country Club; club's crest in relief, half-dollar sized, from Valentine's Day tournament for women, 1927, few Pinehurst medals in circulation, **$1,800, OS**

- Sterling silver Maltese cross with circular center piece from Hastings and St. Leonard's Golf Club, floral scroll engraving, 1898, **$850, OS**

- Scarce silver hallmarked medal embossed on obverse, Bruntsfield Links, crest to the border, Short Hole Golf Tournament and crown embossed, also figure of a golfer, **$185, MM**

- Nine-karat hallmarked medal embossed on the obverse with golfing figure and on reverse engraved British Legion, East Lothian Open, 1927, **$135, MM**

- Set of 4 rare Gulmarg Golf Club silver (1) and bronze (3) medals in retailer-fitted case, Charles Packer and co. London. The silver medal is hallmarked Birmingham 1921, and each medal is embossed on the reverse with golf club and course. Competitions include the Indian Army Cup, Open Championship, and The Fane Davies Cup. Winner details engraved to rims, **$185, MM**

- Two silver hole-in brooches incl. London hallmarked brooch with crossed golf clubs and pearl golf ball and letters N.D.G.C., plus a silver marcasite brooch with crossed golf club and pin flag, **$125, MM**

- Four sterling silver medals, including two large inscribed English medals, ca. 1907 and 1918, **$400–500, WR**

- American Golf Association sterling medal 1905, suspended on gold-plated watch chain, **$600–800, WR**

- Sterling silver vesta case with enameled golf scene, fine condition, **$800–1,000, WR**

- Two English 18-karat gold medals, ca. 1920s, **$400–500, WR**

- Four Foreign Bronze medals, Gulmarg (Kashmir, India), Liguanea, Luffness New, and Walton Heath, **$100–150, WR**

- U.S. Amateur Championship Medallion, ca. 1890s by John Frick Co., New York, copper, uninscribed, **$2,000–2,500, WR**

- Two turn-of-the-century medals: bronze with golfing figure, large sterling 1905 medal, **$250–300, WR**

- Two medium-sized pre-1900 British medals: women's bronze award 1894, and gentleman's silver medal 1893, **$300–350, WR**

- Sterling silver Goodnow Choice Score Trophy medal, dated 1919, uncommon, **$90–100, WR**

- Two 15 karat gold scratch medals from the Manchester Golf Club, 1921 and 1923, **$300–350, WR**

- Twelve English sterling silver spoons and one sterling silver stamp box, very good, **$15–200, WR**

- Two sets of gold-plated cuff links, one set decorated with crossed clubs and ball, the other embellished with clubheads, **$250–300, WR**

- Unusual tie bar, ca. 1930s, in shape of golf badge and clubs, 14 karat gold and platinum, **$300–500, WR**

- Enameled cigarette case with etched scene of three golfers, gold wash interior, **$150–250, WR**

- Six Alvin silver plate stirrers in bag, in shape of irons in their original leather golf bag, uncommon, **$150–250, WR**

- Sterling silver on bronze cigarette box, ca. 1912, very good condition, **$200–300, WR**

- 1930 English Golf Championship bronze medal 1.37" by Bally and Sons, Manchester, **$150–175, WR**

- Three medals: bronze circular medal 2.37" awarded to H. W. Beveridge 1900 at Tooting Bec Golf Club, bronze medal 1.65" suspended from ribbon and bar from Royal Cromer Golf Club, and bronze 1894 Cheltenham Golf Club medal 1.25", **$1,000–1,200, WR**

- English sterling silver collar medal 1.5" diameter hallmarked Birmingham 1918, golf scene in high relief, **$200–225, WR**

- Circular sterling silver vesta case 1.75" diameter by Asprey & Co., Birmingham, hallmarked 1906 with enameled golf scene, **$1,350–1,500, WR**

- English brass matchbox 2" high x 1.15" with gold wash interior, front opening hinged lid decorated with a hand-colored illustration, .75" diameter of a solitary golfer and caddie, **$500–600, WR**

- German 1920s cast-iron decorative glass frame 7$^{1}/_{2}$" x 5$^{1}/_{2}$", **$125–150, WR**

- American sterling silver souvenir spoon 4", handle decorated in relief with a golfer in knickers, the stem decorated with a bag of clubs, **$135–150, WR**

- Sterling silver stamp case with raised golfing figure, ca. 1900, **$150–200, WR**

10 BEAUTIES IN GOLD AND SILVER
Trophies

The bidding began at a modest 500 pounds sterling.

Then it went to £600, £750, and £1000.

A few bidders at the Chester, England auction dropped out, expecting the action to become very serious soon.

It did.

Reflecting the generally held belief that auction bidding is only for seasoned collectors—that the unschooled should only attend these sales to learn about pricing trends—the checkbook war suddenly heated up in earnest.

"1200 pounds," came the call from the audience.

"1400 pounds," stormed another bidder.

"£1800."

"£2000."

"£2200."

A hush fell over the gallery as the bids continued to soar. The spectators eyed the two respected collectors, known for their large, eminent holdings—and aggressiveness—waiting to see if either one of them would blink. Students of the "game," well-versed in searching for provenance and judging an object's historical value, both men re-

Pen holder and inkwell. *Photo courtesy of Old Sport Golf.*

mained poker-faced. Neither of them wanted to reveal any emotion, or their fascination with the trophy/presentation piece that was perched on a stand in front of them.

"It was absolutely stunning, painstaking workmanship that went far beyond most trophies and other golf awards," recalls Wayne Aaron, still sounding as if this silver inkwell with a piece of intricately detailed statuary and two silver-tipped ram's horns had the power to cast a bewitching spell.

"This memorable piece was presented to a general retiring from the Gordon Highlands clan, and while I was struck by the novelty of it, since there were two symmetric horns instead of one, was [*sic*] the love this troop of soldiers had for their general to commission such a magnificent item (in 1870). That was clear from the inscription. They went to several craftsmen to get everything perfect, and that spoke volumes to me."

Finally anteing up about £5,000 for this prize, Aaron was also impressed by "the nice big silver hallmarked snuffbox with a lid that could be raised. This was delightful looking, plus there was a lovely hallmarked silver statuary of a period golfer. All sorts of artisans (a silversmith, an engraver, and clubmaker) worked on this presentation piece. It essentially had everything the collector wants in terms of craftsmanship."

That "everything" meant a variety of charms. Along with the homage to a beloved general, there was the historical overture symbolized by those ram's horns (probably supplied by the clubmaker). As Aaron emphasizes, "Old clubmakers inserted a piece of ram's horn under the leading edge of the bottom of a clubface. So here was an item that related to the early, wonderful heritage of clubmaking, a detail that later evolved

Inwood Country Club cup. *Photo courtesy of Old Sport Golf.*

Sterling inkwell. *Photo courtesy of Old Sport Golf.*

into the Scottish tradition (of golf club workmanship). I've seen deer horns, single ram's horn awards or trophies, but having two horns made this one all the more extraordinary."

Struck by the award's beauty, Aaron felt compelled to match every bid by his chief competitor at the auction, Jim Santy, the owner of the Cambridge Golf Antiquities shop. This art lover was also enamored with the inkwell's alluring novelty, and he hoped to display it at his Pebble Beach, California, gallery (located next to the famed links). But bowing to one of the cardinal rules of auction buying (maximum allowances must be set for every item before attending the actual sale), Santy decided to stick to his predetermined budget, and he finally waved a white flag.

"It was a spectacular art object, one that sadly got away." says Santy, still regretting that he didn't pull the trigger. "Collecting can be like that. I don't know if I'd call it a mistake, a sort of buyer's remorse. The piece definitely went at too low a price. It's easily worth about $15,000. I should've kept bidding, You just have to stop at times."

Aaron has also had to learn how to cope with "ones that get away." Forced to sell his legendary collection for financial reasons, he warns potential enthusiasts "to not be blinded by materialism, to not covet one possession after another. Just enjoy the historical and aesthetic impact of an item, and understand you're not really the owner of these things. You are merely taking care of them. You're a guardian of history."

To fully appreciate the luster of ceremonial plaques, trophies, or any other sort of award, memorabilia collectors must fully immerse themselves in the history and evolution of golf. Mere aesthetics or gold or silver content pale in comparison to historical significance when appraising the value of these artifacts (except, of course, if these items are intended for mere display—and many collectors do opt for this more affordable route). What matters most (to the serious collector) is *association*, a connection to a major professional or amateur event (which makes the true cachet pieces extremely scarce), and also to a fabled player from a bygone era (age is a prime determinant of value).

Essentially, valuable trophies go beyond mere radiance. While many of them emit a seductive, blinded-by-the-light appeal, the truly collectible mementos have an even greater kilowatt power and magnetism. Those prizes are the ones worth pursuing all over the golfing world, for they tell richly textured *stories*.

"Harry Vardon is credited for the overlapping grip, but it was really great amateur John Laidlay who invented it, and I have this fabulous polychrome bronze that honors him," says Aaron, who's slowly rebuilding a collection. "It's just a beautiful piece of statuary with Laidlay wearing a red coat, a traditional Scottish paneled tweed hat, and sporting his big mustache. Very true to life, this piece does what a trophy is supposed to do. It takes you back to a certain time period."

This bronze isn't merely a tribute to one of golf's forgotten heroes. Besides being highly coveted, this statue stirred Aaron to do further research about Laidlay's life, and in the process, he discovered that this British Amateur Champion never got his rightful recognition from the golfing world.

Aaron has spent thirty years burrowing into the past to explore the exploits of golf's most illustrious ghosts. He revels in unearthing information about those legends, for these historical hallmarks enhance the spiritual—and financial—value of his mementos. Knowing how an award was won, and under what circumstances, makes them "come alive," so merely owning a trophy or proudly displaying one was never enough of a satisfaction for him. Looking beyond an award's silver content, or ornate design, he feels trophies are an invitation to study distinct time periods, and to "fully capture their spirit."

"I had two important and attractive trophies that were awarded to Jerome Travers [the 1915 U.S. Open Champion] and Walter "Old Man" Travis [1862–1927], the multiple winner of the U.S. Men's Amateur Championship [1900, '01, and '03] and the North & South Men's Amateur Champion [1904, '10, and '12]," says Aaron without a hint of boasting. "One of these was absolutely fabulous, a cranberry cut glass over glass piece with a silver overlay that Travis won in a club championship at the Nassau County Golf Club in 1902. It was important to me because he's one of the really historic figures of golf, a man I learned so much about when I did my research, and discovered just how important he was.

Chicago Golf Club trophy. *Photo courtesy of Old Sport Golf.*

A bronze plaque 10″ x 6″ marked "Tiffany & Co." on 14″ x 10″ walnut shield dated 1917, presented by the Whitehall Club to Siwanoy Country Club. $400–500. *Photo courtesy of Old Tom Morris Golf, L.L.C.*

"A transplant from Australia, he was one of the first Americans to go to the UK, where he won the British Amateur Championship in 1904 [the first overseas player to win the event] at Sandwich. He won that event with an aluminum headed [and center-shafted] putter called 'The Schenectady.'

"The interesting aspect of this story, and why the trophy is so intriguing, is that the Brits were thoroughly frustrated that a foreigner, especially an American, could beat them for the first time at their own game. The trophy became synonymous with this feeling.

"Travis's success on the battlefield of golf speaks for itself. He was so effective with this putter that the Honorable Royal & Ancient reacted to the fervor generated by the win. They examined the putter and said it was illegal. Immediately after Travis returned to the States they outlawed the putter. I learned all this by doing research, lots of reading, and that's the beauty of trophies, they spur you to find knowledge."

The R & A eventually rescinded the ban on The Schenectady, and honored Travis in 1952. That recognition was richly deserved, and now that this once-criticized golfer has won new acclaim, Aaron feels honored to have owned a trophy "this champion competed for, enjoyed, and appreciated."

"The trophy gave me the impetus to learn more about this often overlooked champion, and to pull together the history of the man," explains Aaron. "It's a beautiful piece of artwork, and that aesthetic appeal should also factor into the buying of trophies. This is clear glass, cut glass over the top of it, and then silversmiths worked on it. They did this lovely silver filigree overlay on the top of the piece. There's just so much here, so many factors affecting the value. The aesthetics, the wonderful, even provocative history, and Travis's actual playing for this award. It's an extraordinary piece."

Having done his homework (instead of just buying "pretty" silver pieces to make "ego statements"), Aaron can display the Travis trophy in a way that truly honors him. He can show the award to fellow collectors, speak informatively about the scorn Travis endured, and discuss his being accorded a rightful place in the game's upper echelons. The trophy consequently has a second life. It's much more than a "dead" wall decoration.

"It's the 'look at me' syndrome," insists Jim Santy. "Much more of an ego statement than a medal, impressive silver trophies satisfy the public's craving for something that attracts attention. People like to have something that serves as an exclamation point to their collection. An attractive trophy does that, so my best advice to a new collector is to buy things they like looking at. If you're in this for fun, and not to have the world's greatest collection of sterling silver pieces, just get a few attractive pieces in the $2,000 to $3,500 range."

Avid trophy hunter Bob Burkett is also in a position to offer a few sterling words of advice. After amassing a collection of over 160 of the game's most distinguished pieces, he's considered to be one of the world's leading experts in the trophy realm. It's not the precious metals or cut glass that fascinates him. He's another history buff.

"One of my most significant items is a 6-inch, heavy sterling miniature of the first President's Cup, a trophy won by Walter Travers that's studded with marquee names like Jerome Travis, Charles Blair MacDonald, and other greats," says Burkett. "The earliest names on there date back to 1899–1900, and those markings give the trophy a dramatic link to the past. The beautiful engraving, the artwork, highlights the fact that the most important golfers of that era competed for this piece. They admired it, overcame obstacles to win it, and my having it takes me right into their living rooms where they displayed the thing. That's why collecting trophies is fun, very exciting. It's a magic carpet ride back into the past."

That ride, though, can be a bumpy one. While fake trophies aren't common (particularly the more elaborately styled and higher quality items), counterfeits do exist.

"The workmanship is just so superb in the better pieces, it becomes incredibly expensive to fake them," insists Burkett. "Duplicating them faithfully wouldn't leave a lot of room to make a lot of money on the item. Collectors just have to remember that if they're prepared to spend $5,000 to $10,000 on a trophy, they should have taken the time to acquire some expertise. Once they do that they'll be able to easily spot fakes, for these phony pieces don't have the sharp lines, the clarity of better ones. Fine quality trophies have a noticeably better strike, finer details that are easy to recognize."

A set of six silver-plated cups with tray by Wallace, ca. 1900 with knickered golfer logo. $300–400. *Photo courtesy of Old Tom Morris Golf, L.L.C.*

A sterling silver toast rack with gold wash. A sterling silver trophy hallmarked Birmingham 1917 with a rabbit on top of a mesh golf ball holding a club. A silver plated cigarette case with etched scene of three golfers. A sterling silver on bronze cigarette box ca. 1912, very good condition. *Photo courtesy of Old Tom Morris Golf, L.L.C.*

Burkett also maintains that the workmanship is typically of much higher quality on sterling than on silver plate. "Sterling has much more value than the plate, as it was the metal of choice for the higher echelon clubs. I'd only buy plate if it's old or from a famous club. Whatever the metal, all bets are off if the piece is something won by Willie Park, Bobby Jones, or someone of that ilk. Then it's [sic] sky's the limit."

Particularly proud of owning a trophy Jones won at the tender age of twelve, Burkett adds, "He won this marvelous silver water pitcher at the Cherokee Country Club Invitational in Tennessee. About 10" to 11" high, this piece really celebrates his boyhood, his coming of age, and showing his potential for greatness. It really speaks to me. It's a bit of history, and very handsome."

Another silver piece owned by Burkett, while stunningly carved, mirrors the more problematical aspect of British-made sterling awards. At 15 inches high, this 1911 trophy from the St. George's Club is certainly dramatic looking, as the top part is an ornate, highly detailed depiction of St. George slaying a dragon.

But buying beautiful, bewitching trophies crafted in Great Britain can also be risky. Particularly if collectors go into that market niche blind, or without studying the special hallmarks and engraving dates that characterize trophies from the United Kingdom.

"You must be able to read and understand hallmarks," Burkett strongly advises. "These markings give you the true age of a trophy, rather than the date of the engraving. I have seen a trophy dated or engraved in the 1880s that was really made much earlier than that. It was presented as a trophy long after it was made and had greater value as a silver piece than the trophy itself.

"Usually the hallmarks and engravings are within a year of each other. If the dates correspond, then you know the silver piece was created as a golf trophy. When the trophy says 1930 and the trophy is dated 1885 you obviously have a forgery on your hands. All the British goods have hallmarks [the maker's name, dates of production, where the piece was produced, all become evident through these hallmarks] and to understand them, collectors must read a few books. With the U.S. trophies, it's a little easier to know what's genuine. These pieces are just marked sterling, and you can get a good sense of the date by becoming familiar with the styles that correspond to a certain era."

If an assortment of trophies dates back to the same time period, and the historic value of them is similar, Burkett advises "go for the piece that's the most aesthetically pleasing. The one with the better appearance is usually of finer quality."

That injunction is not meant to lessen the critical importance of historical association. Burkett feels "history is the spirit of this entire collecting game. In trophies you have to go for history every time. It's this vital connection to the past that makes these pieces worth collecting."

Yet this savvy collector also realizes that an exquisitely crafted trophy or presentation piece offers its own charming satisfactions—that in this glimmering world of sterling and chiseled glass it's often possible to "have your cake and eat it too." Or to seize a historical moment, or to also revel in the glories of an exceptionally beautiful piece.

"I have this stupendous crystal wine decanter given to Walter Travis that is just extraordinarily unique," raves Burkett, who bought the piece fifteen years ago for $6,000 and would never dream of parting with it (now it's valued at $20,000). "It's in the shape of a duck, and about the size of a mallard. The head is sterling silver. You flip the top of the head open and that allows you to pour the wine in. There's a handle on the back of it, and you pour the wine out. It seems as if the wine is coming out of the duck's beak. It's just a one-of-a-kind beauty, a decanter that dramatizes what trophy collecting is all about—finding tributes to history that are true works of art."

Equally impressed with artifacts symbolizing "golfing's most remarkable accomplishments," trophy dealer Art DiProspero has pursued and sold prized objects for the last twenty-five years. Well-versed in the distinct rules governing the trophy market, he offers the following suggestions.

"Condition is very important. You want to be able to read the inscription. In reproductions the clarity isn't there. The strike must be distinct. You want a bold, well-defined strike that's really distinct. Everything must be very legible, for that's part of the beauty."

Thinking of some of the fine pieces that have passed through his hands, DiProspero quickly adds, "The more ornate the trophy the better. Elaborate pieces are much tougher to forge. Collectors are more likely to get fooled on old, wooden-shafted clubs than on ornate gold or silver-hallmarked trophies. Yet buyers must still be aware that there are fakes out there. They do appear.

"Another danger sign is a perfectly clean trophy. That raises a question mark for me since the patina has to be there. Trophies that are old and authentic have that special patina. Beware when it's not there."

Obviously wanting to be protective of his clients, DiProspero has a long catalog of danger signs. He goes on to say, "It's also reassuring when papers, some sort of documentation accompanies a piece. I want to know where the seller got the item. I don't want to buy something that comes out of thin air."

To emphasize the importance of provenance, DiProspero alludes to a P.G.A. gold medal which has been further glorified by a decorative array of diamonds. Insisting this medal was acquired directly from winner Paul Runyon, he continues, "The medal comes with a letter done in longhand fountain pen by the golfer. That letter tells the story of how he won. It's a $30,000 to $35,000 medal, but with the letter it's probably worth $50,000. That's the added value of having certifiable provenance."

David Berkowitz, another well-known and reputable dealer, is also a veteran of the "trophy wars." Feeling that the values of pieces in this market will remain high for the foreseeable future (due to the scarcity of marquee-named items), he recommends, "Don't always assume that only trophies from top-echelon clubs and winners of major events are the most collectible. A low-amateur trophy from the Masters is a phenomenal piece. Very few amateurs play in the Masters so the scarcity kicks in to make this type of trophy very desirable.

"For the guys who simply want beautiful display items, there are a lot of events and clubs that award gorgeous trophies. Don't fixate on the majors, the Harry Vardons [one of his prizes sold for $15,000 a few years ago], or a Walter Travers [$25,000-plus for a significant artifact]. While these are rarely available, you can get very handsome trophies for $1,000."

Besides cautioning award enthusiasts to avoid trophies with broken parts, or that look "worn down," the extremely experienced Berkowitz punctuates his advice with a reminder that could apply to any area of golf collecting.

"New collectors can't rush in and start acquiring a lot of trophies. You must know a little about the game. Read a few books. Find out what pieces have sold for, and where prices seem to be headed. Above all, keep in mind that while condition is very important, trophies are the exclamation point to golf's greatest historical events. In this collecting niche, history is key."

The prices of golf collectibles fluctuate. The following values are estimates offered by various experts:
MM—Mullock & Madeley
WR—Will Roberto
OS—Bob Burkett's Old Sport Golf

- Rare silver trophy, Harry Vardon Cup, hallmarked Birmingham 1927, presented by Vardon and played over his home course South Herts Golf Club, won by Charles Buchan, engraved South Herts Golf Club, 1927, first prize, removable silver lid, **$10,900–11,000, MM**

- Fine silver trophy, presented by Lytham & St. Anne's Golf Club, awarded for best aggregate prize, spring meeting, 1931, bowl-shaped, silver hallmarked, Birmingham made, 1927, decorated floral base, **$550, MM**

- Silver putter cigarette case walking stick, 1900. Spring-loaded hinged lid to reveal space for six cigarettes and fitted to a dark stained black shaft, possibly ebony, 34", **$1,750–1,865, MM**

- Henry Cotton, Wentworth Golf Club, small silver trophy, decorated with crossed golf clubs, 1936, mounted on plinth, **$300–375, MM**

- Sterling silver trophy $10^{1}/_{2}$" high by Cartier in the form of a fluted vase, atop three balls engraved B.B. C.C. 1954, **$200–250, WR**

- Sterling silver trophy hallmarked Birmingham 1917 with a rabbit on top of mesh golf ball holding a club, **$300–400, WR**

- Fine continental silver putter cigarette case walking stick ca. 1900 and stamped 800 to the neck. The hinged lid is finely engraved, and when opened it reveals space for six cigarettes. Fitted to a decoratively stained shaft fitted with a stainless steel tip, overall 34". **$1,000–1,100, MM**

- South Herts Golf Club silver cigarette box hallmarked Birmingham 1937, the lid engraved Spring Meeting Four Ball v Bogey makes an ideal jewelry/trinket box, **$75, MM**

- Fine silver golfing cocktail set comprising silver hallmarked Birmingham 1928, golf bag stand c/w 5 matching silver hallmarked golf club cocktail sticks, **$425–460, MM**

- Sterling silver inkwell in the shape of a mesh gutty ball with three golf clubs leaning against it, 4½" diameter base, 4" high, captain's prize at Anson Golf Club, 1895, **$1,500, OS**

- Copper and pewter three-handle trophy from Chicago Golf Club, 11" high, dated 1906, **$2,500, OS**

- Sterling silver two-handle Cup, 4½" high, inscribed "First Annual Tournament of the Central New York Golf League, 1897," historic early American piece, unusual to find a "first" of any trophy, **$2,200, OS**

- Electroplated trophy from Inwood Country Club (NY), 16½" high, with clubs down both sides as handles, features enamel and bronze medallion, trophy presented 1924, **$750, OS**

- Pen holder and inkwell of electroplated nickel, made in Sheffield, England, inkwell in shape of mesh gutta-percha ball with original ink containers inside, 6½" high, presented in 1893 at Selkirk Club, **$2,200, OS**

- Two biscuit tins with decorative lids, one featuring the "MacDonald Boys" from the Scottish Portrait Gallery with MacDonald tartan sides, enamel and metal inlaid lid featuring golfer playing a shot, **$75, MM**

- Twelve pieces of jewelry, most sterling silver, including Tiffany & Co. key ring, a large-14 karat white gold brooch, **$400–500, WR**

- Five fine jewelry pieces, including 14-karat pendant with pearls from Hawaiian Open, 14 karat U.S.G.A. seal on gold chain, **$600–800, WR**

- Set of twelve sterling silver British demitasse spoons, ca. 1930s, **$300–350, WR**

- Three jewelry items, two Ryder Cup belt buckles from The Belfry, **$80–100, WR**

- A plated, lidded trophy 24" on plastic plinth for the Bristol, CT, City Championship with winners engraved from 1928 through 1931, **$300–350, WR**

- Bronze plaque 10" x 6" marked Tiffany & Co. on walnut shield dated 1917, presented by Whitehall Club, **$400–500, WR**

- Plated cocktail shaker trophy 10" engraved 1924 Wallingford Country Club **$100–125, WR**

- Two plated trophies 22" on plastic plinths, one unmarked with male figure, one with female figure from the Tam O'Shanter Golf Club dated 1968, **$300–400, WR**

- Silver plated two-handled trophy mug 4½" from Innis Arden Golf Club dated 1901, **$150–175, WR**

- Fourteen sterling silver Indian teaspoons with the crest of the Royal Calcutta G.C. Bombay, **$900–1,000, WR**

- Mesh pattern Silvertown gutty ball matchstick holder, hallmarked silver rim with crossed long nose clubs for legs, **$900–1,200, WR**

11 THE POOR MAN'S VAN GOGHS AND RENOIRS
Postcards

Old Tom Morris, the Patron Saint of St. Andrews and of British golf, was a likeable, peaceful fellow. This esteemed player, clubmaker, and course architect just wasn't the type to ignite a war.

Yet once a Morris surfaces—and that's not very often—a ferocious duel begins, and the "blood" flows. No expense is spared in trying to nab a portrait of this old master from the past.

The same aggressiveness is displayed in the war over a miniature Bobby Jones photo. Impelled by the scarcity, fine artwork, and Jones's stature in all collecting niches, a dogfight ensues between aficionados. They all want a piece of history, a postcard bearing the Jones likeness.

"Tom Morris stands out in this world, he's the Babe Ruth in terms of collectibility," says postcard savant Lew Lipset, who's been studying the distinctive style and postmarks of these paper keepsakes since 1999. "Morris is clearly a rarer item [at times costing upwards of $500] since most of his postcards are from the turn of the century [even earlier ones exist]. But Bobby Jones is right up there as a cachet item. A photograph of him on a card, say with Walter Hagen, could easily sell for $150 to $200. For that kind of money you can find a really attractive card with Hagen putting and the legendary Jones standing nearby. That's quite a moment in history."

That's the beauty of pursuing postcards. Whether photographs of the game's immortals, or "oil painting" styled depictions of famous golfing meccas such as Pinehurst, Royal St. George's, St. Andrews, Troon, or Carnoustie, postcard collecting offers the average man a way to own a veritable art collection.

Yale Eleven, unique golf card, 1905, $100.
Photo courtesy of Lew Lipset.

Aerial view of Monterey peninsula,
California, linen card from 1930s, $15. *Photo
courtesy of Lew Lipset.*

Biarritz Golf Club, France. French champ
Armand Massy is shown, early 1900s,
$200–300. *Photo courtesy of Lew Lipset.*

Harry Vardon and James Braid, b/w photo
card, 1908, $400–500. *Photo courtesy of
Lew Lipset.*

The average price of a respectable vintage postcard is only $15 to $25. In that very accessible price range the budget-minded art lover can find an alluring 1930s picture of Pinehurst that looks like it was hand-painted, an equally retro *The Game of Golf* from the Oilette Remarque Series postmarked 1907, and vividly colored landscapes from Britannia.

If the collector takes a slightly heftier financial swing, she or he will be able to land a handsomely colored Molar & Lang postcard of British great J. H. Taylor driving a ball in 1910 into the next borough ($150), an art print of Harry Vardon by the very popular Raphael Tuck (golf's own Raphael) that resembles a painting in a wooden frame ($100), and a cameo photo of Samuel Morse (the founder of Pebble Beach) cu-

Tom Morris color postcard, 1905, $500.
Photo courtesy of Lew Lipset.

View of St. Andrews, 1920s, $50–75. *Photo
courtesy of Lew Lipset.*

riously wearing a Yale U. football jersey ($50 to $100), which Lipset insists, "it's just a
very interesting piece that takes you back into another era.

"The joy of collecting these cards is not only their relative affordability," continues
Lipset. "They're also real art, period pieces that can be enjoyed without worrying
about forgeries [low budget items don't attract counterfeiters] and all sorts of complications. You can just look at the postcard and determine its condition [stain marks,
creases, ragged corners, tears, etc. all lower values] very easily."

Collectors still face a *fateful* decision. Do they go after "virgins" in absolutely original
condition? Or do a few historical markings, such as a personalized note, and a postmark, make the card more—or less—valuable and authentic?

"There are collectors who want the card as close to original as possible, to have the
same pure condition as when it was issued," explains Lipset. "Yet I favor postmarked,
or cards with a personal message written on them. This is especially desirable to me
when the message is pertinent to the picture on the card. There are instances when
the message pertains to golf and that gives the card an added dimension."

Finding most of his cards on eBay or on other Internet sites (they can also be unearthed at golf trade shows and in antique shops), Lipset further notes that "a postmarked card gives you information. It tells you the date, gives the card a historical
reference point. More information is often more appealing."

Insisting that he wouldn't avoid acquiring cards that are in questionable condition if
"the subject matter is intriguing," Lipset is particularly drawn to the British legends—the masters who made history, and their storied playing fields.

Open Championship, Alex Herd, 1902 British Open Champion, and Alex Kirkaldy, early 1900s, $150–200. *Photo courtesy of Lew Lipset.*

Golf Club House, St. Andrews. Tom Morris holds flag stick, 1910–15, $150. *Photo courtesy of Lew Lipset.*

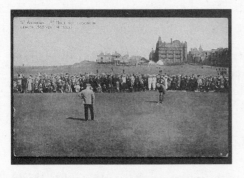

First hole at St. Andrews, unidentified golfer, b/w, 1915–20, $75–100. *Photo courtesy of Lew Lipset.*

Dog and views of Carnoustie Golf Club, "metamorphic" card, 1910, $75–100. *Photo courtesy of Lew Lipset.*

"I have this wonderful four-card set of scenes from St. Andrews in a wide range of pastel colors. The bottom two-thirds of the card depicts the course, while the top third is a color cartoon drawing. They're very unique, British-made by the Art Publishing Company of Glasgow, and each one was only $30 to $50."

By avidly combing the Internet, Lipset found an equally well-priced "homage" to the Olympic Club in San Francisco (a U.S. Open site). "This 1940s card has a 'real' glossy photo of the club, and a more realistic photograph is usually rare and more valuable than the painted landscape variety."

A longtime baseball card collector with an eye for valuable paper materials, Lipset is also a passionate fan of "personality" postcards.

Augusta National with Bobby Jones putting, post 1935, $300. *Photo courtesy of Lew Lipset.*

Hagen-Jones Championship Golf Match at St. Petersburg, Fla. club, 1920s, $200–300. *Photo courtesy of Lew Lipset.*

"One of my Tom Morris cards is this superb black-and-white photo picturing him playing golf with Leslie Balfour. There's a postmark dated August 24th, 1903, so this [$25] card definitely has some history. There's excellent writing on the front and back, capturing the spirit of the era and the importance of the 'King' [British Open Champion in 1861, 1862, 1864, 1867, the designer of Prestwick and Muirfield in the British Isles, and the professional at St. Andrews]."

Leafing through a postcard album filled with protective plastic sheets that shield photos of "golf's royalty," Lipset continues, "In just fabulous condition, I paid $200 for this Bobby Jones that shows him putting at Augusta National. The club was founded in 1934, so I'm guessing this black-and-white photo was taken at some point in the 1930s. It's a great shot, one that beautifully captures him, the moment, one of golf's cathedrals, and Jones's unique aura."

Jones may well be the Prince and Morris the King, but Lipset, recalling his boyhood travels in the back seat of the family sedan, still favors cards that evoke a spirit of place in another, long-ago time period.

"Jones, Hagen, and Morris are certainly evocative of another era, men attached to real history," says this passionate paper collector. "But postcards epitomize travel, discovering distant places, and postcards at their best are a type of escape, a look back at a certain time period.

"That's definitely true of a card I have that was published by the Homestead Pharmacy, which was connected to the Homestead Resort in Hot Springs [Virginia]. In

Myopia Hunt Club House, Hamilton, Mass. *Photo courtesy of Lew Lipset.*

Oakland Hills Country Club, Birmingham, Mich. Site of the 1937 National Open Golf Championship. *Photo courtesy of Lew Lipset.*

Shinnecock Hills in New York, site of first U.S. Open, 1910, $30. *Photo courtesy of Lew Lipset.*

Caddy Master and Caddies, Pinehurst, ethnic card, glossy b/w, 1920s, $100–150. *Photo courtesy of Lew Lipset.*

this 1930s color-tinted photo there are eight black caddies just sitting around on a hill, their bags behind them, and a white guy on the edge of the picture. They're dressed in caps, golf pants, and most of the caddies are smiling. The photo has a Depression-era look, and that picturing of another era is the essence of old postcards. They put faraway places and other time periods at the average guy's fingertips."

♀♀♀

Tom Morris comes alive in a series of striking sepia-toned photographs, while various European resorts evoke a timeless elegance that stirs thoughts of the Great Gatsby.

Pinehurst Country Club Terrace. *Photo courtesy of Lew Lipset.*

Valentine's Series of comic cards, set of 6, 1910, $200. *Photo courtesy of Lew Lipset.*

All this magic is palpably felt when thumbing through William Anderson's formidable postcard collection, the thousands of three-by-fives that's arguably the largest assemblage in the world.

"The beauty of postcard collecting is their history, they won't break the bank, and the opportunity for always finding something new always exists," says Anderson, a college history professor who has traveled to England and Scotland several times to unearth rare early-1900s cards.

"Once you start buying $10 cards it's easy to be seduced. You start working your way up, and buying more expensive cards. You also have to be concerned that new sophisticated copying machines will [*sic*] be able to [fraudulently] reproduce cards. But collecting cards still remains a way for the poor man to acquire many miniature Picassos."

Predictably a lover of history, the professor has focused on turn-of-the-century cards popularizing golf in Great Britain.

One of his favorite "artistic" sets (most postcard sets are a series of six cards) is Raphael Tuck's "In the Open"—a greenish, sepia-toned collection featuring such masters as J. H. Taylor, Harry Vardon, and Jack White. Dating back to 1907–08, cards from this scarce series can sell for up to $500 each.

Another exquisitely photographed, similarly priced set comes from the Valentine publishing company. Its "Famous Golfers" series features "Old" Tom Morris and other notable players. This set was produced in smaller numbers than the Tucks, and is consequently more difficult to find.

"Player Must Not Ask for Advice," North British Rubber Co. ad for golf ball, 1910, chick in corner of card, $30–40. *Photo courtesy of Lew Lipset.*

Golf Caddies, Homestead, Hot Springs, Va. Ethnic card, 1910, $75–100. *Photo courtesy of Lew Lipset.*

"Some Tom Morris cards are common [in the 1900s, postcard collecting was the national mania in Great Britain], yet the best ones can definitely sell for $500," says Anderson, who began collecting in 1988 (this niche is still relatively undiscovered). "He appears in a number of series, such as my 'Wrench' set, which pictures him on the tee at St. Andrews with Harry Vardon. When you find a rare card like this one, condition isn't the key factor. There are collectors who don't want writing on a card, but I like to read sentiments on a postcard. They can be quite interesting."

Feeling that a used card is less likely to be a reproduction, Anderson continues, "If you have a postmarked 1902 card there's no need to worry it's a fake. Plus a postmark adds to the historic value. If there's a mention of golf in the message, the card is even more attractive.

"Postcard collecting gives you a sense of many picturesque and inviting worlds. I have a lot of cards from the Equinox in Manchester, Vermont. One very rare set features black-and-white photos taken during the 1914 Amateur Championship. One double-sized card (valued around $200) shows all of the participants, including the great Francis Ouimet. There aren't too many early American cards that picture tournaments."

As Anderson admires a Valentine series that pictures Vardon, Taylor, and James Braid at the historic International Match between England and Scotland in 1905, he says: "These views [each is valued at $200] of them making shots from a distance aren't very easy to find. But that's the joy of collecting postcards. All collectors love to track down items for that's the exciting part. It means discovering the history and story behind the card."

He enjoyed the pursuit of the Fletcher series. "I also have the original envelope they came in," he said, which adds to their value, which is between $3,000 and $4,000 according to dealers. He is also delighted by a set of twelve Valentine "Golfing" cards that picture St. Andrews golfers in the 1890s.

Yet in terms of a card's telling one of those delightful or historical "stories," Anderson has one clear favorite.

"When a postcard is autographed by the personality that's pictured, it takes on a lot greater value, both historically and financially. I have a black-and-white card of J. H. Taylor that was personally pictured for him. It shows him putting on the 9th green in the final round of the 1913 British Open Championship at Hoy Lake.

"On the back of the card he wrote a message to his son-in-law, asking him if he remembered their playing with Ted Ray (the runner-up in the Open that year). That's a card with a great story, and collectors should know, there are cards out there with all sorts of wonderful stories."

The prices of golf collectibles fluctuate. The following values are estimates offered by various experts:
MM—Mullock & Madeley
LL—Lew Lipset
WR—Will Roberto

- Twenty early b/w postcards, incl. ten of mostly golf courses, incl. a colored card of Abnaki Club House Lyndonville, Newquay, Bournemouth, Cromer, Routenburn G.C. near Largs, the putting green Dunbar, plus two coastal scenes and one garden scene and 10 x various the majority from the early 1900s incl. glamour, Gibson girl, humor, portrait, greetings, and flip-up souvenir cards. **$185, MM**

- Five humorous color postcards publ'd by the North British Rubber Co. with advertising text on the reverse ". . . makers of The Chick, Big Chick, Clincher, Diamond Chick, New Hawk and Osprey Golf Balls." ca. mid-1920s, **$170–185, MM**

- Six early postcards of Golf Courses and Clubs of U.S.A. and Great Britain, incl. color card of Greenore via Holyhead, plus 5 b/w incl. Newquay, Burnham-on-Sea, American: Cherry Valley Golf Club Garden City, Long Island, Belfairs Golf Club Leigh-on-Sea, and Pochefstroom Links and Club House India, **$185, MM**

- Fifty-four instructional cards by Scientific Recreation in the original pictorial box, autographed by "Lighthorse" Harry Cooper, **$500–550, WR**

- Bobby Jones Sweetacres Champion Chewing Gum card, **$400–500, WR**

- Robert Tyre Jones Famous Golfers number twenty-seven from the series of fifty, **$250–300, WR**

- Eight postcards, Augusta National, Hagen-Jones, ex-President Taft, Tom Morris, and others, **$400–500, WR**

- A 1903 postcard of Willie Park putting apparently on the first green of St. Andrews as A. Kirkaldy watches, **$100–125, WR**

- Bobby Jones, Men of the Moment in Sport by Churchman, **$250–300, WR**

- Yale Eleven, unique golf card, 1905, **$100, LL**

- View of 16th hole at Cypress Point, with golfer Alister MacKenzie, linen card, 1930s, **$75, LL**

- Aerial view of Monterey peninsula, California, linen card from 1930s, **$15, LL**

- Augusta National's 18th fairway, Albertype card, very few cards showing course, late 1930s, **$150–200, LL**

- Biarritz Golf Club, France, French champ Armand Massy is shown, early 1900s, **$200–300, LL**

- Harry Vardon and James Braid, b/w photo card, 1908, **$400–500, LL**

- Tom Morris color postcard, 1905, **$500, LL**

- Golf Club House, St. Andrews, Tom Morris hold flag stick, 1910–15, **$150, LL**

- Open Championship, Alex Herd, 1902 British Open Champion, and Andrew Kirkaldy, early 1900s, **$150–200, LL**

- View of St. Andrews, 1920s, **$50–75, LL**

- First Hole at St. Andrews, unidentified golfer, b/w, 1915–20, **$75–100, LL**

- Turnberry Lighthouse and Golf Course, 1910, **$25, LL**

- Dog and views of Carnoustie Golf Club, "metamorphic" card, 1910, **$75–100, LL**

- Coral Gables Golf Club and Gene Sarazen, 1920–30, **$50–75, LL**

- Augusta National with Bobby Jones putting, post-1935, **$300, LL**

- Hagen-Jones Championship Golf Match at St. Petersburg, Fla., club, 1920s, **$200–300, LL**

- 18th Hole at Olympic Club in San Francisco, rare view of club, 1940, **$50, LL**

- Shinnecock Hills in New York, site of first U.S. Open, 1910, **$30, LL**

- Life Saving Crew at 10th hole at Pinehurst in North Carolina, "ethnic" card, Albertype, 1920, **$75–100, LL**

- Caddy master and caddies, Pinehurst, ethnic card, glossy b/w, 1920s, **$100–150, LL**

- Sunningdale Golf Links in Surrey, England, with airship flying overhead, 1910–20, **$30–40, LL**

- Valentine's Series of comic cards, set of 6, 1910, **$200, LL**

- "Player Must Not Ask for Advice," North British Rubber Co. ad for golf ball, 1910, chick in corner of card, **$30–40, LL**

- Golf caddies, Homestead, Hot Springs, Va., ethnic card, 1910, **$75–100, LL**

12 A LONG LIST OF HEROES
Comic Books, Movies, and Other Treasures

Poor Mutt!

He's lying on the floor, taking a nap, and Jeff is up to usual mischief. He's placed a golf ball on Mutt's nose, and is getting ready to take a whack at it with a wooden club.

Superman is also being attacked. A villain has grabbed an iron, and is taking a ferocious swing at America's Man of Steel.

The list of fabled comic book characters who have "taken up the game" is a long one: Buster Bear. Mickey Mouse. Minnie Mouse. Donald Duck. Beetle Bailey. The Chip and Dale chipmunks. Casper the Friendly Ghost.

Then there's the much-beloved Archie. He, like the rest of these American icons, has been pictured on the cover of a comic book with either a club, ball, or in some setting relating to golf.

It hardly matters how foolish any of these characters look in absurd, out-of-date golf attire, or if their swing was straight out of The Three Stooges. Just find a comic book cover with some pictured item of golf paraphernalia, and that could very well mean a profitable collectible score.

"When I first started collecting comic books there were three or four of us looking for such items as a 1920s *Mutt and Jeff,* a *Superman,* a 1940s *Babe Ruth Sports,* or a *Fox and Craw,*" says golf course designer Michael Hurdzan, who also has a vast golf book library, scores of movie posters with delightful artwork, and about 7,000 antique clubs. "Now the comic book area has gotten a lot more popular, for people are realizing that these are fun images, easy to store, ubiquitous, plus the art work is really terrific."

Original signed H.C. Fisher five-panel Mutt
and Jeff cartoon, dated March 5, 1917.
$400–500. *Photo courtesy of Old Tom
Morris Golf, L.L.C.*

Don't be confused. Golf doesn't have to be the main focus of these "literary" escapades. Bugs or Donald simply needs to be pictured with a stick, ball, or in some form of game attire, and that makes the comic a golf collectible. And possibly even a valuable one!

"When I first started collecting comics in the late 1980s, early 90s, I paid $50 for some issues that are now worth thousands of dollars," says Hurdzan, who has over 500 comic books. "Comics are usually $2 to $20, and they don't have to be in great condition. A Famous Funnies #1, for example, is worth an enormous amount of money in whatever condition [about $18,000]. It's all about rarity."

Comic books are also a safe investment. Unlike autographs and featherie balls, this is one niche that hasn't been discovered by counterfeiters. "No one's forging comics," insists Hurdzan. "Too much effort would be involved, and for the most part, comics remain very affordable."

Hurdzan still advises new collectors to be cautious, to first buy "the cheap stuff" before graduating to the $50 and $75 comics. Yet he's confident that enthusiasts will reclaim a slice of their childhood by collecting *Supermans* and *Archies*. "A slice alive with fun pictures that never stop delighting me," he notes.

Just one last word of caution.

Comic books are habit-forming. Once you surrender to their intoxicating charms, Batman and Robin might just have to come to your rescue.

Dennis the Menace comic. *Photo courtesy of Michael Hurdzan.*

Donald Duck comic. *Photo courtesy of
Michael Hurdzan.*

Buster Bear comic. *Photo courtesy of Michael Hurdzan.*

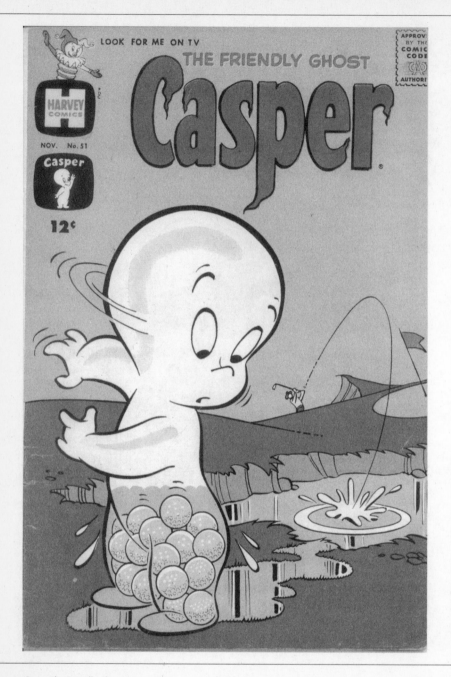

Casper the Friendly Ghost comic. *Photo courtesy of Michael Hurdzan.*

Freak Brothers Comic. *Photo courtesy of Michael Hurdzan.*

Jughead and Archie comic. *Photo courtesy of Michael Hurdzan.*

Kit Carter comic. *Photo courtesy of Michael Hurdzan.*

Popeye comic. *Photo courtesy of Michael Hurdzan.*

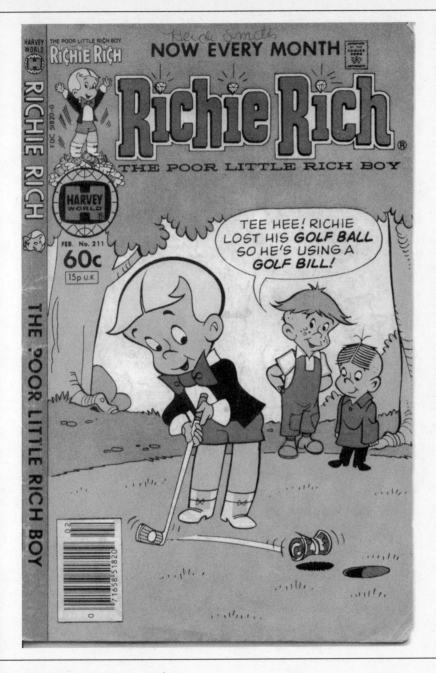

Richie Rich comic. *Photo courtesy of
Michael Hurdzan.*

Porky & Bugs comic. *Photo courtesy of Michael Hurdzan.*

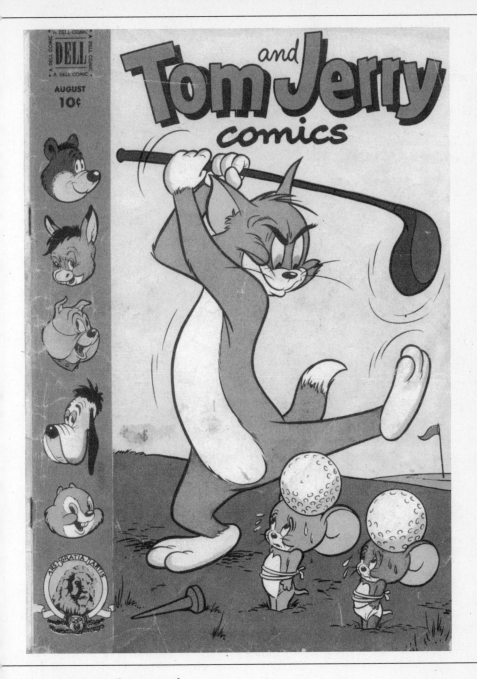

Tom and Jerry comic. *Photo courtesy of Michael Hurdzan.*

Wendy the Witch. *Photo courtesy of Michael Hurdzan.*

Young Scotland Quadrille. 1890s sheet music would start at $350 and go up to $500 or more. *Photot courtesy of Michael Hurdzan.*

Since this 1899 poster is very much about golf and love, it would value about $150–225. But it is not too colorful. The age gives it the value. *Photo courtesy of Michael Hurdzan.*

A genteel 1900 look at golf and girls. $25–35. *Photo courtesy of Michael Hurdzan.*

A 1902 piece with good color. $200–300. *Photo courtesy of Michael Hurdzan.*

"Catch on March" is a 1902 piece with great color and a rather risqué golf scene. $250–275. *Photo courtesy of Michael Hurdzan.*

Written in 1923 and colorfully graphic of a different period in golf. $75–100. *Photo courtesy of Michael Hurdzan.*

1924 piece during the roaring 20s and the golden era of golf. A cute piece worth about $50–75. *Photo courtesy of Michael Hurdzan.*

A popular 1928 production with about 8 songs with almost the same front sheet, so very common. Value about $20–25 each. *Photo courtesy of Michael Hurdzan.*

A movie poster for Ben and Valerie Hogan's life story *Follow the Sun* by 20th Century Fox, ca. 1951. *Photo courtesy of Old Tom Morris Golf, L.L.C.*

Very difficult to find—especially one signed by Hogan (lower left corner). Signed about $1000 or more. *Photo courtesy of Michael Hurdzan.*

Because it is Bing Crosby, expect to pay about $75–100 for this sheet music. *Photo courtesy of Michael Hurdzan.*

Nearly everyone knows Ike's love of golf so this should sell for $50–75. *Photo courtesy of Michael Hurdzan.*

Caddyshack poster. The classic golf comedy that some say is the best golf movie ever. $25–50. Photo courtesy of Michael Hurdzan.

Caddyshack II poster. A poor substitute for the original movie, and the poster is not sought after except by determined collectors. $15–20. *Photo courtesy of Michael Hurdzan.*

This is an American Express poster where Tiger plays Karl the gopher in some TV spots. A little more difficult to find, but lots of copies on eBay. $30–40. *Photo courtesy of Michael Hurdzan.*

An unsuccessful TV movie, but the poster is really hard to find. Original poster in excellent condition is about $75–100. Copies are worth about half. *Photo courtesy of Michael Hurdzan.*

Happy Gilmore is becoming a classic, but this poster still only sells for around $25. *Photo courtesy of Michael Hurdzan.*

Not really a man's golf movie so poster is not widely sought. $10–15. *Photo courtesy of Michael Hurdzan.*

A fun movie with some collector interest but not a lot. Original poster about $25 and a copy about $15. *Photo courtesy of Michael Hurdzan.*

Stroke of genius came out this year so there are lots of posters available. Original could fetch a price of $25, a copy $15. *Photo courtesy of Michael Hurdzan.*

Sheet Music

Sing a happy tune. Whistle, play the piano, or start dancing.

There's Nothing Like a Game of Golf (ca. 1890) or a *Young Scotland Quadrille* (published in 1890) to lighten your heart—and your checkbook.

Golf-inspired sheet music (which first appeared in the 1890s) often has a lively beat, coupled with absolutely wonderful artwork. Yet this is an area of collecting, according to Hurdzan, "that's seeing new price rises."

This versatile collector-cum-course designer anted up $510 for this ditty ten years ago, mainly because the red, green, and white artwork attracted him. Music was then an undiscovered art form. Few people cared about golf tunes. Now all this has changed. And so have the prices.

"Even though the rarities are soaring in price, the music is delightful, real golf history. Owning these song sheets [mainly waltzes, two-steps, and marches] lets you imagine people having a good time in a picturesque setting. People are using golf to enliven things. Anyone who wrote these songs would have to have a real passion for the game, and that makes owning them a lot of fun."

So strike up the band, tune your favorite piano, and expect a good time. That is, of course, if you're able to find one of these extremely scarce items (usually $300 to $500, but more common ones are $20 to $30), and can afford to reach those high C notes.

The prices of golf collectibles fluctuate. The following values are estimates offered by various experts:
MH—Michael Hurdzan
WR—Will Roberts

- *Casper the Friendly Ghost,* with golf balls splashing into a bunker, 1962, **$5–10, MH**

- *Donald Duck,* Walt Disney Comics, a 1953 comic with Donald and his nephews, **$5–10, MH**

- *Dennis the Menace,* Dennis atop a golf trophy, 1974, **$2–5, MH**

- *The Fabulous Furry Freak Brothers,* scarce, **$75 in good condition, $225 in mint, MH**

- *Jughead with Archie,* this comic series often does golf scenes, 1999, **$2–5, MH**

- *Target,* character Kit Carter fights off the villain on the cover of this 1948 comic, rare, **$175–225, MH**

- *Popeye,* in swing mode, very scarce, 1947, **$125, MH**

- *Porky Pig and Bugs Bunny,* fairly common golf themes, 1972, readily available, **$25–35, MH**

- *Rags Rabbit,* rare cover from 1953, **$75, MH**

- *Richie Rich, The Poor Little Rich Boy,* very common, 1982, **$5–10, MH**

- *Tom and Jerry Comics,* popular in the 1950s, common, **$5–10, MH**

- *Wendy the Good Little Witch,* these comics featured golf covers from 1963–1973, common, **$12–15 depending on condition, MH**

- Bobby Jones *Golf Series*, set of six instructional films, tru-vue viewer complete in original case, **$300–400, WR**

- Four LP records: *Tommy Armour Tells You How to Play Your Best Golf All the Time, Songs Fore Golfers, Caddyshack, Arnold Palmer Golf,* **$80–90, WR**

- Coca-Cola advertising tray circa 1920s, **$800–1,000, WR**

- Three vintage glass "Magic Lantern" slides; two are from the *Golf in Many Climes* series (India and China), **$180–200, WR**

- Two film items: a reel of *Play Better Golf* by J. Victor East and *"Chick" Evans' Golf Secrets* by Brunswick records, complete five-record set in original illustrated box ca. 1921, **$300–400, WR**

- *Follow the Sun* movie poster, signed by Ben Hogan, **$1,000, unsigned $250, MH**

- *Stroke of Genius* movie poster, 2004, original poster **$25, MH**

- *Caddyshack* poster, **$25–50, MH**

- *Dead Solid Perfect*, unsuccessful TV movie, but poster in excellent condition, **$75–100, MH**

- *The Legend of Bagger Vance* movie poster, original **$25, copy $15, MH**

- *March of the Golfers*, sheet music cover, 1902, good color, **$200–$300, MH**

- *Catch On March*, 1902 sheet music with great color, **$250–275**

- *Tomorrow's My Lucky Day*, cover featuring Bing Crosby and Bob Hope, **$150–200, MH**

- *With Your Plus Fours On*, 1923 sheet music, **$75–100, MH**

- *Straight Down the Middle*, sheet music cover featuring Bing Crosby, **$75–100, MH**

13 STAKES IN TIME
Innovative and Affordable Tees

Most of them are quite undistinguished looking, just trumpet-shaped wooden pegs. They're stuck in the ground, and the clubface takes a whack at them and the ball. Nothing all that esoteric or highly crafted. They're just plain tees.

Then there's sand tee molds, weighted tees with tethers, and a variety of funnel-shaped, ivory, applesauce (yes, applesauce), spring plunger, avidly sought Ransoms, Paradise, and even the noxious-sounding *Nigger Head* tees.

These scarce and often curious-looking items are the crème de la crème in the tee world. Once yesterday's junk, barely noticed by even the most ardent collectors, tees have had such a price renaissance and explosion that they're today's gold.

"Once the attraction of tees was their low cost, they were the most affordable golf antiquity," recounts one of the world's most ardent collectors of tees, Lee Crist, who since 1987 has amassed over 37,000 of these artifacts. "Now those fifteen-cent tees are selling for $3, and my *Alexander* sand mold that goes back to 1890 [probably a one-of-a-kind piece made of balsa wood] is worth $5,000 to $7,000, while my Ransoms are $600 to $800. The price escalation has been unbelievable."

Attributing these wild price jumps to the "utter craziness of golf collectors," tee enthusiast Paul Biocini says, "The rarity of some tees is also driving this phenomenon. Sand tee molds dating back to the early 1900s are just impossible to find. They're part of the game's history, mirroring the attempt of inventors to develop the perfect ball holder and that evolutionary process is of great interest to collectors. Golfers have money and they spend it."

A brown Bakelite sand tee mold by Keystone Mfg. Co., Chicago; an early aluminum sand tee mold with external spring application; an English brass sand tee "mould" producing either a high or low tee by Ransomes, Ltd.; an English brass sand tee "mould" producing either a high or low tee by Ransomes, Ltd. *Photo courtesy of Old Tom Morris Golf, L.L.C.*

Yet the question still remains: How does the fledging tee enthusiast spend his money wisely?

The Great Tee Master Crist strongly suggests that the first point of departure is "learning your history." That essentially means returning to 1899, when a dentist named G. F. Grant patented a funnel-shaped tee with a tapered stem and a rubber collar (the added flex ensured it wouldn't break on club contact). There were earlier tees made in Great Britain, but the Grant (one is now worth about $50) ignited a

Sterling Tether Tee, Reddy Tee, 1920. *Photo courtesy of Paul Biocini.*

The Top Not Tee (1920s), featured a wire stem and a wooden top. *Photo courtesy of Paul Biocini.*

competitive war, as dozens of would-be inventors (along with several Northeastern button factories) scrambled to devise their own "perfect" tees.

One of the most popular tees to evolve from this burst of creative gamesmanship was the *Reddy Tee*, which was developed by another dentist named William Lowell (why dentists were at the forefront of these historical breakthroughs remains one of golf's great mysteries). The *Reddy* (when purchasing this tee, make sure the box says manufactured by Niebolo) was made of wood, and came in red, green, or white. As Crist explains, the green version was the most popular since "it didn't look messy on the teeing area."

During this halcyon period of development, when America's most brilliant minds were looking to profit from the game's surging popularity, the tether tee was another big hit. Almost impossible to lose, this stroke of genius featured a piece of yarn or a fluffy ball at the end of a string. Weighted down in this manner, the tee wouldn't fly very far when struck, and wouldn't disappear like many errant hit balls.

Crist delights in talking about these fluffy accessories, and his myriad assortment of other "novelties," such as sponge, leather, brass, rubber, ivory, water-soluble applesauce tees, and even those that "were impregnated with grass seeds" which would plant grass when they dissolved.

Yet his most prized possessions are the sand tee molds that were developed in the late 1800s and early 1900s to essentially "clean up the game."

Recalling that golf originated along the Scottish and English coasts, Crist animatedly says, "Courses were always close to the water, and there would be a hole dug

Made by the makers of the "Reddy Tee" Nieblo Mfg. Co., N.Y., 1920s. *Photo courtesy of Paul Biocini.*

Wire medal tees, Multi Products Corp., Plainfield, N.J., 1920s. *Photo courtesy of Paul Biocini.*

Celluloid tees (new plastic), Amsterdam N.Y., 1920s. *Photo courtesy of Paul Biocini.*

Wood tee, 1925. *Photo courtesy of Paul Biocini.*

where the caddy could dig out sand to make a tee. They would squeeze their fingers and pinch the sand to create an elevation higher than the regular ground. These mounds of moist sand were also created by putting sand into a caddy's leather pouch and adding a few droplets of water to keep everything moist. It got a little messy."

Then came a revolutionary "no fuss, no dirty hands" idea. Some brilliant inventor realized a child's beach bucket could be inverted on a golf course to form sand tees.

"Various sand mold shapes were developed, which allowed golfers to dip into a supply of sand located next to the teeing area, and to build either a high mound, or a low

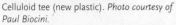

Celluloid tee (new plastic). *Photo courtesy of Paul Biocini.*

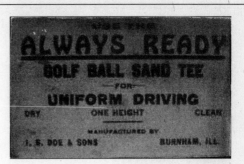

Always Ready Golf Ball Sand Tee. *Photo courtesy of Paul Biocini.*

one," says Crist. "Usually shaped like whiskey jiggers, some held an ounce of sand, others a half ounce. I have one from Scotland called the *Alexander* that's made of balsa wood, and there's no way I'm going to part with it. This is real history."

This mold aficionado also treasures his *Ransom* Sand Tee Cups (once given to groundskeepers as promotional items, these were produced from 1885–89, which were produced in various shapes, and sell for $600 to $800. His vast, unparalleled collection also includes a *Douglas* cylindrical sand tee gun (ca. 1910–20) that's spring-loaded (this totally eliminated the need for a golfer to scoop sand with his fingers).

"That very good-looking, stainless steel spring plunger is considered another evolutionary item, for there was a stationary piece that was packed into the sand, and by pressing a button, the sand was unloaded," explains Crist. "These types came about in the 1920s, and now a spring-loaded *Keystone* sells for about $550, while the *Douglas* is worth about $1,800."

Along with appreciating his encyclopedic array of sand molds (thirty-two different varieties), Crist has twenty-odd rubber weighted tees (one end, of say a $150 *Manhattan*, had a cup where the ball could be mounted). He understands these molds are not Impressionist paintings, but still says, "Tees are a historical item. If a collector acquires a respectable number these antiquities make a very nice display. The only problem is that new enthusiasts should know that the really desirable sand tee molds are very scarce. Most are just gone."

It's still enjoyable to search for interesting tees that have survived the onslaught, and to also collect tee boxes.

Wood tee. *Photo courtesy of Paul Biocini.*

24 Celluloid tees, L.A. Young Co., Detroit, Mich., 1920s. *Photo courtesy of Paul Biocini.*

Besides cultivating the bona fides to be known as Mr. Tee, Crist is also a Box Man. Appreciating the classic artwork of tee cartons and cloth bags, he's acquired scores of patterned boxes filled with their original contents.

"You've got to judge the printing on the box, and go for those with the best designs in the most superb condition," advises Crist, whose favorites include a 1930s *Red Zinc* box (with eighteen tees, priced at $200), the *Reddy Tee* container ($85), and Gold Medal ($150). "There are a lot of gimmicks in tees [he has a 1900 spring steel item called *The New Principle* that looks like an alligator's mouth], the collector can go for those or the ones with a real historical aura [tees with advertisements have little value]. But whatever the choice, be wary of fakes. The crooks have discovered tees."

Forgers have predictably focused on one of the market's most valued rarities, those questionably named *Nigger Head* tees. In the last six to eight years scores of boxes depicting an African-American with a tee stuck in his head have been widely reproduced—and fraudulently sold as originals.

"Because it's the number one box collectors must have, the crooks offer all sorts of phony and expensive reproductions," notes Biocini, who has been collecting golf items sine the 1970s. "You can tell a fake by determining if the writing on the box is fuzzy ["You Can't Hurt the Tee" is written on an orange and white box], and the print can be off center. It's terrible that they used a stereotype of a tough black fighter to promote these very solid wooden tees [there was also a rubber, or tether tee model]. Yet these boxes are still very prized, historical artifacts [one in excellent to mint condition with ten tees is valued at $350], even if they are in shockingly bad taste."

Medal Zinc tees. *Photo courtesy of Paul Biocini.*

Days golf tee. *Photo courtesy of Paul Biocini.*

Far less controversial, *Reddy Tee* boxes are similarly priced ($300 to $350) and attractive. Less apt to be forged, these white and green packages contain either the company's longer tees or a shorter variety.

The generic tee box usually costs about $125, but there's nothing common about *Paradise*. Extremely difficult to find, yet still worth the hunt, this white *Paradise* tee box is artfully detailed with two rubber red and blue dice. Attractively priced at $175, these dice were hooked together with a string (or tether), and as Biocini explains, "there was an indentation, or essentially a cup on top of them, so you could tee up your ball. Every inventor in the 1920–30s was trying to devise the perfect holder, the one that reduced friction and caused less friction [*sic*]. It was crazy! There was even the *Magnet Tee* [priced at $375], one you could pick up with your putter without having to bend down.

"People think of tees as just wooden pegs stuck into the ground. They have to think again. There may be 4,000 designs of what you hit a golf ball off. New collectors just have to be wary of phony boxes, search for the best condition, and know that from goblet-shaped to teardrop and rubber cylinder styled pieces, there's a vast tee universe to be discovered."

The prices of golf collectibles fluctuate. The following values are estimates offered by various experts:
MM—Mullock & Madeley
LC—Lee Crist
PB—Paul Biocini
WR—Will Roberto

- Fine and rare Douglas Golf Patent Sand Tee, silver-plated, stamped patent, appears unused and comes in original maker's box, tissue paper wrapper, **$1750–1850, MM**

- Keystone Bakelite sand mold, 1928, egg crate with twelve molds, spring loaded, rare, **$550–600, LC**

- KD sand mold, aluminum spring loaded, 1928, mint, **$500–650, LC**

- Douglass, stainless-steel sand mold spring loaded 3", very rare, **$1,800 LC**

- Alexander, bell-shaped wooden tee, two known to exist; handle on top, 1890, very rare, **$2,000–2,500, LC**

- Ransom, 1890–98, brass sand mold, shaped like a whiskey jigger, **$700, LC**

- Nigger Tee in an original box, contains eighteen tees, 1926, made by Philport Brokerage Co., mint, **$700 LC**

- Red Head Peg Tee, two-piece celluloid tee, red head, cream-colored shaft, twelve tees, checkerboard box, 1920, **$200–225, LC**

- Rex Tee, made of zinc, red box with white lettering, "cited 'King of the Tees,'" 1930, **$300 LC**

- Scottie Tee, Scotsman with floppy hat pictured on the box, sitting on tee, British made, 1930s, fairly rare, **$300–325, LC**

- Burke Sturdy Tee, tee on the box, brightly colored graphics, eighteen tees in box, plastic tees, **$175–200, LC**

- Stay on Line, standard wooden tee with a directional wing, plastic, 1996, **$7, LC**

- Perfect Tee, made of rubber, 1927, **$125, LC**

- Manhattan Tee, a weighted tee, cup on end to hold the ball, rubberized lead weight, 1915, **$150, LC**

- Bloxsom Tee, four rubber little prongs used to set ball, ca. 1880s, very rare, **$200–225, LC**

- Fore UP Tee, tripod shaped, can be adjusted to various heights, 1950s, **$45–$55, LC**

- The Rev Tee, a "swivel" tee, made of plastic and metals, ca. 1930s, **$165, LC**

- Magic Tee, a swivel tee, made of spring steel and has a metal base, 1927, **$175–225, LC**

- Forma Tee, paper tee comes in box, two wings inserted into tee to set the ball, thirty-six tees in a box, 1918, **$300, LC**

- Novel Tee, paper tee, the tees come in a booklet with an attached string, 1918, **$175–200, LC**

- Right Height, PLA-Wood Products Corporation, cloth bag holds 100 wooden tees, ca. 1940s, **$75, LC**

- Leedall Golf Tee, cloth bag with 100 tees, 1945, **$75, LC**

- Brown Bakelite sand tee mold by Keystone Mfg. Co., **$500–600, WR**

- Early aluminum sand tee mold with external spring application, **$500–600, WR**

- English brass sand tee mold producing either a high or low tee by Ransomes, Ltd., **$400–500, WR**

- Three tee boxes: Gold Medal, Champion large size, and Longdrive. Some tees in each box, **$100–125, WR**

- Two patented pressed cardboard Blue Ring Colonel tees by St. Mungo Mfg., a tethered rubber Brook Bond Tee, six paper crown tees by Tufts-Lyons Arms, and full decorative box of twenty-four "Longdrive" tees ca. 1920s, **$200–250, WR**

- A booklet of 24 Paper Golf Tees with decorative cover advertising Vat 69 Scotch whiskey, **$250–300, WR**

- English brass sand mold producing either a high or low tee by Ransomes, Ltd., **$400–500, WR**

- Typewritten, signed letter dated 1935 on the full-color illustrated letterhead of the Rite-Hite Golf Tee Co., sample tee enclosed, **$35-40, WR**

- J. B. Hailey Company, British made, 12–20 tees, 1940s, very rare, **$75, LC**

- Rite pencil Teem picture of a tee, looks like someone is writing with the tee, 1928, **$15, LC**

- Pee Gee Tee, advertisement, "tee to use with practice golf ball," 1954, **$12, LC**

- Morley Yellow Tee, made by Morley Button Manufacturing Co., 1928–30, **$15, LC**

- Brass Tees promoting Bob Curry's Shell Service station, in a matchbook package, 1932, **$155–200, LC**

- Always Ready sand tee mold, 18 tees, 1920s, very rare in orange box, **$900, PB**

- Nigger Head Tee, orange and black box, wooden tees, box contains 10 tees, 1920s, **$450, PB**

- Walter Hagen Tee, black and yellow box holds 24 celluloid tees, 1926, **$400, PB**

- Top Not Tee, made by Top Not Tee Co., orange box contains 12 tees, 1925, **$250, PB**

- Perfect Sand Mold, made of brass, made in U.S., 1910, **$1,200, PB**

- K-D Old Mold, sand mold tee, made of aluminum, 1920, **$400, PB**

- Reddy Tee, green and white box contains 18 tees, made by Nieblo Manufacturing, 1928, **$100, PB**

- Days Golf Tee, tethered with chain, rubber tee, weighted base, 1915, **$250, PB**

- Tethered tee made of sterling silver, 2 tees, entire unit including tether is made of silver, 1920, **$150, PB**

- Perma-Tee, spinner tee made of aluminum, with metal side arm, 1918, **$300, PB**

- Excel Tees, made of rubber, weighted on one end, covered with rubber, 1950s, **$75, PB**

- Rex Tee, made by Jack Shipman, made of zinc, "King of All Tees," 18 tees in a box, 1928, **$200, PB**

14 GOING FAR BACK INTO TIME
One Man's Quest

The search typically begins in a few English or Scottish pubs. A few words are exchanged with an innkeeper, some patrons, and those conversations invariably lead to finding a long-retired pro, a club secretary, and perhaps even a greenskeeper.

Once contact with these men is initiated, tips are furnished that take this Great Adventurer to the homes of the golfers' distant relatives. There a common fraternity is kindled; camaraderie struck that shows a mutual respect for the game's lofty traditions. Only then, once this American proves he is worthy of owning, or preserving, a certain keepsake for posterity's sake, is a monetary transaction possible. Investment potential and profits are never the prime concern. History is.

"There's nothing like the search, the putting together of two and two to make four," exclaims Joseph Tiscornia, the preeminent collector of pre-1885 golfing memorabilia. Solely focusing on these very specialized and particularly rare artifacts, he sits next to an 1850s black and white engraving of a golf scene in his home, and excitedly adds, "The chase for finding these objects is absolutely terrific. It's just very rewarding to pore through documents, go to factories, museums, and golf courses, talk with experts, and to do detective work.

"It's just as satisfying to find things accidentally, to be looking for one item, and to find something serendipitously. Usually that type of discovery adds to the value of an object since it wasn't known to exist. But the real satisfaction is not money. After spending years on one of these hunts, the real thrill is the intellectual fulfillment, finding something from the 1800s or before that adds to the game's history."

Books and newspapers from the 1700s.
Photo courtesy of the Joseph R. Tiscornia Collection.

Living in a glorious time capsule, where such prized items as paintings of Old Tom Morris, books from the 1700s, 1800s clubmakers' tools, a putter crafted by Hugh Philp—the "Antonio Stradivari of clubmaking"—and lustrous British Open medals compete for attention, Tiscornia has taken numerous excursions into the past. He's unearthed the rarest 19th century photos of Great Britain's golfing elite, found a Tom Morris–crafted baffie spoon (a wedge-styled club) that was probably "plucked" by immortal clubmaker Allan Robertson after winning a bet, and discovered a 1566 printed compilation of the acts of Parliament which state in 1457 "that football and

Tom Morris tobacco "bogey roll" case.
*Photo courtesy of the Joseph R. Tiscornia
Collection.*

golf be utterly cried down, and not be used." As Tiscornia exults, "that's the first known *printed* word (or mention) of golf."

All of these unique items attest to Tiscornia's seemingly insatiable desire to acquire knowledge about his beloved game, "to put everything under a microscope, and to know their historical significance" in golf's evolution. Unlike the mere "trophy hunters" who spend thousands, if not millions of dollars, simply accumulating rarities without researching their provenance or importance, this former tennis pro-*cum*-health club owner with a B.A. in biology is driven ("all collectors can become obsessed at some point; you have to somehow realize collecting is not the most important thing in life") to unearth objects that resonate with "rich stories."

More than merely stocking his new home with 18th- and 19th-century engravings, signed Tom Morris receipts, and iron-headed clubs from the 1700s, he's the relentless self-termed "searcher," the "scientific" antiquarian/alchemist, ever trying to conjure instant magic from those two-plus-two connections.

Among all those "storytellers," or memorable museum-worthy objects that have a definite dynamic quality ("they spur you to do more investigations, to make more connections"), Tiscornia's favorite prize is an 1898 brass "bogey roll."

Why he's fascinated by this oval-shaped pipe-tobacco case is obvious. Once owned by the "Patron Saint" of British golf, the legendary Tom Morris, it's marked with the initials "TM."

"After doing a little research, I found that it was given by Reginald C. Hodder to Tom in 1898," relates Tiscornia, emphasizing this point by eyeing a photo of Morris that shows an oval-shaped bulge in his sports jacket. "I went to St. Andrews, saw Hodder's name there. He was friends with Tom, who would've kept a chunk of raw tobacco in the bogey roll, and sliced off some shavings with a penknife.

"Tom's one of my favorite people, a Victorian golf hero [(1821–1908)] who was a ball-maker, clubmaker, course designer, and four-time winner of the Open Championship. He was a scholar, a Renaissance man, but that's only part of this fabulous story."

In Tiscornia's world, where memorabilia must provide insights into their original owner's character or habits, this means that his initial musings are only half of that two-plus-two equation.

There's still more math to be done, stepping back into time that gives that brass keep-sake an added, even richer dimension.

"Tom kept a shop alongside the 18th fairway on the old course at St. Andrews, and I visited his great-granddaughter there," animatedly recalls Tiscornia, who's been an ardent collector since 1988. "I went into the second-floor parlor above the shop where Tom would open the window and look out at the 18th green. As I was sitting by that window, in that room all made of pine, I saw an oval water stain on the windowsill where Tom would've sat. I put the case on that stain, and it matched perfectly. It was the first time in 100 years that the bogey roll and the stain were put together. What a connection! Making it was absolutely wonderful."

Other collectors may not discover similarly exciting brass cases or 19th-century watercolor paintings. Yet Tiscornia's tale underscores the importance of going past mere price tags, appreciating the emotional or intellectual value of objects. Too many collectors, according to this internationally respected expert, just acquire items to fill up shelves for bragging rights, "for prestige or bravado." Armed with a limitless checkbook, they "don't particularly care about what an object is or means," and "never piece things together, get the knowledge that adds to the joy of collecting."

The savvy enthusiast also looks for possible bargains. Tiscornia feels collecting golf memorabilia is a very "young, dynamic, and fast-changing hobby. There are so many [existing] things that haven't been found yet. There are discoveries every month." This fluidity offers the promise of finding exciting, new discoveries. Yet since serious collecting only began forty years ago, it retains a mysterious element that makes accurate pricing difficult for many antique dealers.

"If you do your homework, it is possible to go into an antique shop, and to find something that the dealer didn't realize was significant," insists Tiscornia, referring to a 1690s painting of two children playing a golf-like game. "Remarkably, I paid very little for it, one of the earliest golf paintings. A collector just has to know more than the

John Gray lofting iron, ca. 1860s. *Photo courtesy of the Joseph R. Tiscornia Collection.*

dealer. Antique shops can be a very good place for finding stuff since these dealers don't often know much about golf memorabilia."

Tiscornia's expertise certainly comes into play during his pursuit of the world's premier clubs. On either the walls of his home or office, he displays such magnificent rarities as a John Gray iron headed "lofter" from 1865, three clubs from the late 1700s, fifteen to twenty clubs from 1800–1850 that were used during the feather ball era, ten Tom Morris creations, and of course, that "Stradivarius," a Hugh Philp–stamped putter with a thorn head and hickory shaft that was made in the 1820s. Hand-polished by the "only man known to make a perfectly balanced putter," this delicate piece has such a fine finish, Tiscornia excitedly says, "there's no doubt about it, Philp was the best craftsman of clubheads [his work was so exceptional, Philp became the clubmaker to the Society of St. Andrews in 1819, or what was later known as the Royal & Ancient]. He did absolutely beautiful work."

With more than 100 choice clubs on display, it's impossible to catalog all of these glorious finds. Suffice it to say, Tiscornia has diligently put together a selection of artifacts that rivals most Scottish museums.

In one key respect, however, he's outtrumped them with a piece of wood from the mid-1400s. "Found under a house this piece of conifer with lead on it has been carbon-dated, and is the first known wooden-headed club," insists Tiscornia. "It's the part of a club that would be connected to the shaft, and has a square toe to it. It's an amazing find. I trust the person who got it to me [a "must" when buying rarities], a well-established dealer in antiquities. He knows that time period, and it's during that

Wooden-headed clubs made by Tom Morris. *Photo courtesy of the Joseph R. Tiscornia Collection.*

era that they were playing all sorts of games in Holland. The head is definitely from a 1400s golf club."

That transaction was relatively simple. No complicated, drawn-out search and just a few phone calls to agree on a price.

More typically, Tiscornia's historical knowledge is tested during extended chases that demand patience, negotiating skills, grace, and charm. One doesn't get very far by

Earliest known golf club (head only), ca.
1400s. *Photo courtesy of the Joseph R.
Tiscornia Collection.*

merely waving a checkbook. As he's shown, a great degree of subtlety must also be employed.

"I have quite a number of fabulous medals, like an 1821 piece presented to D. Wiley, the winner at the Caledonian Golf Club, and an 1828 medal given to Samuel Aitken at the Bruntsfield Links in Edinburgh," says Tiscornia, proudly pointing at these prominently displayed awards. "Yet my best medal took three years to track down, an 1883 British Open medal won by William Fernie at Musselburgh."

Those pilgrimages to Scotland began with a "rumor." Tiscornia heard through his network of fellow collectors (cultivating such contacts is a must for exchanging information, and for finding singular items) that "a family member of an old golf pro [Fernie was the pro at the Royal Troon Golf Club] might have some old golf memorabilia."

Tirelessly combing through phone books, visiting pubs, and going door-to-door in various towns for two years, Tiscornia traveled to Scotland six times to simply locate this relative. Then he faced the more ticklish challenge of convincing Fernie's great grandson (over the course of a year's time) to sell him the gold medal.

"The new enthusiast must know that really choice items don't always come easy, one must be prepared to do a little legwork and to be very patient," advises Tiscornia. "I had to do a lot of research, and once I started talking with the great-grandson, he made it clear that he wanted this very early medal to be with someone who appreciated its history, and his great-grandfather's legacy [the first Open was held in 1860, and medals weren't awarded until 1872]. The lesson here is obvious. Money isn't always the dominant factor in acquiring memorabilia. Patience is sometimes far more important."

Even after securing this prize that's adorned with crossed clubs and a shield, Tiscornia continued his historical studies. He learned that Fernie had twenty Top Ten finishes in the Open, proceeded to obtain the family's genealogical chart, and later acquired a photo showing this champion wearing his medal. Tiscornia once again made a storytelling connection.

"Collecting isn't just about fulfilling acquisitive needs, making great finds," says Tiscornia. "Serious collectors are just caretakers of this rich material. These items don't really belong to us. We're just caretakers, saving things from being destroyed. The medal should be displayed, exposing Fernie to the world."

Another recently discovered wonder is *Angliae Notitia: Or the Present State of England. First part. Together with divers Reflections upon The Ancient State thereof.* An encyclopedic 1684 book by Edward Chamberlaine, these reflections charmingly list the Royal Court's personnel roster, from sword cutters and "operators for the teeth" to gunners, rat killers, and a golf club maker (David Gastier).

"No one has ever heard of Gastier as being a golf club maker," notes Tiscornia. "I need to find out who he is. It's fascinating that they put him on the last page after the rat killer. Yet the king must have had a connection to France since the French played a game called Pall Mall which was similar to croquet. Most likely Gastier made mallets, so he was brought to England. I need to find out more about him. So you can see that a find like this one inspires more research, and stirs the imagination. That's what I mean when I say collecting shouldn't just be about displayed artifacts. Collecting should also prompt dreams."

In Tiscornia's House of Historical Delights there are numerous books, salted paper, tin- and platinum-type photos (mainly of the Tom Morris clan) and priceless documents that capture the game's early stirrings. Either unceremoniously crammed onto shelves, or stuffed into binders with little regard for preservation, this paper trail dotes on golf's "heavyweights," the legends who continue to charm this consummate connoisseur.

There's an 1854 receipt signed by Tom Morris acknowledging his receiving payment for being the greenskeeper at the Prestwick Golf Club.

Together with a photo of the amateur participants in the "first ever golf tournament" (an 1857 event which featured such stalwarts as George Glennie, John Stewart, and John Dunn) Tiscornia has found the invitation for the celebratory dinner, the menu, and the "drinking poem" that was written for the festivities. "It took me ten years to get all this," he admits. "I didn't know the invitation existed, or the poem. I talked to

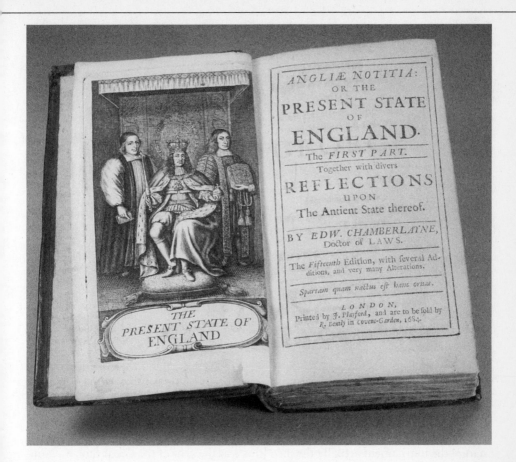

Angliae Notitia, ca. 1684, listing David
Gastier as "Golfe Club maker." (See also
pp. 64–65.) *Photo courtesy of the Joseph R.*
Tiscornia Collection.

many people, and learned there were such items. New collectors must reach out to people."

The greatest amateur of the 1850s, Glennie was prohibited from playing in the 1860 British "Open" (only professionals were permitted to enter and play in the first championship). Rather than becoming angry, he wrote a letter to the Open's organizers stating, "I'm sorry I can't play, but I hope everyone has a good time." This is significant, as Tiscornia relates, since it's the first correspondence that mentions this presti-

A detail of *Angliae Notitia* (ca. 1684), showing a mention of David Gastier as a "Golfe Club maker." (See also pp. 64–65.) *Photo courtesy of the Joseph R. Tiscornia Collection.*

gious British event (the Glennie Medal is now presented to the winner of a St. Andrews tournament).

Intent on flushing out "historical truths," this time-traveling sleuth next turns towards a scoresheet from the weather-plagued 1881 British Open, and insists, "they got it all wrong." Sounding very assured that his "evidence would set the record straight," he quickly adds, "according to the official records eleven of the twenty-two golfers who started the tournament actually finished [this was the year of the Great Storm]. Nonsense! Not too many people know it, but sixteen people finished. I'm sure the R & A would love to have a copy of this scoresheet." As new collectors will learn, it's quite acceptable to be a little self-congratulatory after unearthing a unique prize.

Clearly the Anglophile, continuing to talk about the vaunted Open, he thumbs through a binder, and is soon staring at a "pretty important" document, the Open's "Magna Carta."

"When they started the Open Championship there was only one club that held the event, the Prestwick Golf Club," explains Tiscornia. "After they held thirteen championships there, other clubs got involved, like St. Andrews and Musselburgh (Mary, Queen of Scots reputedly played there in 1567). Those three rotated the championship for many years, then other clubs wanted to get involved, and all this happened during the 1890s. They all got together and rewrote the rules for the championship, determining how much prize money would be awarded, who would contribute the money, how the courses would be rotated, things like that. Those rules were written in 1893–94."

(Front) Receipt for greenskeeper's wages paid to Thomas ("Old Tom") Morris, formerly of St. Andrews, by the Prestwick Golf Club, Scotland, in November 1854. *Photo courtesy of the Joseph R. Tiscornia Collection.*

Pausing, Tiscornia, in an even flatter voice, adds, "Here they are, the original handwritten rules that govern the championship. This is a true Holy Grail. The original rules."

Leafing through that binder, Tiscornia eyes an 800-pound Royal Bank of Scotland check signed by Tom Morris ("a fortune in those days"), a photograph showing him sitting in automobile at St. Andrews in 1903, and a caustic 1938 letter from Sam

(Back) Receipt for wages paid to Tom
Morris, greenskeeper, by the Prestwick Golf
Club, November 1854. *Photo courtesy of the
Joseph R. Tiscornia Collection.*

1857 photograph of players in the Grand National Golf Tournament. *Photo courtesy of the Joseph R. Tiscornia Collection.*

Ryder to the reigning British Open champion Henry Cotton. Congratulating him for refusing to go to the U.S. for a challenge match, the founder of this goodwill international competition wrote, "Bravo Cotton. Let them damned, conceited Yanks come to us—You'll get little there but promiscuous women and idiot men."

That revealing, decidedly collectible letter is Ryder's spin on freedom, his approving Cotton's novel golf stance. Then there's Tiscornia's veritable "call to arms" letter, what can be dubbed British golfer's "Declaration of Independence."

Page one of amateur George Glennie's
letter regarding the 1860 "Open"
Championship. *Photo courtesy of the Joseph
R. Tiscornia Collection.*

It must be recalled that up until the late 1890s professional players represented themselves. There were no unions, no endorsement deals, no appearance fees. Golfers simply earned their incomes through prize money. Or they became featured attractions at exhibitions, where the money was always greater than in the Open or other prestigious events.

These pros ultimately banded together and employed an attorney to represent their financial interests. As Tiscornia describes this effort, "This lawyer went to the Open's

Second page of George Glennie's letter
about the 1860 "Open" Championship.
*Photo courtesy of the Joseph R. Tiscornia
Collection.*

ruling committee, and essentially threatened a boycott of the 1899 championship. He
told them 'if you don't raise the prize money they won't play.' This letter [in his hand]
on Royal and Ancient letterhead talks about the 'trouble arising' because of the small
clubs [those apart from the ones regularly staging the Open] giving money to the professional for exhibitions. It also states the five 'important' clubs will get together to
discuss the attorney's demands. Sure enough, the big-name Open clubs raised the
prize money, and this is the first letter hinting at the formation of a P.G.A.-type association."

1881 (British) Open final results scoresheet.
Photo courtesy of the Joseph R. Tiscornia Collection.

Rules for conducting the (British) Open
championship, ca. 1890s. *Photo courtesy of
the Joseph R. Tiscornia Collection.*

played alternately in Scotland and England on the following Greens successively commencing as already arranged in 1893 at Prestwick vizt Prestwick St Andrews Hoylake, & Sandwich these being the greens generally considered best suited for the Competition.

2. That in order to provide the Prize money (say £125) each year required all the Clubs in Scotland & England be invited to contribute annually —

3. That the Clubs on whose green the competition takes place should subscribe £10 & the other Clubs not less than £2 annually.

4. That the prize fund should be administered by a Committee of 8 members to consist of 2 members to be appointed by each of Prestwick Hoylake St Andrews & Sandwich Golf Clubs. The Chairman to have a casting vote.

Second page of rules for the (British) Open championship, ca. 1890s. *Photo courtesy of the Joseph R. Tiscornia Collection.*

Tom Morris and friends, posing in the fast car in St. Andrews. *Photo courtesy of the Joseph R. Tiscornia Collection.*

During those early, halcyon days of Old Tom, Willie Park, Fernie, and other distinguished Open competitors, the golf ball was undergoing revolutionary transformations. Students of the game now keep a chronological record of that evolution from wooden balls to featheries to post–World War II dimpled balls, and Tiscornia has amassed over 100 of these representative collectibles.

Letter written by Sam Ryder. *Photo courtesy
of the Joseph R. Tiscornia Collection.*

To introduce this assemblage, he stands in front of one of his most valued artworks, and notes, "This little Dutch piece, the *Den Kolf Ballen Maaker*, the Golf Ballmaker, is probably from a book. It's a wood engraving [ca. 1700s]. I just love it."

Delightedly discussing its vivid details, he goes on to emphasize, "You have to enjoy looking at what you collect. See what artwork is available, educate yourself, get a few art books, and set a budget. Then decide what you really like, and focus on a category,

Pages one and four of a letter indictating
early thoughts on a Professional Golfers
Association, 1899. *Photo courtesy of the
Joseph R. Tiscornia Collection.*

engravings, oil paintings, watercolors. A savvy collector specializes. You must have a
focus and you shouldn't just buy what's rare. Art has to be enjoyed."

The aesthetic appeal of a ball fashioned out of wood is somewhat questionable,
yet that doesn't prevent Tiscornia from introducing his collection with obvious
gusto.

Pages two and three of a letter concerning the formation of a Professional Golfers Association, 1899. *Photo courtesy of the Joseph R. Tiscornia Collection.*

"Dating to pre-1600, this boxwood ball was found under a house in a trash pit. It may have been a child's ball. In early literature there are references to balls made of boxwood. So I feel this is one of the earliest golf balls."

Taking a feather ball out of a glass showcase, he next talks about the laborious process of producing these 1700s–1850s artifacts.

1700s engraving of the golf ball maker.
Photo courtesy of the Joseph R. Tiscornia Collection.

Tom Morris random-cut gutty ball, ca. 1850s. *Photo courtesy of the Joseph R. Tiscornia Collection.*

Gutta-percha balls from the 1800s. *Photo courtesy of the Joseph R. Tiscornia Collection.*

"Even with the boiling of feathers, and stuffing of them into leather cases, these balls didn't last long. The feathers would get wet; the cases would split so gutta-percha was seen as a big improvement. Initially these balls were smooth, but they quickly determined they weren't too aerodynamic. The more golfers hacked them up [with iron-headed clubs, and mis-hits], and put a mark on them, they flew better. Interestingly, that led to golfers sending their caddies out to hack up balls before they were played with."

Hammers were eventually used to create "random pattern" balls, and then the process became far more scientific with the introduction of ball molds. Holding a random-patterned Tom Morris-made ball, Tiscornia says it's one of the valuable artifacts in his collection, and proceeds to display such other rarities as machine-scored balls from the 1860s–70s, along with hand-hammered balls crafted by Robert Forgan.

Meticulously ensuring that his collection features representative samples from every important production era, Tiscornia also has numerous patterned gutta-percha balls (these lasted until shortly after 1900) and rubber-cored balls of various descriptions. Seduced by the game's richly textured history, Tiscornia relishes this opportunity to chronicle the different hallmarks of ballmaking, such as the "curing" of gutta-percha, putting "molds into a press," and the "aerodynamics of dimples."

Yet in terms of pure storytelling, balls pale in comparison to most of his antique golf clubs. One of the most charming tales concerns that "plucked" baffie spoon, and the legion of British legends who once owned it.

As Tiscornia relates, this club, which produced a baffing sound when it hit the ground (and broke relatively often), was made by Old Tom Morris (Tom Jr. was also

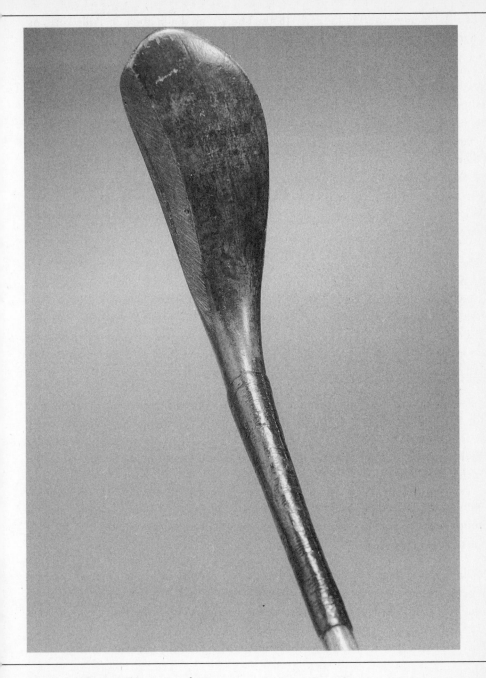

Tom Morris baffy spoon. *Photo courtesy of
the Joseph R. Tiscornia Collection.*

a British Open winner) in the early 1850s. There is no doubt about its fabled origins. On the top of the club, "T. Morris" is inscribed in very large letters.

Admittedly "guessing" that Morris crafted the spoon for himself—"this definitely adds to its panache"—Tiscornia continues, "Tom and Robertson, the best feather ballmaker of his era, and a terrific golfer, most likely played a match and Allan won the bet. In those days that meant he got to 'pluck' a club [meaning he was able to select a club of his choice from Morris's holdings]. Afterwards he presented it to Willie Dunn [a famous 1840–60 player who was the greenskeeper at Blackheath and Scotland's North Berwick], who in turn gave it to Mr. David Lewis, a gentleman golfer who belonged to the North Berwick Golf Club. He subsequently gave it to Willie Park Jr. [noted ball- and clubmaker, who designed the bulger driver, and won two British Opens].

"There are just so many wonderful connections here. Some of the best pieces I have are not my most costly ones, but those that really demanded a lot of research and knowledge. This club, that changed hands so often, I got at an auction in St. Andrews. All the experts and big collectors were there. They didn't recognize how important this baffie spoon was. I did simply because of my research. All my clubs have a story to tell, it's just a matter of finding out what the story is. That's what makes club collecting exciting, not monetary values."

Purposely pursuing clubs that can be traced to distinguished owners, or to reputed club makers, Tiscornia also proudly displays a putter belonging to Morris crafted by George Daniel Brown ("Tom played with it in memory of his son young Tom who liked to play with that style"), and three long-nosed woods made by the venerable Patrick family.

John Patrick started producing highly coveted clubs in the 1840s. They only made a limited number of long noses, yet Tiscornia has still managed to devise his own version of a family tree.

Again emphasizing the point that new collectors should avoid the mere stockpiling of items for a more systematic approach, he stresses, "It's very nice when you can put some general theme together. Here you have three clubs from the Patrick family, one from 1840s [John Patrick Sr.], 1860s [John Patrick Jr.], and 1870s (Alexander Patrick). This is terrific. It's very unusual to have three clubs made by the same family."

Journeying further back into time, Tiscornia is equally charmed by his "no-named" iron-headed clubs from the 1700s. These "general" or oval-shaped bunker irons were produced by blacksmiths who also made armaments for royalty. Their exact lineage remains unknown, since clubmakers didn't start to put names on their pieces until the 1790s. But despite their crude, almost menacing appearance, Tiscornia still appreciates them as rare works of art.

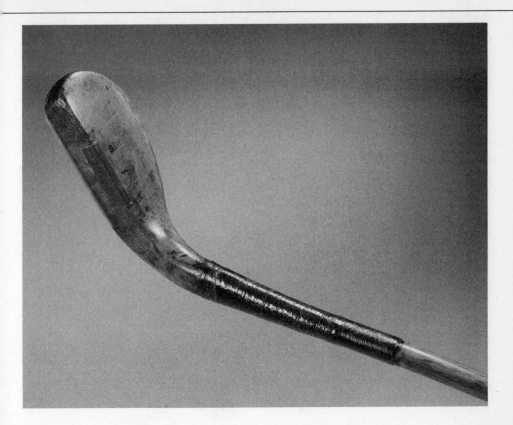

Tom Morris putter, made by George Daniel
Brown. *Photo courtesy of the Joseph R.
Tiscornia Collection.*

Owning a world-class array of clubs isn't satisfaction enough for this impassioned
historian. He's also assembled dozens of the original tools that were used to craft early
golf equipment.

From various types of planes and chisels, to the ram's horn (an extremely hard, protective material) that was used in conjunction with wood, he's constructed a veritable
clubmaking shop in his home, complete with an 1800s workbench.

241

Tools used for making clubs and balls in the
1800s. *Photo courtesy of the Joseph R.*
Tiscornia Collection.

Discovering these items during ten years of visiting assorted English and Scottish
shops and auctions, he describes how they were used to produce legendary objects,
then begins to work on a piece of wood. Much like a Civil War buff who's steeped in
Gettysburg and Bull Run folklore and has devised his own battle plans, Tiscornia is
no longer the mere collector. Now totally enveloped by the process of boiling a piece
of ram's horn, putting it into a press, and seeing "genius" unfold, he's now crossed
into another dimension. Into his own field of dreams.

"Young collectors should know that they can take the hobby wherever they want to," advises Tiscornia. "They can spend millions of dollars, or a few dollars, but whatever direction is taken, studying the history, and doing the research lets you put two and two together. That's the key to the most enjoyment, knowing the essence of things [in many instances he puts objects under a microscope to confirm their origins]. To really understand how these tools worked, how a piece of wood became a golf club, that's terrific. You want artifacts to come alive."

That stirring, pulsating quality is dramatically apparent in one of his most appealing artworks, Charles Lees's *Evening on Musselburgh Golf Links*. A 1914 engraving of a painting done in 1859, it's an amusing, vivid depiction of assorted golfers looking at a ball from different angles, apparently hoping the ball will drop into the hole. Tiscornia acquired this print for very little money about seven years ago, and has seen a similar engraving (there are only three known to exist since the plate was destroyed in Germany during World War I) recently sell for five figures. But instead of savoring this triumph, this relentless searcher is again hoping to work more magic.

"There's an oil painting of this very important print, and no one knows where it is," he explains. "The painting was reportedly last seen in Canada. It's just disappeared. The new collector has to know that in this ever-changing hobby there's always the promise of finding something the [*sic*] unexpected. I hope to. That oil painting is around somewhere, and I will find it."

As Tiscornia hunts for that painting with his typical flair and determination, he's already landed quite a number of other exemplary works. Prominently displayed on one wall of his house, there's a copy of a Morris portrait that was originally done in Edinburgh in 1904–05 ("cantankerous Old Tom didn't like to travel," laughs Tiscornia, "yet in his 80s at the time, he had to make several trips to the studio"). It's a very famous Sir George Reid oil painting that hangs in the Royal & Ancient clubhouse. The face is terrific, very detailed."

Continuing to praise this engraving, particularly the fact that both Morris and the artist have signed it, Tiscornia suggests, "Old Tom's signature is the most collectible other than Bob Jones's. I've authenticated Tom's signature. Those items signed by him are obviously worth more than those pieces signed by family members. It's very hard to tell the difference."

How can this master historian discern those minute distinctions? After years of study, and examining untold items, Tiscornia has a practiced eye. He's seen enough genuine material to separate what's real from the fake and illusory.

Yet even this meticulous maestro doesn't strictly depend on his own eyes. "Once the value of what you're collecting goes up, there's more incentive for forgeries and fakes,

Charles Lees's depiction of golf on
Musselburgh links in 1859. *Photo courtesy of
the Joseph R. Tiscornia Collection.*

and reproductions to be made. That's true in any hobby. That's why I use a microscope to examine golf clubs [reproductions are a thriving industry], and a black light
when it comes time to examine paintings.

"The black light can tell me if paintings have been overpainted and touched up. It
will tell me if a golf hole has been added to a scene. This will happen occasionally.
You have to be aware no matter what you're collecting. Paintings can be reproduced."

Photograph of Old Tom Morris at St.
Andrews, signed by Morris. *Photo courtesy
of the Joseph R. Tiscornia Collection.*

Earliest golf engraving. Golfers at
Blackheath, near London ca. 1790. *Photo
courtesy of the Joseph R. Tiscornia Collection.*

1850 engraving of "The Grand Match" at St. Andrews. *Photo courtesy of the Joseph R. Tiscornia Collection.*

Numerous reproductions have been made of Samuel Abbott's *Society of Golfers at Blackheath* (earlier a notorious site outside London where black plague victims were buried), yet Tiscornia's 1790 copper plate engraving of this fabled work is undeniably genuine. "This is golf's first engraving. There were maybe fifty impressions from that copper plate, and I'd guess there are fifteen left. I just love the caddie, the bottle of whiskey in his pocket, the old golf clubs. It's anyone guess where the original painting is. It was rumored to have been lost in a fire in India, but I'd just love to find it still intact."

Tiscornia goes on to praise the detail of a watercolor depicting St. Andrews's Old Course, Flemish painter David Teniers's late 1500s painting of two children playing with what looks like a golf club, and an 1850s engraving titled either *The Grand Match* or *The Golfers* that pictures a host of wealthy gentlemen cavorting at St. Andrews. As this afternoon of gazing at art treasures winds down, he will also highlight the pleasures of collecting original saltpaper photos (especially an 1857 photo of the participants in the "first golf tournament," staged at St. Andrews).

But once this tour through history ends, Tiscornia will undoubtedly be compelled to make a few phone calls, contact fellow enthusiasts, and even plan another trip to Scotland. Obviously a *completist*, that type of collector who must reach totality, he has to do more research. For as he remarked, his collection is alive, continuing to confront him with question marks and to weave its own mysteries.

He'll be busy this evening, wondering, "Just where is that painting? What ever happened to Abbott's *Blackheath Golfers*, and what can I do to find it?"

15 SCULPTURED TREASURE
Bronze Statues

Turning paper into bronze was no easy feat.

Golfer and illustrious sculptor Hal Ludlow first had to trek to several courses to watch the Immortal One in action. In a series of 1903–04 sketches, he pictured the swing that would eventually propel Britain's Harry Vardon to six British Open titles (along with one U.S. Open victory), and to later renown as "the game's first international celebrity." Yet these depictions were just the beginning of Ludlow's labors. To style "real art" that would capture Vardon's power and grace, this soon-to-be famous artist turned those drawings into impeccably detailed bronze statues—highly collectible 5-inch to 8-inch pieces that showcase the hand of genius.

"These Ludlow bronzes have real heft, substance, and they're just beautiful with their flowing lines, dark brown patina, and faithfulness to Vardon's likeness," says Tom Chisholm, who has assembled fifteen of the world's most coveted golf statues. "People of that era felt Vardon had picture-perfect form, and Ludlow's work, which immortalizes that swing [the club is bent back, in the finished position], is much more than a lifeless statue. It has real energy, a dynamic power that connects me to the 1900s."

About 800 to 900 of those bronzes were produced (most of them are no longer extant), and while Chisholm's 5-inch statue (worth about $12,000) is dwarfed by the larger, $25,000 pieces, this ardent collector is still exultant about discovering a "hard-to-find" Ludlow. "I had to search very hard for this piece, and new collectors should know that finding 'gold' takes patience, and help from experienced people," he cautions. "Whenever things are rare and pricey that's an invitation to the counterfeiters and

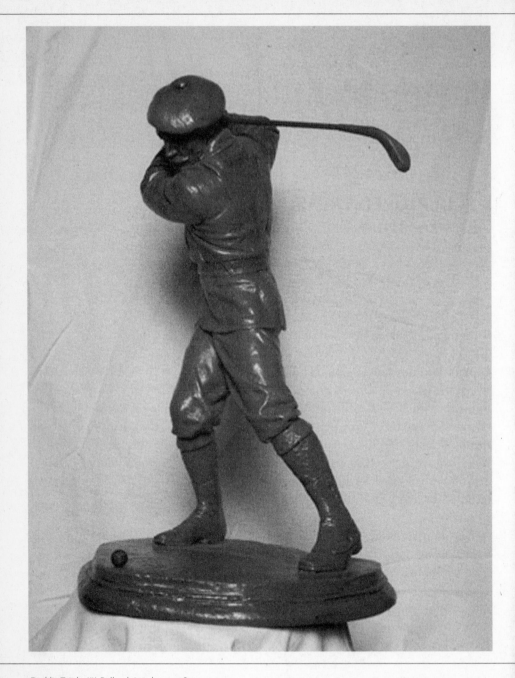

Freddie Tait by W. Rolland, London ca. 1892.
Plaster. British champion killed in Boer War
about 1900. Approx. 24″ h. *Photo courtesy
of Will Roberto.*

A cast-iron paperweight in the form of a
dimple ball atop a spoked wheel advertising
Hockensmith Wheel & Mine Car Co. $100–
125. *Photo courtesy of Old Tom Morris Golf,
L.L.C.*

the less reputable. That's why I strongly recommend working with dealers [who often offer bronzes on a consignment or guaranteed money-back basis] and getting their counsel. They know what [artist] markings to look for, how to spot a real piece. Only experienced dealers well-versed in the business can look at a bronze, its markings, and tell if it was made by a sculptor with a real pedigree or by some fake. That distinction can mean thousands of dollars."

Though the prices of bronzes are certainly influenced by the sculptor's notoriety, the key determinant in assessing collectibility or pricing is a piece's association to a specific golfer. Bronzes such as Ludlow's Vardon statues, which can be directly linked to one famed player, are typically far more valuable than generic items. Chisholm certainly enjoys his *Putter Boy* (ca. 1950s–60s), a bronze depicting a young golfer wearing a big floppy hat and holding a putter that was used as a trophy at Pinehurst (worth about $1,100 to $1,200, as they are fairly common). Yet he admits that bronzes honoring golf's elite, such as metallic likenesses of Ben Hogan and Bobby Jones, are often more prized than pieces picturing a classical golfer, or some form of the golf swing.

"The artist isn't all that important when it comes to a Bobby Jones, or say a Tom Morris," insists Chisholm. "The value comes from the mere fact that it's a named golfer. Go for players. Gorham [of sterling silver fame] did make some bronze statues of Jones in the 1920s and if you can find one, it certainly has value because of this signature name. These Jones pieces are usually $10,000, and very beautiful. Knowing who the golfer is definitely adds value to a bronze."

Most bronzes aren't cheap. Chisholm feels the new collector should acquire one quality piece at the outset, and be prepared to enter this very specialized niche with a

A cast iron door stop ca. 1920s. $300–400.
*Photo courtesy of Old Tom Morris Golf,
L.L.C.*

Old Tom Morris ca. 1890s by Robert Crerar.
8″ high on plinthe, in solid silver. *Photo
courtesy of Will Roberto.*

$3,000 to $4,000 budget. Only then, he insists, "will you be sure of having something that will retain its value."

Chisholm has acquired most of his bronzes at auctions, but again sounding a cautious note, he admits, "Only really daring collectors should go to these sales by themselves. I prefer to have a knowledgeable representative do my bidding. Auctions can be very dangerous; places where you can easily go spend wildly, so I prefer to commission someone who's a lot wiser than I am. Someone who really knows the ins and outs of bidding at auctions."

Most of Chisholm's favorite bronzes have been acquired at auctions, including a "very substantial" 17-inch, long-skirted representation of Glenna Collette, a 1900s U.S. Women's Amateur champion, and an unsigned French piece that pictures a golfer in customary knickers. Both of these statues date back to the early 1900s, and that historical lineage prompts Chisholm to say, "Unless a piece has been dragged by a car, and looks like it, beginners should always buy old pieces. A few dings or scratches on a statue are okay. They are not going to break, so even if a bronze needs a little repair, go for it. You won't find totally pristine bronzes."

Chisholm is far more concerned about unscrupulous sellers who try to pass off pot metal or cast metal statues as authentic bronzes. "There's nothing wrong with good pot metal statues, you just must know they're not the same as bronzes valuewise," says Chisholm, who has served on the U.S.G.A.'s library committee. "An old pot metal piece can definitely be worth thousands of dollars, yet there are sneaky people who try to make these [usually lighter] statues look like bronzes with a phony patina.

Young Tom Morris by Trevor Faulkner
ca. 1990s cast by Alex Kirkwood and Sons,
Edinburgh in solid silver. Approx. 12″ on
plinthe. *Photo courtesy of Will Roberto.*

The distinctions between pot metal and bronzes are pretty easy to spot, but new collectors must still be vigilant."

And careful that the striking aesthetics of these three-dimensional objects don't leave a lasting, overpowering spell.

"I really would like to have this very handsome, 19-inch bronze of John Ball, the first English-born player to win the British Open [1890] who also won a record eight British Amateur titles," confesses Chisholm, ruefully. "The piece depicts his backswing, Ball in knickers, and it's very rare. I thought a lot about buying it, but since it goes for $30,000 to $40,000, I finally decided against it. That was tough. That bronze was so bewitching I'm still thinking about it."

♀ ♀ ♀

Greeting visitors to his loft space that is filled with the rarest golf clubs, books, and balls, a solid silver 6-inch high Young Tom Morris sits on a shelf under a protective glass sphere. An ode to the glories of silversmithery, this one-of-a-kind commemorative is a fitting welcome to the artistic wonders that abound in this elegant sitting room.

Alongside Morris, an equally detailed bronze figure is sporting a polychrome, red flowing jacket, black-and-tan shoes, and pants with a silverish sheen. A tribute to legendary British amateur John Laidlay, this prize, situated next to his shoes and an autographed piece of Laidlay's correspondence, is visually striking, and also a bit provocative.

Golfer—bronze by Antoine Bufill ca. 1890s.
Approx 18″ h. *Photo courtesy of Will Roberto.*

The figure's hands are separated on the club, reminiscent of the "Vardon Grip," and while Laidlay, not Vardon, is often credited for originating that grip, there's no dispute over the statue's artistic value. Only four of these bronzes, with a well-defined, caramel-colored face, were crafted in 1895 by G. Gonella of Dundee, Scotland. Representative of statuary at its evocative, lifelike best, this true rarity was acquired a decade ago through "a little chicanery" for $32,000. It is now worth about $100,000.

"I knew the bidding for this very historical item would be fierce, so I used a little trickery at the auction," admits attorney Will Roberto, who despite lacking the financial resources of many elite collectors, has assembled many of golf's rarest pieces.

"Everyone knew I was going to be bidding on the statue, and I didn't want people running me wild. What I did was to bring some friends to the auction, told them to bid to a certain amount, and in effect, I disguised what I intended to do to the very end. That way I could determine the most interested parties at that sale, their degree of interest, and only at the end did I take over the bidding. Auctions can be very risky propositions for the uninitiated. The beginner should keep his hands in his pocket, let an experienced dealer or representative get involved in the real action."

Statuary like that exquisitely detailed $10,000 Young Tom Morris, produced by the same company (Kirkwood & Sons) that crafts medals for the Royal & Ancient Society, and an 1892, 2-foot high plaster likeness of Freddie Tait (a British amateur killed in the Boer War) called the *Golf,* have long impressed Roberto. He admits to "not being able to draw a straight line even with a ruler," so the meticulous workmanship that brings turn-of-the-century golfers to life stirs his aesthetic sensibilities.

Johnny Ledlay by G. Gonella, Dundee, Scotland ca. 1895. Red coat of the honorable Company of Edinburgh Golfers (Muirfield) won 2 British Amateurs. Approx. 16″ h, polychrome bronze. *Photo courtesy of Will Roberto.*

"Whether it's a whimsical plaster, a pro shop display item [of a Scottish golfer] worth about $500, something for $100, or my Young Tom, statuary to me is fine art, more alive than photos or paintings," insists Roberto. "Turn-of-the-century castings were mainly gifts given to distinguished golfers, or served as celebratory mementos for clubs, so not too many were made. That rarity makes the hunt for them more exciting, and keeps values high."

Another attribute that attracts many collectors to bronze, silver, and even plaster castings is their "security," or authenticity.

Roberto's $5,000 bronze of Old Tom Morris, with accentuated beard, and scrupulously sculptured pocket watch, demands such laborious workmanship that reproducing or counterfeiting statuary usually proves too costly.

"It just takes thousands of hours to try and fake a statue, a huge outlay of cash at a foundry, so beginners don't have to worry about counterfeits," insists Roberto. "There aren't that many great historical statues to fake, plus not that many top-echelon collectors pursue statuary."

Yet even if statues are a generally "safe" specialty, collectors must still be concerned about condition. Here there are no blanket rules.

Pointing to Laidlay's flaming red jacket (the 1800s color of the Honourable Company of Edinburgh Golfers, otherwise known as Muirfield), which is dotted with several black spots of missing paint, Roberto says, "These chips are common in polychrome bronzes. Buying a less-than-perfect piece, while hoping to get an even better example in the future, entails the risk of being stuck with one of them. But there's still no way I'd turn this Laidlay down. When an item is this rare, you must go for it."

Numerous other statues flank the Laidlay. There's an Old Tom Morris standing on the Sauken Bridge at St. Andrews, a $100 "1800s" golfer that was used by the Johnnie Walker Distillery as a promotional item, and Antoine Bofill's *The Golfer*. A reproduction of a 1900s casting now in a Scottish museum, this 1½-foot tall piece depicts a player in plus fours and cap who seems to be awkwardly holding a club with a baseball grip. It's quite striking and worth upwards of $3,000.

Yet as Roberto advises, "Statues can't just be investments. They must speak to people," and that's the palpable impact of the entire Laidlay display.

"The statue is of course special, yet that framed letter Laidlay sent to a journalist denying he was the true inventor of the 'Vardon Grip' [another famed British golfer named J. H. Taylor insisted Laidlay was its pioneer], gives the piece much more resonance," reasons Roberto. "He admits in the letter he copied it from a very good amateur, and said that he really didn't mind if Vardon got the credit for it. Together, this letter and statue make a beautiful combination."

But even without revealing, or emotion-tinged letters, statues still make a statement. One that's powerful enough to evoke the past, and to transcend time's usual limitations.

The prices of golf collectibles fluctuate. The following values are estimates offered by various experts:
MM—Mullock & Madeley
GLP—Golf Links to the Past
WR—Will Roberto

- Bronze figure of Harry Vardon (in the style of Hal Ludlow) 5½" high, **$1,750–1,850, MM**

- Bobby Jones limited edition bronze by Chapel, a full bronze of Jones blasting out of a bunker sits on a stainless steel base with a multiple-toned patina finish, stands 19" tall, weighs 30 pounds, limited to 500 bronzes, **$4,000, GLP**

- A. W. Tillinghast sculpture, bronze of famed architect who designed Baltusrol and Winged Foot, in a cold-cast edition of 350, 18" tall, **$395, GLP**

- Ben Hogan sculpture, by renowned artist Ron Tunison, stands 16" tall and mounted on a base, **$395, GLP**

- Miniature bronze Austrian figure, 3", ca. 1910, mint, **$900–1,200, WR**

- Pair of bronze bookends, two repoussé scenes figure at top of swing, bag of clubs, ca. 1916, very good condition, **$500–750, WR**

- Cast-iron door stop, 8" high by Hubley Mfg., ca. 1920s, **$300–400, WR**

- Male and female bookends by Bradley & Hubbard, and a statue 7.25" by approximately 7.25" on metal base ca. 1930s, **$150–200, WR**

- Metal ashtray, cast-iron golfer with movable golf ball head, ca. 1930s, **$150–200, WR**

- Two statues, one 10" high on marble base and one 14$^{1}/_{2}$" on granite base, **$150–200, WR**

- Cast-iron paperweight in form of dimple golf ball atop a spoked wheel advertising Hockensmith Wheel & Mine Car Co., **$100–125, WR**

- Ben Hogan bronze by David Earle Goodrich, circa 1980s, **$2,500, WR**

- Harry Vardon bronze by Hal Ludlow, circa 1899, several sizes, **$1,000–2,500, WR**

- John Laidlay bronze by Gonella of Dundee, Scotland, ca. 1890s, **$35,000–75,000, WR**

- Nude golfer by Adolph Wein, ca. 1900, 17$^{3}/_{4}$", **$3,000–5,000, WR**

- Young Tom Morris by Trevor Faulkner, ca. 1990s, **$3,500 plus, WR**

- John Ball bronze by Alex Macleay, 19" high, ca. 1893, **$2,000, WR**

- Golfer 19" high by Antoine Bofill, ca. 1895, **$20,000, WR**

- Nicklaus, Palmer, Bobby Jones, and other molded figures by Albert Pettito, ca. 1980s, **$100–350, WR**

- Horace Hutchinson 26" bronze by William Tyler, ca. 1890, **$35,000, WR**

- Old Tom Morris and other figures in solid silver by Garrard in London, **$3,000–8,000, WR**

16 GOLF'S REMBRANDTS
Alluring Artwork

Inspired by man's heroic attempt to tame menacing courses, the world's most revered artists have long been captivated by golf's magic. They've pictured wondrous Scottish seaside links, artfully depicted red-jacketed aristocrats at play, and stroked canvases that picture the very essence of the game: man's struggling with bunkers, foreboding hillsides, and other nerve-rattling torments.

Ever since Lemuel Francis Abbott pictured William Innes, the Captain of the Society of Golfers at Blackheath, England, in 1778, the game has attracted the palettes of numerous art-world luminaries.

From Sir George Reid's portraits of Old Tom Morris to Norman Rockwell's stabs at golf subjects, and Charles Crombie's humorous watercolor cartoons highlighting man's inevitable struggles with the golf ball, the collector has a bounty of choices. Will it be a 19th-century Charles Lees landscape, another "blue-chip" like a Sir Henry Raeburn portrait, or a far more contemporary work from America's master of all sporting events, Leroy Neiman?

Whatever suits your aesthetic sensibilities, when assessing the desirability of a painting or print, collectors must realize that the value of art objects wildly fluctuates. Many artists are in and out of vogue, and that the "emotive power" (or investment potential) of different works changes over time (as collector tastes and market conditions always vary).

"Mistakes can easily be made valuewise," insists golfiana lover Jim Espinola. "So the safest collecting strategy is to buy art that you like to look at. That way you can at least live with the work on your wall."

Blackheath Golfer after L. F. Abbott ca. 1900, matted and framed. *Photo courtesy of Old Tom Morris Golf, L.L.C.*

A photogravure of Old Tom Morris after J. Michael Brown. *Photo courtesy of Old Tom Morris Golf, L.L.C.*

Robert Tyre Jones, Jr. after Dwight D. Eisenhower. *Photo courtesy of Old Tom Morris Golf, L.L.C.*

To avoid those mistakes when assessing a Crombie's "Rules of Golf" stone lithograph that charmingly captures the emotions of the game, a Charles Malzenski contemporary landscape, or a canvas by premier Irish impressionist John Lavery (an 1856–1941 artist, his work typically sells for six figures), Director of the U.S.G.A. Museum and Archives Rand Jerris advises, "Go slowly. Work with dealers who can authenticate items. Above all, however, buy what you like. Don't just think about investment values."

Continuing to sound a cautionary note, Jerris counsels, "Even when working with a dealer, use an ultraviolet light on paintings. Areas that show up dark under UV are repairs. You can see the extent of overpainting. There are ways to determine if something has been added to a painting. This is far cheaper than sending paintings to a lab

Evian Les Bains: The Wonderful Savoy Spa,
poster by François Geo, ca. 1930s, matted
and framed. *Photo courtesy of Old Tom
Morris Golf, L.L.C.*

Poster by Genes, framed, ca. 1930s,
advertising Dieppe as the beach closest to
Paris, with golf as a prominent attraction.
Poster has some folding marks. *Photo
courtesy of Old Tom Morris Golf, L.L.C.*

Dick Mayer for Chesterfield Men of America
ca. 1950s, matted and framed. *Photo
courtesy of Old Tom Morris Golf, L.L.C.*

where they can be analyzed for additions [there are instances when a solitary golfing figure or a hole with a flag are added to a canvas to make it a "golf collectible"]."

Jerris feels that British watercolorist Arthur Weaver is "arguably the most collected, popular artist" (in the $5,000 to $7,000 range, Weaver is particularly known for painting courses). "Weaver is still working in the style of the great 19th-century watercolorist and people enjoy that," says art historian Jerris. "There are always people who value photo-realism and Weaver comes close to that."

Phillip Morris & Co. Ltd. Inc., cigarette advertisement with U.S. Savings Bond War Defense logo, framed. *Photo courtesy of Old Tom Morris Golf, L.L.C.*

An F. Earle Christie print of a well-dressed woman with golf club. *Photo courtesy of Old Tom Morris Golf, L.L.C.*

A Coca-Cola advertising tray ca. 1920s, $800–1000. *Photo courtesy of Old Tom Morris Golf, L.L.C.*

Collectors also value the few golf paintings done by American icon Norman Rockwell (these works are also in the six figures), John Hassall (1868–1948), who did a series of whimsical prints, and of course Crombie (his work is fairly accessible, selling for $4,000 to $7,000 at auctions).

No matter who the artist, Jerris says, "My greatest concern is true condition. A lot of cosmetic work can be done to make art look better than it is, so I worry more about how much a piece has been altered than about forgeries."

Jerris is equally concerned by art that's "heavily promoted." "You want longevity," he insists. "Art must have a track record, so be wary of things that get very hot. Values can go through the roof, but then they become less significant, and values sharply decline. So avoid paintings that don't have a long historical timeline, what's fashionable short-term."

Admiring Charles Lees's (1800–1880) *The Golfers* hanging in the U.S.G.A.'s Golf House (a depiction of a St. Andrews match), Jerris further advises collectors to "find paintings where the colors are still bright, not faded out. The blues, purples, and reds are very sensitive to light, very subject to fading, so try to get paintings that are not washed out."

As a general rule watercolors are much more fragile than oil paintings, so Jerris concludes, "Oils can be displayed for many years without prompting much concern. Just look at the back of a painting to see if it's been relined. Look for signs of physical intervention by taking a picture out of its frame to see if the canvas has been tacked

A James Douglas watercolor of Reis Golf
Club, Wick, Caithness. Well executed. *Photo
courtesy of Old Tom Morris Golf, L.L.C.*

with small nails onto a stretcher. Look for a second set of stretcher holes, and see if the
canvas has been cut and glued onto another surface. The back of a painting can be as
important as the front.

"Collecting art can be very exciting and rewarding, but you just have to be patient,
and to take precautions. If you're careful, art becomes a whole lot of fun."

An early print titled the "Golf Girl", ca. 1900. A very colorful print. *Photo courtesy of Old Tom Morris Golf, L.L.C.*

An F. W. Stark watercolor, signed, dated 1927, "Every Putt Pleases Somebody." Bold colors, hilarious expressions on the greenside observers faces. *Photo courtesy of Old Tom Morris Golf, L.L.C.*

Travel Posters

The French Riviera. Fashionable Swiss Alps resorts. Royal Troon, Gleneagles, other famed Scottish seaside escapes, and of course, the Sistine Chapel of golf, St. Andrews, the home of the Royal & Ancient.

All of these inviting locales, evocative of the charmed sporting life, are not distant fantasylands, reserved for the idle rich.

They are also wonders to be visually savored, landscapes and other graphically stunning scenes that are delightfully captured by illustrious artists in collectible stone lithograph golf posters.

A relatively affordable niche for new enthusiasts, investment-worthy, aesthetically pleasing images of storied golf resorts can be acquired for $1,500 to $2,000. Rarer, Art Deco depictions of St. Andrews and other British Isle meccas are pricier (a St. Andrews poster recently sold for $25,000), as the demand for these "Railway" getaway posters is now intense. Yet poster collecting, which combines art, history, glamour, and a love for the game, is still seductive—and for the most part, attractively priced.

Just be prepared for a little hard work, as discovering rare travel posters demands patience, arduous searches (or legwork), and networking with art dealers (make sure they are well-established and accredited).

"You can try to find lightning in a bottle by yourself, but knowledgeable dealers know values, and have the eye to judge the best quality images with the greatest clar-

An F. E. Hieridge framed and matted watercolor, "Nilgeri Hills, So. India," mat notation "looking towards Mysole from City Golf Clubhouse." Scene depicts two players on green, possibly two caddies lower right. Bird's eye maple frame. Signed. *Photo courtesy of Old Tom Morris Golf, L.L.C.*

A William Rainey framed and matted watercolor (1856–1936). "Hard approach at the 15th (Try Again Sir!)." Signed lower right. Scene shows golfer playing from deep bunker with bag-toting caddie. Landscape and figure painter, water colorist and illustrator. *Photo courtesy of Old Tom Morris Golf, L.L.C.*

ity," says New York attorney Robert Sidorsky, a collector who exhibited many of his most valued posters at the U.S.G.A.'s Golf House in Far Hills, NJ.

The luminous stars of that exhibit were British Railways posters from the 1920s and 1930s that promoted the splendors of such legendary golf resorts as Cruden Bay, North Berwick, Gleneagles, and St. Andrews. In striking maroons, blues, yellows, and greens depicting majestic scenery, beaches, and knicker-clad, tam-o'-shanter-wearing golfers, the Great Gatsby spirit of these playlands is vividly captured by the masters of this art form. The Rembrandts of posterdom—Maxwell Parrish, Tom Purvis, and Frank Newbould—had unrivaled talent for picturing the freedom-loving élan of the Jazz Age.

"Seashore images by Purvis, Newbould, and other big-named artists commissioned by the British railroads to promote their hotels are the top of the [poster] market," insists Sidorsky, a collector for twelve years, as he gazes at a 4-foot by 3-foot horizontal image of Cruden Bay done by Purvis. "Very influential in the field, Purvis developed a certain style of a flat, bright montage of color. Horizontals are also rarer than verticals (26 inches by 39 inches usually), and more desirable. This Cruden Bay [featuring a woman golfer in a windblown hat and a caddy in a kilt set against varied hues of green and yellow] is just a wonderful [$10,000] classic."

Ever in pursuit of those historical destinations that were brilliantly colored by marquee artists ("the key to value is the resort's cachet, the clarity of the image, and the artist's reputation"), Sidorsky has assembled so many classics, he's been forced to display them in his house on a rotating basis.

"One of my favorites is this *Number 4 Colonel Cottontail, Swears by the Drier Side*, done by Frank Newbould, which whimsically promoted the less rainy east coast of Scotland," says Sidorsky, holding a poster that shows a rabbit in yellow golf attire standing alongside a goose who is evidently watching a ball in flight and yelling "fore." "It just has a lot of energy, humor, and Newbould was one of the real trailblazers of the Art Deco, flat color style."

The long-eared Colonial (part of the valuable "East Coast Frolics" series), as well as Sidorsky's *Le Touquet Paris-Plage* (a resort on France's north coast) with a fabled red caddy, red flag, and red golf bag, and a minutely-detailed promo of Gleneagles, *Palace at the Gate of the Highlands* ("the more people, beaches, clubhouses, and other details boost the value of posters"), are in predictably exemplary condition. Connoisseurs have devised a lettered grading system where A means mint or near mint quality, and nearly all of Sidorsky's lithographs fall into the A category (B usually signals minor fraying, and C posters are badly worn).

"When posters have been restored or repaired it definitely affects the value," explains Sidorsky. "Beginners must be wary about items said to be in original condition that have actually been restored. They must also be able to tell the difference between reproductions and true vintage posters. Most reproductions are smaller, and have colors that aren't as bright."

Paper quality also distinguishes authentic classics from reproductions, but confessing that "these technical paper and ink issues are a little too complicated for most collectors," Sidorsky has relied on dealers (mainly from the art world) to acquire his showpiece items.

Purchasing articles through these experts not only assures him that posters will be authentic. This approach also serves as a deterrent against frenetic impulse buying, and gives buyers the time to fully study what's available in the marketplace.

"The most important key to buying is patience," says Sidorsky. "You can't just buy things quickly and haphazardly. Working with the right people helps give the new collector time to thoughtfully consider what to buy. You must be discriminating. Don't just buy posters that are rare. Go for things you really like looking at, items that will give you pleasure."

By working with well-connected dealers, Sidorsky has amassed a formidable collection of A-condition British Railway masters. Yet the poster world is not just $3,000-to-$5,000 scenes of white façade, *grande dame* hotels sitting alongside azure blue firths that were commissioned by either the London & Northeastern Railway, or the Caledonian Railway.

Along with more affordably priced scenes of the French Riviera and Swiss Alps resorts, most notably done by Leonetto Cappiello and E. Courchinoux (French railroad posters are typically more abstract and playful than their British counterparts), Sidorsky also pays tribute to America.

In his "hodgepodge" of visually thrilling "stuff," there are several reminders of America's vaunted literary tradition.

During the 1890s and 1900s literary magazines such as *Harper's* and *Scribner's,* influenced by such celebrated French postermakers as Jules Cheret and Henri de Toulouse-Lautrec, commissioned leading American artists to style golf images. The game was just starting to become popular in the U.S., and by enlisting the likes of a Maxwell Parrish or Edward Penfield, these magazines hoped to reach a middle-class audience with "English gentlemanly" aspirations.

Displaying a poster that flaunts a blazing red TRUTH logo, Sidorsky says, "This magazine liked to show fashionable couples, so to promote the publication they pictured this woman in an elaborate flowery red hat holding a golf club. Such an American poster is in lesser demand than British lithographs [the market for British and French posters is more developed than items from America]. Yet collectors shouldn't buy things just because of their monetary value. Images should also be fun."

It will cost a collector $5,000 to own an authentic Harper's *Golfing Calendar* by Ed Penfield, a playful depiction of a golfer sitting cross-legged in *de rigeur* jacket and hat. This "ritzy" Gatsby-looking figure is clearly poised for some glamorous action, and that's the allure of these portrayals. They're approachable, fun-filled leaps into the past, that Sidorsky emphasizes, "never fail to stir the imagination."

"They just have this undeniable power to delight, charm, and to evoke visions of another age."

The prices of golf collectibles fluctuate. The following values are estimates offered by various experts:
MM—Mullock & Madeley
WR—Will Roberto
GLP—Golf Links to the Past

• Charles Crombie's *Rules of Golf Illustrated,* 1st ed., 1905, twenty-four color prints, needs rebinding, minor stains, **$750–850, MM**

- *The Drive*, Douglas Adams antique hand-colored lithograph, depiction of the Caernarvonshire Golf Club in Conway, Wales, the artist's proofs were printed for this 35" x 26" framed restrike published in 1894, **$1,500, GLP**

- Old and Young Tom Morris original oil, by renowned artist Greg Rudd, **$12,500, GLP**

- *The Sandy Carry at Pine Valley's Third*, by Michael Miller, original painting ca. 1929, depicts the bunkers and green, 36" x 48", **$12,000, GLP**

- *18th Hole and Del Monte Lodge at Pebble Beach*, original painting by Michael Miller, rocky beach and Pacific Ocean are prominent features, 36" x 48", **$12,000, GLP**

- *Hell's Half Acre, Pine Valley's 7th Hole*, by Michael Miller, circa 1927, original painting, depicts numerous sand hazards leading to the green, 36" x 48", **$12,000, GLP**

- *Golfer in a Red Coat*, original oil by Sir John Watson Gordon; John Taylor, the subject of this oil, was the captain of the Honorable Company of Edinburgh Golfers, this is a 100-plus-year-old copy of the original and the artist is unknown, **$8,500, GLP**

- Harry Vardon original oil painting, painted by Arthur Miller, depicts Vardon's swing, **$2,500, GLP**

- 1997 *U.S. Open Championship–Congressional*, 15" x 27", limited edition in color, **$500, GLP**

- 1996 *18th Hole Royal Lytham*, limited edition print signed by artist Linda Hartough, 15" x 27", **$350, GLP**

- 1996 *U.S. Open Championship–Oakland Hills*, limited edition print of this Donald Ross course signed by artist Linda Hartough, **$300, GLP**

- 1994 10th Hole *Dinna Fouter Turnberry*, by Linda Hartough, 15" x 27", **$1,200, GLP**

- *The Golfers* by Charles Lees (1800–1880), arguably golfdom's most famous canvas picturing a golf match in St. Andrews in 1847, this reproduction is 40" x 27", **$3,600, GLP**

- *The Bunker* canvas transfer art, painted in 1894 by Charles Edmund Brock, one of golf's most famous paintings, limited edition (125) reproduction, 22" x 28", **$750, GLP**

- *Golf Is Not the Only Game on Earth* by Charles Dana Gibson (1867–1944), print with caption. (Gibson created the characters known as "Gibson Girls"), unframed, **$149, GLP**

- *National Golf Links of America*, hand-signed limited edition pen and ink print of storied clubhouse, **$125, GLP**

- 1995 U.S. Open Print, played at Shinnecock Hills, 23½" x 15½", **$75, GLP**

- *Ben Hogan Tournament Victories*, each of his wins listed by year on this sepia-toned lithograph, image is 16" x 20", **$80, GLP**

- *Payne Stewart—Tribute to a Champion*, Stewart's 1999 U.S. Open victory at Pinehurst No. 2, 17" x 32", **$75, GLP**

- *Arnold Palmer, A Masters Farewell*, 19" x 22", **$70, GLP**

- *Pebble Beach 7th Hole*, 12" x 24", **$48, GLP**

- *The Blackheath Golfer,* color lithograph from engraving by V. Green, ready for framing 20¾" x 15¼", famous print of William Innes, Captain Blackheath Golf Club, first printed in 1790, **$65–120, MM**

- *The Golf Hills* (*Black Hill Golf Course*) by Adolf Dehn, 9¾" x 13½", limited edition etching, number 23 of 100 signed by artist, dated 1952, framed, **$400–600, WR**

- *Walter J. Travis*, 14" x 9" hand-colored illustration by Edward W. Kemble, ca. 1910, matted, **$60–70, WR**

- Original signed H. C. Fisher, five-panel *Mutt and Jeff* cartoon, dated 3-5-17, framed, **$400–500, WR**

- *Ben Hogan*, limited edition print signed by artist Edward Kasper, matted with Hogan signature, in inlaid burl frame, **$400–500, WR**

- *The Golfers*, after Charles Lees 15" x 24", identification key on backing, by Frost and Reed, ca. 1951, matted and framed, **$175–200, WR**

- *Blackheath Golfer* after L. F. Abbott, ca. 1900, matted and framed, **$400–600, WR**

- Seriograph of 12th hole at Augusta National, 39¾" x 29½", **$600–800, WR**

- Limited edition print of Bobby Jones winning the British Open at St. Andrews, by Currier & Ives, 11" x 16", ca. 1930, **$700–800, WR**

- Arnold Palmer poster by Leroy Neiman, 18" x 23", signed by Palmer, **$200–250, WR**

- Shinnecock Hills Poster, 1986 U.S. Open, signed by winner Raymond Floyd, **$200–250, WR**

- Two framed prints: *The Memorial Tournament* after Nick Leaskou, limited (500) signed, and *Fore,* a modern poster of old golf equipment, **$200–250, WR**

- *Ben Hogan* poster, ca. 1950s, signed in pen by Ben Hogan, matted and framed, **$300–400, WR**

- *Royal & Ancient Clubhouse at St. Andrews*, matted and framed color print 16" x 22", hand signed by the artist Arthur Weaver, **$250–300, WR**

- Original serigraph of Jack Nicklaus by Hiro Yamagata, depicts Nicklaus during the 1980 U.S. Open at Baltusrol (in New Jersey), number 75 of 200, **$7,500–10,000, WR**

- *Royal Country Down Golf Course, Playing to the 11th Hole* after Michael Brown for the Life Association of Scotland, 9" x 14", framed, **$400–500, WR**

- Eight matted and framed Brauer prints with original cardboard envelope: *The History of Golf*; eight original lithographs by Bill Brauer, **$200–300, WR**

- Twenty paper items including a *Li'l Abner* series of five prints, **$100–150, WR**

- *Robert Tyre Jones, Jr.* after Dwight D. Eisenhower, $10^{3}/_{4}$" x $13^{1}/_{4}$", **$300–350, WR**

- *Cypress Point View from the 15th hole*, $16^{1}/_{2}$" x 22", limited edition (750) after Arthur Weaver, 1974, signed and framed, **$200–225, WR**

- *Evian Les Bains, The Wonderful Savoy Spa* after François Geo, $38^{1}/_{4}$" x $28^{3}/_{4}$" poster ca. 1930s, matted and framed, **$2,000–2,250, WR**

- *Hyeres* after Roger Borders, 39" x $24^{3}/_{4}$", poster ca. 1930s, matted and framed, **$2,000–2,250, WR**

- *Cannes La Ville des Sorts elegants* after SEM 38" x $25^{1}/_{2}$", poster ca. 1930s, **$2,250–2,500, WR**

- *Dick Mayer for Chesterfield Men of America*, $21^{3}/_{4}$" x $25^{1}/_{2}$", ca. 1950s, matted and framed, **$200–300, WR**

- Phillip Morris & Co. Ltd. Inc., cigarette advertisement with U.S. Savings Bond War Defense logo, 28" x $20^{1}/_{4}$", framed, water damage, **$750–850, WR**

- *Jack Nicklaus*, original oil painting 36" x 30", Nicklaus is holding the 1980 U.S. Open Championship trophy, painted by Nigel Cooper, **$400–500, WR**

17 JOY IN A BOTTLE
Precious Glassware

Reminiscing about his lost love is difficult. The pain is etched in his voice, and the words come hard, as if they're opening up an old wound.

Such angst is understandable. Uniquely styled glassware exerts a bewitching effect on collectors, and the turn-of-the-century pieces Kevin McGrath once owned were exceptional ruby-cut prizes.

"The beautiful clear-glass trophies I owned belonged to Walter Travis, glass with silver overlays [and plaques] that were wonderfully crafted in Europe," recalls McGrath, a leading auctioneer of golf antiques who conducted the first U.S. sale of memorabilia in 1988. "One of those [1897–98] trophies was an absolutely stunning greenish color, but you just can't collect and sell. Too bad, those [$15,000] pieces were remarkable."

Delightful glassware is also available at considerably lower prices. While hand-blown glass trophies are "buried" in elite collections, McGrath feels "very attractive" items like the Tiffany lamps that were once awarded by Pinehurst at the North South Open, are available at moderate prices ($300–$1,000).

These decorative pieces include jugs, ball-shaped whiskey decanters (many 1920s decanters, priced from $400 to $500, contained six small glasses), water tumblers, and trophies with silver overlays depicting early 1900s golfers.

New enthusiasts will pleasantly discover that even finely executed glassware can be acquired for $100 to $200. As McGrath says, "This is one area where you just don't need to have a lot of money to put together a handsome collection."

Yet collecting glassware does present one major challenge: Worthwhile items are in exceedingly short supply.

"Forget about finding pieces with lineage," insists McGrath, "Those connected to big name players just [don't] appear. In the 1900s, 1920s, each tournament tried to outdo the other, and these beautiful works have been squirreled away. Even if a pinnacle piece is being sold, the top collectors compete for it [privately], and so most stuff disappears before it hits the market."

Finding attractive glassware is still possible, however. The beginner must simply remain steadfast and hopeful (isn't that at the heart of all collecting?), and follow McGrath's advice.

"Before you get heavily involved in buying anything, wait a little, look around, see what you really like," says this seasoned market observer. Have the patience to read a few books, call up a few dealers, and as you check out their reputations, you also need to see examples of glass, the craftsmanship in this area. Later on go to auctions, but remember, you don't have to spend a lot of money to build a nice collection."

As new collectors study those books and attend auctions, they will learn about pricing trends, which makers are highly regarded, and will certainly develop an eye for condition.

"When buying quality glass or other golf collectibles, the serious collector often goes to Scotland, England, and that's a whole different world in terms of condition's importance," warns McGrath. "In the U.S., condition is everything in determining values. Not so abroad. People there believe a family might have loved a piece so much, they went to the bother of repairing it.

"That's fine, but if a piece of glass is cracked it only brings a fraction of the price [of an undamaged piece]. Minor chips though, say on the edges, that shouldn't influence the price much. Cracks are the killer, while a decent-sized chip affects the value 15 to 20 percent. You have to keep all this in mind. But go to those auctions, learn how to judge quality, and go for pieces as close to mint as possible. Above all, enjoy what you're looking at. Have fun."

The prices of golf collectibles fluctuate. The following values are estimates offered by various experts:
WR—Will Roberto

- Set of two T. G. Hawkes & Co. Crystal decanters, Corning, NY, ca. 1900, etched glass golfing scenes, sterling silver caps with inner glass stoppers, in original wicker basket carrying case, very good, **$1,800–2,000, WR**

- Leaded glass bottle 10", ca. 1910, with painted overlay of two golfers and ceramic stopper in the shape of Scot and golfer motif bronze bookends (damage), **$700–1,000, WR**

- Jim Beam commemorative whiskey bottles, including Crosby and Sahara, **$400–600, WR**

- Red glass cocktail shaker, 11", with silver golfers, ca. 1920, good condition, **$200–300, WR**

- Three fine glasses: pink Cambridge glass, etched golfing scene, ca. 1925, two tumblers, hand-painted golfing scenes, **$250–300, WR**

- Pair of glasses with different beautiful hand-painted image of golfer in plus fours, vest, ca. 1920, fine, **$250–300, WR**

- Crystal inkwell with silver lid and mounted golfer, silvermaker's hallmark, to lid, excellent condition, **$600–800, WR**

- Green glass decanter 8³/₄" high with sterling silver overlay depicting a period golfer, no stopper, **$600–800, WR**

- Small etched glass ashtray in a metal holder in the form of a basket, **$50–75, WR**

- Glenmore Whiskey bottle, hand-painted "The 19th Hole" scene, purportedly by George Broadhurst, **$40–50, WR**

18 IN THE CLUBHOUSE
Buying Items and Preserving Them

Join the Golf Collectors Society. That's the first step towards determining what to collect and how. Joining this society will immediately bring you into a world of fellow enthusiasts who know the collecting world and its nuances.

Knowing these collectors (through a society directory and informative newsletter), and sharing their excitement will help you find various items, alert you to trade shows and other gatherings, and provide valuable contacts with sellers, dealers, and auction houses.

By attending these sales events and working with dealers, collectors ultimately develop an understanding of values and condition. Demand and rarity account for much of an item's value, but condition is often crucial in assessing the worth of a particular artifact.

Once that "eye" for condition has been developed (by seeing lots of stuff and following the precepts of the experts that made this book possible), collectors must preserve their collectible no matter what its price.

Regarding paper items, Mark Emerson recommends, "Keep programs in acid-free plastic envelopes that can be taped close to airtight and then stored in boxes that are free of light. Letters, postcards, photos, and other paper golf items usually can be stored in acid-free sleeves found at office-supply or hobby stores. Then the sleeves can be put in three-ring binders and organized by category. If any paper item is going to be framed, professional framers should always use completely acid-free matting materials and conservation glass. Even after that process, these pieces should be kept out of direct sunlight."

An Osmond Automaton Caddie, all original.
$750–1000. *Photo courtesy of Old Tom
Morris Golf, L.L.C.*

A wicker golf bag, all original. $800–1000.
*Photo courtesy of Old Tom Morris Golf,
L.L.C.*

Will Roberto has his own safeguards for preserving the beauty of his assorted treasures. "You do as little as possible," he says referring to his long-nose woods. "You can lightly spread a coating of linseed oil, but make sure none of it touches the face or sole of the club. This prevents the lead weight from oxidizing. The less moisture on these clubs the better. You don't want the face of clubs to darken so try to avoid all moisture.

"If you don't use linseed oil then try a damp cloth with just a drop of Murphy's Oil Soap. You just want to get the dust off a club. You don't use a dripping wet cloth. Use another damp cloth to wipe any remaining soap remnants off the club, and finally a dry cloth after setting the club aside for about an hour.

"Depending on the color of the finish, cherry, oak, walnut, whatever, spread a slight amount of Briwax on the wood, but none on the face or sole. Let it dry for a few minutes, and then wipe it off. Use a light or dark wax to restore the finish to hickory shafts. Don't touch the grips. If they are coming apart, go to an art shop, and find some sort of preservative.

"As for storing them, I like to mount them horizontally in display cases. This keeps them from warping, and lessens their exposure to moisture. Moisture is the killer."

Roberto goes on to say that "rust is the number one enemy of old irons." He advises soaking old irons in motor oil, yet understandably warns against "soaking the shaft in this oil. If you really want to get rid of rust, soak them in oil for weeks, then wipe them down. Do not rub aggressively. If the club needs a lot of work, send them to a professional. You want to remove rust, but if a club is really covered with it, the better strategy is to send the club to a restorer."

A leather trunk, brass fittings, containing a canvas and leather golf bag. $300–350. *Photo courtesy of Old Tom Morris Golf, L.L.C.*

A wooden Seminole Golf Club cart barn sign with seven *Rules for Seminole Speedway.* $100–125. *Photo courtesy of Old Tom Morris Golf, L.L.C.*

He's even more wary of cleaning or handling balls. "Leave them alone," he counsels. "Even a damp cloth can take the paint off that's been there for 100 years, and that will kill their value. I don't do a thing with balls, and that's the same strategy I follow with pottery and statues, and the pages of books. To play it safe, don't touch them. Go to the experts."

Roberto goes to other sorts of experts when selling items. When he wants to "move" one item to secure enough cash for another purchase, he will sell a club or ball through his own private network of collectors that he has developed over time. This same approach is followed by Mark Emerson, who cites Donald Trump and his *The Art of the Deal* that inspires him to keep moving in business. "When it comes to selling golf memorabilia, timing is very important," insists Emerson. "Understanding the market, where prices are at, the highs and lows, that should dictate any sort of liquidation. You must have a feel for current market conditions, and you will get that understanding by talking to dealers and attending auctions.

"Most collectors develop relationships with other collectors, dealers, and auction houses in order to buy and sell. Experience should guide a collector as to where to attempt to sell certain objects. Just like with all collectibles, some things gain in popularity while interest in others diminishes. 'Feeling' the market and selling at the right time has a good deal to do with one's proceeds. Selling privately can be quicker and more profitable, as there are no commissions to pay and there is no time lag for the seller's funds to arrive from the buyer."

Profits can be made in golf collectibles, but it's far more enjoyable to preserve and treasure them. They are true history.

Appendices

NETWORKING WITH THE PROS
Collector Links

Antique Golf Clubs from Scotland
www.antiquegolfscotland.com/antiquegolf/main.php3
An informative and well-illustrated Web site with historical insights and online auction.

British Golf Collectors Society
www.britgolfcollectors.wyenet.co.uk
A trip to England and Scotland is imperative for collectors. Learn the basics of collecting by joining this organization.

Bob Burkett, Old Sport Golf
One of the leading authorities in old clubs, trophies and medals.
770-493-4344. Can also be reached through *www.oldsportgolf.com*

Lee Crist
An avid collector of tees and a leading expert in this collecting niche.
814-693-9636

Art DiProspero, Highlands Golf
Experienced dealer who has long helped clients acquire scarce and valuable items
P.O. Box 300
Watertown, CT 06795
860-274-4203

Dick Donovan
Longtime book dealer who specializes in finding rare editions of golf's most treasured volumes.
607-222-3431

Jeff Ellis Golf Collectibles
www.antiqueclubs.com
Jeffery B. Ellis is a leading authority on collectible golf clubs. He represents collectors at auctions, authenticates clubs, and is the author of *The Clubmaker's Art*.
P.O. Box 843
Oak Harbor, WA 98277
360-675-7611
e-mail: jegc@whidbey.net

Mark Emerson
An autograph and photo expert who authenticates material for collectors. When it comes to paper, he's the best in the business.
561-747-5457
e-mail: memerson@adelphia.net

Jim Espinola
An experienced pure collector more than eager to share his tips and knowledge with other enthusiasts.
978-459-7165

George Fox, PBA Galleries
www.pbagalleries.com
One of the most knowledgeable auctioneers of books and documents in the golf world. Company does online book auctions.
133 Kearny St.
San Francisco, CA 94108
415-989-2665
e-mail: online@pbagalleries.com

Chuck Furjanic
A writer and authority in pricing golf collectibles.
P.O. Box 165892
Irving, TX 75062
972-594-7802

C. Gibson & Company
www.mtechpub.com/golf
An attractive site offering an extensive collection of artwork, figurines, affordable clubs and books.

800-335-6851

e-mail: gibson@mtechpub.com

Golf Classics

John Bonjernoor is a reputed book dealer who can find out-of-print classics

P.O. Box 250

St. Clair Shores, MI 48080

313-886-8258

e-mail: jbonjernoor@comcast.net

Golf Collectors Society

www.golfcollectors.com

Members receive a newsletter with useful information on golf history, upcoming sales, and collecting tips. Contact Karen Bednarski.

P.O. Box 3103

Ponte Vedra Beach, FL 32004

904-825-2191

e-mail: kbednarski@golfcollectors.com

Golf's Golden Years

Knowledgeable dealer David Berkowitz issues a valuable catalog and represents collectors at auctions around the world.

847-934-4108

Golf Links to the Past

www.golfspast.com

Eddie Papczun's Web site offers investment tips about collectibles, golf gifts, historical overviews, and dozens of photos that will provide new collectors with fascinating insights into the golf world.

800-449-4097

e-mail: sales@golfspast.com

George Lewis, Golfiana

www.golfiana.com

A leading book dealer.

P.O. Box 291

Mamaroneck, NY 10543

914-698-4579

e-mail: findit@golfiana.com

Lew Lipset

www.oldjudge.com

A "paper" collector who has an encyclopedic memory of prices. He operates a Web site where collectors can leap back into time with programs and other golf memorabilia.

P. O. Box 5092
Carefree, Az 85377
480-488-9889
e-mail: llipset@aol.com

Mullock & Madeley
www.mullockmadeley.co.uk
One of the most expert auctioneers of golf and sporting memorabilia in Europe. Visit their Web site for valuations and trends in the collectible market.
SY6 7DS
UK
44-169-477-1771
e-mail: info@mullockmadeley.co.uk

Kevin McGrath
A widely respected expert in golf collectibles who has staged numerous auctions
781-662-6588

Will Roberto
Avid collector of pre-1875 golf memorabilia who as the president of former Old Tom Morris Golf has conducted numerous auctions. He's also a member of the American and British Golf Collectors Societies.
860-657-3300

Royal & Ancient Golf Club
www.randa.org
Golf on the other side of the Atlantic, an insider's view, St. Andrews, Scotland.
Fife
Scotland
KY 16 9JD
UK
44-1334-460000

Brian Siplo
A partner with Will Roberto and avid collector. He is a renowned photographer of golf memorabilia. Can be reached through British Golf Collectors Societies.
860-657-3300

The Sports Gallery
www.sportsgallery.co.uk
Offers scores of golfing prints, particularly landscapes of famous golfing venues.
44-1436-820-269
e-mail: mail@militaryart.freeserve.co.uk

Joe Tiscornia
One of the most knowledgeable and trustworthy collectors in the world. He's done his homework, and knows pre-1850 material better than most museum curators.

United States Golf Association
Visiting the Golf House with its pottery, clubs, balls, and other memorabilia is a must for every aspiring collector.
Golf House
P.O. Box 708
Far Hills, NJ 07931
908-234-2300

BIBLIOGRAPHY

Biocini, Paul. *Signature Golf Ball Collector's Guide*. Modesto, CA: Paul Biocini, 1995.

Christie's, Glasgow, Scotland, various auction catalogs.

Darwin, Bernard. *Mostly Golf: A Bernard Darwin Anthology*, Stamford, CT: Alisa/Classics of Golf, 1986.

Doherty, Mike. *Golf Classics Price and Identification Guide*. Studio City, CA: Golf Classics, 1978,

Donovan, Richard E., and Joseph S. F. Murdoch. *The Game of Golf and the Printed Word 1566–1985*. Endicott, NY: Castalio Press, 1988.

Ellis, Jeffery B. *The Clubmaker's Art*. Oak Harbor, WA: Zephyr Productions, 1997.

Ellis, Jeffery B. *The Golf Club: 400 Years of the Good, the Beautiful & the Creative*. Oak Harbor, WA: Zephyr Productions, 2003.

Furjanic, Chuck. *Antique Golf Collectibles: A Price and Reference Guide*. Iola, WI: Krause Publications, 1999.

Georgiady, Peter. *Wood Shafted Golf Club Value Guide*. Kernersville, N.C.: Airlie Hall Press, 1996

Gilchrist, Roger E. *Gilchrist's Guide to Golf Collectibles*. New York: Alexander Books, 1998.

Gilchrist, Roger E., and Mark Emerson. *Gilchrist's Who's Who in Golf*. New York: Alexander Books, 2001.

Hotchkiss, John. *500 Years of Golf Balls: History & Collector's Guide,* Iola, WI: Antique Trader Books, 1997.

John, Ronald O. *The Vintage Era of Golf Club Collectibles: Identification and Value Guide,* Paducah, KY: Collector Books, 2001.

Jones, Robert T. and O. B. Keeler. *Down The Fairway*. New York: Minton Balch & Co., 1927.

McGimpsey, Kevin W. *The Story of the Golf Ball.* London: Philip Wilson Publishers Ltd., 2003.

Olman, John M. and Morton W. Olman. *The Encyclopedia of Golf Collectibles*. Florence, AL: Books Americana, 1985.

Olman, John M., and Morton W. Olman. *Olman's Guide to Golf Antiques & Other Treasures of the Game,* Cincinnati, OH: Market Street Press, 1992.

Platts, Michael. *Illustrated History of Golf.* New York: Portland House, 1988.

Watt, Alick A. *Collecting Old Golf Clubs*. Hants, UK: A. A. Watt & Son, 1985.

INDEX